Selected
ALPINE CLIMBS
in the Canadian Rockies

Sean Dougherty

ROCKY MOUNTAIN BOOKS

Front cover: Andromeda Strain on Mount Andromeda. Photo James Sevigny
Back cover: Mount Robson from the NW. Photo Greg Horne
Title Page: N Face of Mt. Alberta. Mt. Columbia in left background.
Photo Urs Kallen

Published by Rocky Mountain Books
106 Wimbledon Crescent,
Calgary, Alberta T3C 3J1

Printed and bound in Singapore by
Kyodo Printing Co (S'pore) Pte Ltd.

Separations and halftones by
United Graphic Services, Calgary

ISBN 0-921102-14-4
The publisher wishes to acknowledge the assistance of the Alberta Foundation
for the Literary Arts in the publication of this book.

Canadian Cataloguing in Publication Data

Dougherty, Sean M. (Sean Melbourne), 1961-
Selected climbs in the Canadian Rockies

Includes index.
ISBN 0-921102-14-3

1. Mountaineering--Rocky Mountains, Canadian
(B.C. and Alta.)--Guide-books.* 2. Rocky
Mountains, Canadian (B.C. and Alta.)--Description
and travel--Guide-books.* I. Title.
GV199.44C22R633 1991 917.123'32043
C91-091535-0

CONTENTS

Climbing Areas

Acknowledgments

No guidebook containing the information found in this book could ever have been written by a single individual. This book owes a great deal to a large number of people who helped bring it to fruition.

Many climbers contributed information as diverse as bivi site locations to the best saunas in the Rockies. Several people even went out of their way to provide a critical review of some of my writing. My thanks to Barry Blanchard, Kevin Christakos, Donnie Gardner, Greg Glovach, Mike Haden, Pierre Lemire, Jeff Marshall, John Martin, Karl Nagy, Andrea Petzold, Ken Purcell, Glen Randall, Ward Robinson, Mike Shaw, Grant Statham, Darro Stinson, Kevin Swigert, Murray Toft, and Ken Wallator. Special thanks to Tim Auger who read, re-read and provided many suggestions about sections of the text; to Chic Scott who not only lent me his "little black books" but also found time in a busy schedule to write the foreword, and to Murray Toft who provided several topos and a photograph from his own publications.

The generosity of some of the leading photographers of the Canadian Rockies led to only a few photographs being taken especially for the book. Don Beers, Glen Boles, Bruno Engler, Greg Horne, Urs Kallen and Leon Kubbernus provided the bulk with Karl Nagy, Grant Statham and Dane Waterman supplying the remainder. I am grateful to Gillian Quinn who kindly provided photographs from the Dave Cheesemond collection.

Information about travel, access, regulations, campgrounds etc. were provided by the wardens and information personnel of the various parks and recreation areas covered by the book: George Field, Kiwi Gallagher and Don Morberg from Kananaskis Country; Roger Tierney and Glenn Campbell from Mount Assiniboine Provincial Park; Tim Auger, Greg Horne, Darro Stinson, Mark Lewidge and Donna Pletz from the Canadian Parks Service; and lastly the information staff at Mount Robson Provincial Park.

Rounding up a lot of the information required the help of several people who have extensive lists of phone numbers. I'm indebted to: George Bracksieck and the staff of Rock and Ice magazine; Dave Harris, editor of the Canadian Alpine Journal; and Jeff Lowe who helped me track down some previously unknown climbs.

With more practical and down to earth issues I was helped by: Grant Gussie who lent me his computer and Mary-Ann Podgorski who let me commandeer her office and computer; Lynn Kristmanson who suggested a whole new way of thinking about alpine climbing; Suzanne Tousignant who provided moral support when I was ready to throw in the towel; Willi and Vincene Muller who kept me well fed and watered as press date loomed ever closer and I got ever thinner, and James Sevigny — a constant alpine climbing companion who has shared countless great adventures on many of the described routes.

Once a book is written it is far from finished. There is proof reading, layout of text and pictures, cross referencing and an infinite number of other important things that need doing. John Martin and Gillean Daffern had the onerous task of proof reading an assortment of versions of the text, and Tony and Gillean Daffern took care of all the important publishing stuff that takes hours of meticulous work — the book would never have made the shelves without them.

Foreword

Canadian mountaineering is coming of age very quickly and at last the Canadian Rockies are taking their rightful place as an international alpine climbing mecca. For many years our climbing guidebooks, written primarily by poorly informed non-residents, left a great void in our mountain world. We have had a long wait for a climber's guidebook worthy of our magnificent mountains. This book will now fill that void.

The author, Sean Dougherty, has collected the most up-to-date information available on virtually all the quality climbs in the Rockies. You will find: an overview of the character and dangers of a particular ascent; a technical route description where required; all the necessary practical information to get you through the towns and campgrounds, and along the highways and trails to the bottom of the routes.

The adventure is still there; one is not led by the hand up *these* mountains. However, there is adequate information for mountaineers with judgement and common sense to successfully reach their summits and not go home disappointed.

Sean himself, considered one of Canada's foremost alpinists, has climbed many of the great routes described in this book. When you combine this experience with his talents as a researcher and a writer you have the right person to write this book. Add in a great sense of humour nurtured at character building bivouacs high on north faces and the result is a fine book which is a classic in itself.

The Canadian Rockies offer thousands of square kilometres of beautiful and uncrowded mountains. The mountains are unpolluted and undeveloped, and thanks to the presence of our national and provincial park systems, which protect much of the range, are a paradise for those who love wilderness and solitude.

So here is your guide to the classic climbs of the range. Use it to explore this great mountain inheritance of ours, then do your best to leave the area unspoiled for the next mountain pilgrims.

Good climbing.

Chic Scott

July 1991

Introduction

In the summer of 1983 I was a newcomer to the Canadian Rockies and wanted to rush off and climb all the routes I had read about in climbing magazines and seen in picture books. However, after a few abortive attempts and some minor epics it rapidly became apparent that to get up alpine routes in the Rockies you needed to know a little more than where a route went — what about the walk-in, life-threatening river crossings, condition of the rock, avalanche hazard, the best descent route, bivi sites, best time of day and year to make an attempt? The list goes on. And where to get this information? The one guidebook in existence (until now) doesn't exactly get into too much detail about the way in and the way out, and often the information about the way up is incorrect! Furthermore, the issue of route quality is avoided. Certainly, one can argue that there is more adventure in having less information, but we are supposed to be out climbing for fun, not trying to drown ourselves in a river, or thrashing ourselves with serious bushwhacking, or trying to decide the best descent! That isn't adventure. It's a pain in the ass that can get you into a desperate situation. To top all this off, when you discover that the route you are on is a pile of garbage (often about half-way up) you are unlikely to be having as good a time as you had hoped.

The only way to get good, reliable information was to ask the local climbers who had gone through the adventure "ritual" themselves at some time in the past. Unfortunately, getting information this way runs into a few problems, particularly when you can't find someone who has climbed the route or you aren't a local climber yourself and don't know who to ask or where to go to find that someone. Furthermore, there is no guarantee the knowledgeable person will be around when you need the information.

The problems and dangers of having little information about a particular route didn't grab my attention until 1987 when a friend and I were driving south over Sunwapta Pass after the first of a number of annual attempts on a route in the Tonquin Valley. Two guys had just arrived back at their car after an attempt on the Grand Central Couloir. Since it was August and the air temperature was quite high, we figured they would have a tale or two to tell, so we stopped to find out how they had fared. They were visitors to the area and knew the route by reputation, but knew nothing of the best time or conditions to try an ascent. They told us of rockfall, and avalanches and about a harrowing descent. They were just grateful to be in one piece. Finally, they added that they were off to Mt. Alberta later that day to give it a try, which seemed odd to us considering that the storms of the previous few days had put most routes out of condition, as they had just found out. When we enquired why they were going to try Mt. Alberta they said they knew of no alternatives of that calibre. After providing some alternatives which they might find interesting and in condition, we went on our way.

All the way home I was thinking about those guys, the fact they had come here on a climbing holiday, had an epic on their first outing and might well be in for another if they went to Alberta. What a way to spend a holiday, scaring the shit out of yourself, and escaping by the skin of your teeth. It's no wonder that the Rockies have a reputation. By the time we arrived back in Calgary I was convinced an alpine climbing guidebook was necessary, something to help visitors at least, so that people could go out on a route, then go back home and tell tales of a great trip rather than of a series of horrendous epics! A few months later I discovered that Tony and Gillean Daffern of Rocky Mountain Books were also thinking about the same idea, and so we sat down and hatched the project that has ultimately become this book.

To write a guidebook covering *all* the routes up every mountain in the Canadian Rockies would be an admirable task but to a large extent would go unused. There are many great routes in the Rockies but, being honestly blunt, the vast majority are piles of crap that have few, if any, redeeming features. Amongst the remaining routes only a handful get repeated on a regular basis, yet there are many more that deserve to be repeated more often. From the genesis of the book it was decided to write a guide to selected climbs in order to spare people the tribulation of doing a lot of shitty routes when there are so many good ones to be climbed.

The first problem was to decide which climbs should be selected. I originally thought that choosing routes for a book of this nature would be straightforward — first pick the routes that get climbed most frequently, then add the most talked-about routes, and finally include a few routes that everybody ought to know more about. The first two categories were not too difficult to fill, since there is a reasonable consensus as to which routes fit the bill. However, to establish which routes might fall into the final category, I was offered many different opinions from many different people. Route selection was obviously not going to be a trivial affair. To get a variety of opinions I asked a number of people who have climbed extensively throughout the Rockies to suggest routes of all difficulties and types (alpine rock as well as snow and ice) they might recommend to their friends. The final selection is an amalgamation of these opinions. They are all routes east of the Columbia River Valley between Mount Robson in the north and Mount Joffre in the south that are either climbed frequently, offer interesting climbing, take an aesthetic line, or have exceptionally good rock. In each of the different areas described, I have attempted to include routes right across the range of difficulties so there is something here to please everybody, from the extreme alpinist to the mountaineer who enjoys a pleasant scramble to a summit. Hopefully, I haven't screwed up and made any glaring omissions or included routes that are absolutely rank. If I have, I'll undoubtedly be hearing about it sooner than later!

And here it is, at last. It took more than two years of research, mixed with procrastination and then a final year of frantic writing to get it out before the end of 1991. All the information you are likely to need to climb the best alpine routes the Canadian Rockies have to offer is somewhere in the following pages, plus tidbits on renting cars, the nearest 24 hour gas stations and where to go to celebrate your successful ascents. If you find errors or omissions please send them to me care of the publisher.

So get out in them thar' hills and find out for yourself about the Canadian Rockies alpine experience. Have fun!

Sean Dougherty
July 1991

Climbing in the Canadian Rockies is a unique and unforgettable experience, providing all manner of adventure from easy days out to routes that prepare you mentally and physically for almost all eventualities in bigger ranges. The late Dave Cheesemond, who was the driving force behind the majority of the recent extreme routes in the Rockies, was fond of saying, "if you can climb here, you can climb anywhere." Such an accolade arises because of several factors that all play a part, in varying degrees, in making an ascent in the Rockies an experience: objective hazard, rock quality, remoteness and weather which all combine to make some ascents such taxing affairs they have a knack of pushing you to your limits. These features are not mentioned as reasons to put you off climbing in the Rockies, but rather to make you aware of the nature of the climbing so that you are prepared for the occasion and thus more likely to have a successful ascent.

The Rock

The primary consideration for most climbers, particularly visitors to the area, is the type and quality of the rock. Most of the Canadian Rockies consist of limestone of varying degrees of solidity ranging from excellent boiler-plate to plain rotten. In many ways this is similar to the rock found in the Bernese Oberland in the Alps, though unlike the routes in Europe, the Rockies climbs do not see as much traffic and consequently the loose rock is not "cleaned" away to the same extent. Hence, there is a lot of loose rock kicking around on ledges. At times the fractured nature of limestone, makes climbing a demanding cerebral exercise requiring care not to rip off holds since protection and belays can be illusory. This situation occurs quite rarely and in many instances the poor quality of the rock has been exaggerated out of all proportion. The rock on the "Selected Routes" is typically very tolerable — solid, with good protection and belays, and sometimes even approaches the solidity of granite!

Even though the majority of the rock is reasonable, the most common reason that climbing trips to the Rockies get derailed is the rock. The participants cannot handle the lower rock quality compared to granite, gritstone and quartzite. The best method for dealing with this problem is to get some limestone climbing mileage under your belt before attempting routes involving extended amounts of rock climbing. Go do a few of the longer rock routes near Canmore, Banff or Jasper — you'll quickly get the feel for whether you like it or not! This approach is almost mandatory if you intend to get up routes like the North Face of Twins Tower or the North Face of Alberta. The other remedy for the limestone blues is to go climb on the quartzite of the Tonquin Valley. It is excellent rock, giving climbing akin to that found on the crags at Lake Louise, though on a much larger scale.

Objective Hazards

Besides being a factor in the difficulty of a route, loose rock poses a very serious objective hazard. This is an important consideration on almost all routes, but in particular where the rock is above freezing level during the day and below freezing level during the night. This rising and falling freezing level promotes freeze-thaw action that hastens the separation of rock from the parent rock body. Additionally, nighttime freezing fixes loose rock in place and daytime heating, either from direct sunlight or a rising freezing level, melts the frozen bond and sets the rock free. The rockfall hazard sometimes becomes acute if the sun hits the face during the middle of day. Such scenarios are acted out on almost all Rockies faces during the summer months but the NE face of Andromeda is legendary in this regard. Cold nights, low freezing level and an early start are pre-requisites to a safe ascent on routes where rockfall is a major hazard.

The other objective hazards to consider are avalanches and serac collapse. Avalanches are obviously a major objective hazard consideration in the winter months because of the amount of snowfall that occurs in the Rockies. Furthermore, extreme changes of temperature caused by Chinook winds, a warm wind from the Pacific that occurs on a regular basis throughout the winter, create unstable layers in the snowpack. In the summer months many people wouldn't consider avalanches as a hazard since the bulk of the snow has either already avalanched or melted. However, in the early part of the season the hazard still exists. On slopes that face the sun, the snow may be quite firm early in the day before the sun gets to work on it. Later in the day the snow will have softened and could be quite wet. Depending on the depth of the snow, the state of the remaining snow pack, and the amount of free water, this situation can lead to instability and an eventual slide. This is a quite common cause of accidents in the summer months so be aware of the possibility. The onus is on you to appreciate that such a situation may arise on a particular route and to do something

about avoiding it. Familiarize yourself with recognizing potential avalanche terrain, and assessing the threat of avalanche. "Avalanche Safety for Skiers and Climbers" by Tony Daffern is the standard reference book.

Serac danger occurs below glaciers with hanging ice cliffs and is usually very obvious. For example, the North Ridge route on Mt. Temple is very exposed to this hazard. Since serac collapse is totally unpredictable, there are two philosophies to dealing with this hazard: avoid climbs where seracs pose a threat, or climb the routes or sections of routes that are threatened as quickly as possible so as to minimize exposure time. Any serac danger on routes described in this book is brought to the reader's attention.

Conditions and Weather

The weather plays a major part in Rockies climbing since it determines the conditions on the routes. The usual climbing season is July until about mid-September, at which time a major snowfall usually occurs, particularly at higher elevations. In recent years, the time to anticipate an extended period of settled weather has been late July-early August when you can expect temperatures in the mid 20's to mid 30's. This is also the time of year by which the alpine rock routes at higher elevations have dried out and are in peak condition. Around mid August expect some crappy weather that may effectively end the dry conditions for the year. The fall is often a good time to get into the couloirs since the freezing level has sunk low enough that rockfall hazard is reduced. Furthermore, there is often, though not always, an extended period of good weather in the fall known as "Indian Summer". Generally though, by mid-October the first snowfall has reached lower elevations and winter conditions start to prevail.

From November through early February temperatures can reach lows of -30°C or less for periods of a week or more and staying home in front of a big fire with a glass of wine and your lover is probably more beneficial for your health, though a few keeners (weirdos?) shun such pleasures of life and venture forth at this time of year. In some areas of the southern Rockies like Kananaskis Country and the area around Canmore the winter cold is regularly relieved by Chinook winds which can raise the temperature by as much as 30 degrees in one hour! By the end of February and the beginning of March the temperature is usually a little more moderate (around -10 to -15C) and some parties get out and squeeze off the odd winter ascent before the official end of winter. In April the conditions and weather are similar to March though the temperature is on the rise. May is generally a wet month and May/June is usually the time of year when the previous winter's snow pack starts to come down. Which brings us back to summer.

Bear in mind that the area covered by this book is very large and the prevailing weather in one area of the Rockies is not necessarily like that in another. This is a point to note for the many climbers staying at the Columbia Icefield campground. When the weather is the pits at the Icefield, try Banff or Jasper. If it is raining in Banff or Jasper try the Front Ranges, Roche Miette east of Jasper, or the peaks in Kananaskis Country. Generally, the further east you go the better the weather. So before deciding on routes get hold of the weather reports for the various areas and find out what the weather is up to. With a few more phone calls to the relevant information centres you can also find out about prevailing conditions.

Remoteness

A feature of climbing in the Canadian Rockies that is quite unlike climbing in the European Ranges, is the remoteness of the mountains. Many of the routes in the book are reasonably close to a highway but a significant number are at least a day's hike away, and some are several days hike from a vehicle. You are climbing in "wilderness". For example, when you are at the Clemenceau Icefields or in the upper reaches of the Athabasca River you are in backcountry that is a long way back! Climbing in the backcountry can take on mini-expedition proportions not only in terms of time required to do the route but also in terms of self-sufficiency. This requires dealing with all eventualities that may arise on such a trip. It is strongly advised that you register out or leave your itinerary with a reliable person, especially when you go walk-about in the backcountry, so that if you get into difficulties and become overdue the appropriate people can be quickly alerted and act accordingly.

Gear Needed

I assume that everybody venturing forth in the mountains is up on the kind of clothing and gear one needs for an alpine outing. Unless the guide expressly states that you don't require ice axe and crampons you are advised to take them, as you would on most alpine routes elsewhere. For the gear rack take a good selection of Friends and wires, particularly medium to large wires. Also take a good assortment of pins, especially angles and knifeblades. Knifeblades are what you are going to end up using the most but the angles come in very handy. And if you are likely to be staggering about on any icefield don't forget to take a map and compass — a surprising number of people go without!

Grading

Much sooner than later this Medusa had to raise its ugly head. In alpine climbing, thankfully, this is not such a hot topic as in crag climbing. The intrinsic difficulty with grading alpine routes lies in the fact that the grade is trying to reflect comparisons of difficulty between different routes with different types of climbing. For example, alpine rock vs. ice vs. mixed climbing. In an attempt to provide an informative grading scheme, a common practise of splitting the grade into several parts has been adopted instead of trying to include all the information in one single grade. The grades presented here are in one, two, or possibly three parts: an overall grade of I to VI; the technical grade of the hardest climbing given by the commonly used YDS scheme 5.0 to 5.10, and sometimes a third grade, where applicable if the climb involves technical ice climbing, denoted W1 to W5, a system that has its origins with Jeff Lowe.

The overall grade of a route is determined by taking into account many factors including the length of the route in terms of both distance climbed and time taken, the difficulty of the hardest pitch, the sustained nature of the climbing, the availability of escape and the difficulty of retreat. The idea is to give a relative measure of the "magnitude of the undertaking" denoted on a scale of I to VI.

The technical grading denoting the hardest move is the well used Yosemite decimal system. On alpine rock routes the grades in the book should be comparable with local rock climbs of the same grade. Visitors are advised to find out how local standards compare to grades from their own local climbing area. However, where the climbing involves snow and ice, and hence the use of crampons, things are not quite as clear. As an example take a well established 5.7 rock climb. In rock shoes, warm weather and with solid protection it's a 5.7. Now take the same climb except add big boots with crampons, rotten rock, indifferent protection, and toss in some spindrift. It is now a very different ball of wax. Most alpinists don't think of the grade in terms of how difficult it would be with rock shoes, good protection and warm, sunny weather but rather how difficult it "feels". Hence an alpine 5.8 feels like a rock climb of 5.8 though the actual climbing is invariably easier. And yes, it still means you have to be competent at 5.8. Aid climbing grades are much simpler — A2 is A2, just the same as an A2 in Yosemite.

This brings us to the infamous Rockies alpine grade 5.9 A2, the almost universal grade that is applied to anything that is hard! As described above, 5.9 A2 can mean a route with free moves that feel like 5.9 with some A2 aid moves. However, until the 1980's local climbers used 5.9 as the top grade on the local limestone routes. In addition, there is an unwillingness to believe that it is possible to pull off sustained 5.10 in big boots and crampons. Hence, 5.9 has become something of a catch-all grade for routes that seem like 5.9 or harder. Likewise with the aid grading, few local alpinists think they can climb aid harder than A2 (though A3 has begun to appear). Thus, the 5.9 A2 grade applied to a mixed alpine climb should be taken to be difficult to say the least.

Lastly, there is the grade given for ice climbing. Many people may argue, and can argue if they so desire, that inserting an additional grade to the other two just increases confusion. Opponents to this additional grade will undoubtedly insist that the grade for ice climbing is included in the overall grade. My retort is why grade technical rock climbing in a separate grade and not technical ice climbing? This question is particularly relevant now that many of the modern, hard alpine climbs have difficult and technical ice climbing pitches. In an attempt to include the level of ice climbing difficulty you expect to encounter on a particular climb, *where it is relevant*, an ice climbing grade has been included. To avoid confusion with the overall grade (quoted in Roman numerals) I have adopted the scheme introduced by Jeff Lowe that uses Arabic numerals instead of Roman. In all other ways it is the standard ice climbing grading scheme used in the Rockies where routes are graded from 1 to 7. The prefix W is an abbreviated form of WI for "Waterfall Ice", as used by Jeff Lowe. It is abbreviated to W since the I is superfluous.

OK, have you got all that? Good. Finally, I ask you to resist the temptation to compare routes of a particular grade with routes of the same grade in other mountain areas throughout the world, because due to the nature of the climbing in the Rockies, the grades here are likely to mean something quite different. VI's in the Canadian Rockies and VI's in the French Alps, for example, have little in common with each other, other than being difficult. The latter are a totally different kettle of fish and, by and large, are less taxing (mentally if not physically) than the Rockies version of the same grade. The section on "Climbing in the Rockies" provides some reasons as to why there may be a difference. Amongst the routes described here the system is self-consistent, though many of the factors one has to take into consideration resist objective assessment.

Disclaimer

Alpine climbing is potentially hazardous and dangerous. A friend of mine commented that alpine climbers might as well save their time and energy and just lie down on the highway! This facetious yet amusing point of view is not an uncommon sentiment among non-practitioners. Hopefully, this guidebook provides information to help make your time in the mountains a safe and enjoyable experience. However, it is only a guide and will not get you up climbs — that part is up to you. Users of this book must be responsible for learning all the techniques required to climb the particular route they have chosen to attempt. Furthermore, due to changing conditions, this guide may not accurately reflect a particular climb in the prevailing conditions. It is up to you to make all the necessary decisions based on information you have about the route and conditions to hand. This guide is NOT a substitute for experience and judgement.

Once you are in the mountains, most of the approaches from the highway to the routes are on foot. In a few cases mountain bikes can be used, but in most areas, except Kananaskis Country, mountain biking is severely restricted to just a few trails. If this mode of access is allowed to a particular climb it will say so in access notes to that climb.

Outside of the National Parks it is possible to fly into most areas via helicopter and in the case of some icefields by ski-plane. Access by air is a "Pandora's box" of different opinions; you can decide for yourself whether or not it is an acceptable practice. Information regarding this mode of transport is included because it is often used, particularly into remote areas. Helicopters are usually chartered from Canmore (Canmore Helicopters and Canadian Helicopters), Golden (Canadian Helicopters), and Valemont (Yellowhead Helicopters). A ski plane operation flying out of Golden called Amiskwi Air runs charters into the Clemenceau Icefield and parts of the Columbia Icefield outside the National Park boundary. All the local pilots know the restrictions they are operating under, but if there is some confusion as to whether you can fly to a particular place, particularly in a Provincial or near a National park, enquire at a local information centre.

Walk-in Hazards

There are a few potential hazards on the walk-in or walk-out that you should know about: bushwhacking, river crossings and various forms of wildlife, both big and small.

Bush Bushwhacking is sometimes a gruesome necessity that cannot be avoided. The difficulty of getting through the bush varies across the Rockies from quite easy on the eastern slopes of the Front Ranges to desperate on the B.C. side. Thankfully, the majority of routes in this guide are well served by trails but occasionally you will end up doing a route where there are few or no trails. In this case, the best advice is to try and find a game trail or, failing that, pick the easiest line through the bush. Be prepared for thrashing about through slide alder and clambering over deadfall. Rest assured that any bushwhacking will bring out your best qualities!

River crossings are mostly a case of putting up with wet feet. However, there are some routes that require wading waist deep through glacier meltwater rivers. If you know this beforehand a pair of neoprene socks or wet-suit booties are manna from heaven. On the other hand, you could just put up with the excruciating pain of your toes re-warming. Early in the season the rivers are all swollen due to spring run-off and many may be impassable. Later in the year, when water levels are typically much lower, the water level is lower in the morning than in the afternoon so be prepared for more exciting crossings later in the day.

Wildlife: big and small Lastly, it is appropriate to mention something about wildlife. A feature of climbing in the Rockies that gets some people freaked out is bears. Yes, this is "bear country" with both black and grizzly bears. In popular areas close to the highway you are unlikely to come into contact with bears since they are reasonably private animals that enjoy their peace and quiet. Away from the highways and the more popular hiking areas coming across bears or evidence of bear activity is more likely, though still a fairly rare occurence. This is far from a major disaster — bear attacks are very rare since the bears usually amble off. Nevertheless, it is a good idea to know how to behave in bear country to minimize the likelihood of an encounter. You are advised to read a reliable publication about bears and how to deal with them. The Parks Service has a pamphlet called "You are in bear country" that you can pick up from any National Park Information Centre. There is also a book written by local climber and noted authority on bears, Steve Herrero, called "Bear Attacks: Their Causes and Avoidance". It should calm any worries you may have. Some of his recommendations are:

-   Make noise — singing, talking loudly etc. Bear bells aren't loud enough plus they are really annoying to other trail users who don't have them!
-   Travel with others. You make more noise this way.
-   Don't take a dog since it may increase the risk of bear attack.
-   Be alert. The sooner you spot a bear the more alternatives you have to avoid a confrontation.
-   Leave the area as unobtrusively as possible if you see a bear.
-   Avoid food odours and cook away from your tent.
-   Store food in a place out of reach of bears: up a tree or a bear pole (all National Park campgrounds have food hangs). Do not store any food in your tent.
-   If you have an encounter, climb a tree as high as possible.
-   If you are attacked by a grizzly play dead. Curl up and protect your head as best you can. If attacked by a black bear, however, fight back.

The moose is another large animal you might come across. They are much bigger than you and it is wise to give them a wide berth — you wouldn't want to upset one, particularly during the rutting season in the fall. Similarly, bull elk are also potentially dangerous animals during rutting season and are best avoided.

You are much more likely to run into problems with smaller beasties like pack-rats, ground squirrels and porcupines. They have a distinct liking for sweat salts and like to chew on or run off with any sweaty item as well as eat your snack foods and almost anything else they can get their teeth into. Make an attempt to keep things out of their reach or you might wake up in the morning to find a boot is missing. It has happened!

Going to even smaller-sized nuisances, mosquitoes are perhaps the most insidious wildlife you are going to have to deal with. They habituate the valleys where there is wetland, such as the Tonquin Valley, a place synonymous with mosquitoes (and horse flies) in the Rockies. Thankfully, the glaciers are a bug-free escape if the valleys get to be too much. The best defense is a good offence — liberal use of good anti-bug lotion.

Most of the routes in this book are in areas where backcountry use is controlled to some degree. The majority of climbs lie within the boundaries of one of four national parks in the Rockies: Banff, Yoho, Kootenay and Jasper. The remainder are located within either a British Columbia provincial park or Alberta's Kananaskis Country. Any regulations pertaining to these two areas are mentioned in their introductions. To a large extent each of the four national parks have the same backcountry regulations and to save repetition a summary is provided here.

Backcountry use permits

In the national parks it is necessary to get a backcountry use permit if you spend *at least one night* in the backcountry. Permits can be obtained at park information centres. If you are just going out for a day trip then a permit is not required.

There are no problems getting a permit when you intend to use designated campgrounds but there are some guidelines that affect climbers regarding bivi sites at the base of long alpine routes. A backcountry permit for bivi sites will be issued under the following conditions:

1. The party must actually intend to undertake a climb.
2. The climb must be one which *reasonably* requires a bivi in order to get a safe start.
3. The bivi site must be as close to the start of the route as practical.
4. Wherever possible the bivi must be above the alpine zone i.e. off meadows.
5. If a designated backcountry campground is nearby it must be used in preference to a bivi at an undisturbed site.

6. The bivi has to have zero impact on the site i.e. no fires, no tent ditches, and pack out all your litter. Building rock walls is discouraged.
7. A small tent may be used. However, it should be collapsed and all gear preferably concealed if leaving it during the climb.

The long and the short of these regulations is that if there is a designated campground or hut in a location from which you can SAFELY complete a route in a day, the Parks Service will not issue you a permit to bivi at the base of the route. This is particularly relevant to routes at Lake O'Hara, Fryatt and Tonquin.

Registration

A voluntary registration system is provided by the Parks Service for hazardous activities within the national parks. For many years climbers shunned its use, feeling that it was an infringement upon their freedom in the backcountry. However, you are strongly advised to use the scheme. If, for some reason, you get into difficulties, the service is priceless since it may be the only way for rescue personnel to realise you may be having problems.

It is necessary to register in person at either park information centres or at a warden office since registering out for a route is a contractual agreement that requires a signature. Therefore, it is necessary to register during the office hours of the particular office. All overdue registrations are checked out. There are two important considerations to bear in mind when you register:

1. Since all overdues are checked out you must provide a reasonable estimate of your trip time. This may avoid unnecessary use of costly helicopter flights by rescue personnel.
2. You *must* notify the Parks Service upon completion of your trip. This is done by either dropping the registration slip off at one of the warden offices or information centres, or by telephoning the offices or centres. If you are late, phone at your **earliest** convenience. Failure to notify the Park Service of your return or cancellation of a trip is grounds for prosecution.

Rescue personnel will exercise some discretion about when to commence a search. This depends on many factors like weather conditions, amount of time overdue, estimate of the individuals ability, number in party etc. For this reason you must be prepared to spend at least one night out before expecting help to arrive.

Vehicle Permits

There are a few relevant regulations unconnected with climbing but rather with everyday use of the national parks. Vehicle permits fall into this category. All vehicles stopping in a national park are required to have a Park Motor Vehicle Permit — a little sticker that says you paid your entrance fee to the park. These can be obtained at park information centres, from campground attendants (summer only) or at the east entrance to Banff Park (Canmore), the west entrance to Kootenay Park (Radium), east and west gates of Jasper Park (on Highway 16) and the west entrance gate to Revelstoke/Glacier Parks (Revelstoke). You can buy either a one day, four day or annual permit. If you intend to stay for longer than a few days the best bet is to lash out the $26.75 (1991 price) for the annual permit.

Travel Info

Most visitors to the Canadian Rockies will arrive via one of three main routes from three different cities in Alberta and British Columbia: from Calgary via the Trans-Canada Highway; from Vancouver, also via the Trans-Canada Highway; or from Edmonton via Highway 16, the Yellowhead Highway. Each of these three cities are serviced by major airlines, with connections to everywhere, and are the most likely places of arrival for overseas climbers. The major centres in the mountains are Canmore, Banff, Lake Louise, and Jasper.

Getting Around

Cars It is an unfortunate and regrettable fact that having a motor vehicle makes a climbing holiday in the Canadian Rockies a lot more straightforward than having no vehicle. The routes are spread out over such a huge area it takes about a day to drive from end to end. Thus, the benefit of a vehicle should be obvious and you are advised that having a vehicle is the best way to go. For those arriving by air, there are the usual car rental companies at the airports but there are better deals to be had. Check out the Yellow Pages when you arrive and shop around. One of the cheaper outfits is "Rent-A-Wreck" which rents cars that are not brand-spankin' new at very reasonable rates.

Public Transportation For some, the budget may not stretch to a vehicle. If this applies to you, there are other, though less efficient, alternatives. The Greyhound Bus Company and Brewster Gray Line run bus services through the mountains along the following main highways: Highway 1 (the Trans-Canada)

between Calgary and Vancouver via Banff, Lake Louise and Field; Highway 16 (Yellowhead Highway) between Edmonton and Vancouver via Jasper and Valemont. Buses also run along the Icefields Parkway from Banff to Jasper and it is possible to alight almost anywhere by pre-arrangement with the driver. Check with the local bus depot for schedule information. A tidbit for those arriving in Calgary by air — Brewster Gray Line runs a daily service from Calgary International Airport to Banff. Enquire at the tourist information desk in the airport arrival area for more details.

If you intend to climb in the Jasper area, you can also arrive by train, either from Vancover or from Edmonton by VIA rail. The train service in the southern part of the Rockies through Calgary to Vancouver via Banff, Lake Louise and Field was discontinued in 1989.

Hitching There is also the old-reliable standby, hitch-hiking. Hitching in Canada is nowhere near as popular or socially "normal" as in Europe or the USA and can be a real pain-in-the-ass in terms of the time it may take to get from A to B. Many, if not most, drivers are not interested in stopping and moreover, in the summer months they'd be cramming you plus gear into a vehicle already crammed with holiday goodies. However, with a *small* pack the situation is often not so bleak and hitching provides a reasonable, if not efficient, way of getting about. Bear in mind that hitching is not allowed within the city limits in Calgary. This may also be true in Vancover and Edmonton. You'd be well-advised to enquire at a tourist office before you get dinged with a ticket — it happens!

Where to Stay

Camping Camping is the cheapest form of accommodation and the most popular with climbers. Throughout the various parks and recreation areas mentioned in the book are many campgrounds, both backcountry campgrounds and drive-in campgrounds near to highways and towns. In the summer months the mountains are a popular place and sites fill up quickly, particularly on the weekends. Though not always necessary you might wish to book a site in advance, especially in the popular areas. Contact the relevant information centres for more details.

Huts In some areas of the backcountry there is one alternative to camping that may appeal, namely the mountain huts . Visitors from outside the area will find a large difference between the hut system here and those elsewhere. In Europe, for instance, mountain huts tend to be quite large, have a custodian, simple meal service and be regularly served and resupplied by helicopter. By contrast, the mountain huts in the Rockies tend to be quite primitive, leaning towards a philosophy of self-reliance. The log cabins below tree-line are very comfortable, more like their European counterparts, though much smaller. The more recent prefabricated huts above treeline are closer to a bivouac hut style, being simple one-room shelters with minimal facilities. They make a wonderful haven when the weather craps out.

The majority of the huts in the mountains are run by the Alpine Club of Canada (ACC). Huts in the British Columbia provincial parks; i.e. the Naiset Cabins and the R.C Hind hut at Assiniboine and the Ralph Forster hut on Mt. Robson, are run by B.C. Parks. For details read the area introductions to Mount Assiniboine and Robson. Bryant Creek Shelter (no fee) is run by the Parks Service; for details contact a Banff Park information centre or the Banff Warden Office.

The ACC hut system requires advanced booking for all huts. Reservations are made on a person per night basis and must be made through the ACC Facilities Office in the Canmore Clubhouse. There are two types of huts in the system: Class A huts that are typically locked when no custodian is present, and Class B huts which are the high mountain huts. Any person can make a reservation to stay in an unlocked hut or at the Canmore Clubhouse, but only national ACC members may reserve space in locked huts if there is no custodian present. Reservations are accepted up to 6 months in advance, the payment of the first night's accommodation for all persons in the group being a prerequisite to making a reservation. If the reservation is made less than 2 weeks prior to the first night, payment in full is required. In the case of the Clubhouse, this balance may be paid upon arrival. Deposit and payment with Visa and Mastercard is accepted. If you cancel your reservation prior to 2 weeks before the first night you get all your money back but if you leave it to within 2 weeks to cancel you'll forfeit your deposit. Any reduction in numbers is also subject to the 2 week policy.

The huts useful for the routes described in this book fall into the two classes:

Class A Huts: these are completely equipped with foamies, cooking and eating utensils, Coleman stoves and lanterns, and stove complete with firewood. These huts, with the exception of the Abbot Pass hut are locked when a custodian is not present.

Elizabeth Parker (Lake O'Hara)
Stanley Mitchell (Little Yoho)
Wates-Gibson Memorial (Tonquin)
Sydney Vallance (Fryatt Creek)
Abbot Pass

Class B huts: are partially equipped with foamies, Coleman stoves and lanterns. Users have to supply cooking and eating utensils and white gas. These huts are unheated except for the Lawrence Grassi hut.

Neil Colgan (Ten Peaks).
Castle Mountain
Mt. Alberta
Lawrence Grassi (Clemenceau)
Mt. Colin Centennial

Hotels, Motels and Hostels In the towns there are numerous hotels, motels and B & B to suit all pocket books. The best resource for finding out about such accommodation is to contact Alberta Tourism using the toll-free number. Close to the highways are a large number of Youth Hostels which provide a cheaper alternative to motels. On top of this, many of them, particularly the ones along the Icefields Parkway have killer saunas that are the perfect remedy for aching bodies after a tough climb. Enquire at the Information Centres for more information regarding Youth Hostels.

Food, Gear, and other Supplies

In the mountains, Banff, Jasper, Canmore, and to a lesser extent Lake Louise, are the spots where you will find the best selection of groceries and assorted supplies. In addition, these towns have a large range of stores and restaurants, as well as amenities geared towards the tourist industry like book shops which sell maps and all manner of books relating to the backcountry and climbing (guidebooks, for instance!).

Banff has two large climbing stores (Mountain Magic and Monod's) that have all the gear you are likely to need in the Rockies and probably some that you don't need. Jasper doesn't have a speciality climbing shop but Totem Men's Wear & Ski Shop sells a limited range as does Wilson Mountain Sports in Lake Louise.

Stove fuel (white gas and propane) can be readily found at a number of stores and gas stations throughout the Rockies.

After a few days of living off freeze dried food, or whatever your back-country palette can stand, a good meal is a great treat. Canmore, Banff and Jasper have a large selection of eateries, covering a diverse range of foods. There are a large number of bars of course, and for those with a taste for dark beer there are a number of British-style pubs in Banff and Canmore.

Health

Residents of Canada are covered by various provincial health care programs. Climbers from outside Canada are advised to get medical insurance before the trip. There are no necessary vaccinations for a stay in Canada.

Apart from the obvious problems of acclimitisation, the main worry for many people is "Beaver Fever" or more properly *giardia lamblia.* The most common way of getting beaver fever is by drinking bad water. The Parks Service recommends that you boil all creek water for 20 minutes before consumption. However, in practise, high mountain creeks close to their source are unlikely to give you any ailments.

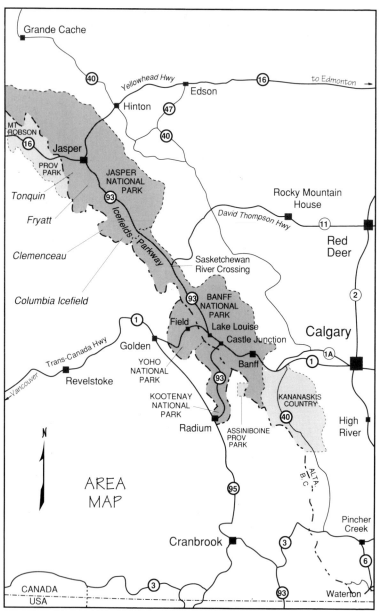

Grande Cache

40

Yellowhead Hwy

16 to Edmonton

Edson

Hinton

47

MT
ROBSON

16

Jasper

40

PROV
PARK

JASPER
NATIONAL
PARK

93

Tonquin

Fryatt

Clemenceau

Columbia Icefield

Icefields Parkway

Rocky Mountain
House

David Thompson Hwy

11

Red
Deer

Sasketchewan
River Crossing

BANFF
NATIONAL
PARK

93

Field

Lake Louise

2

Calgary

Castle Junction

1

Golden

Trans-Canada Hwy

YOHO
NATIONAL
PARK

Banff

1A

1

Vancouver

Revelstoke

93

KOOTENAY
NATIONAL
PARK

KANANASKIS
COUNTRY

Radium

ASSINIBOINE
PROV
PARK

40

High
River

N

95

ALTA
B.C.

AREA
MAP

Cranbrook

3

Pincher
Creek

6

CANADA

USA

3

93

Waterton

MOUNT ASSINIBOINE PROVINCIAL PARK

Mt. Assiniboine	3618 m	N Ridge (normal)	II 5.5	p. 26
		N Face	II 5.5	p. 26
		E Face	V 5.9 A2	p. 28
		E Buttress	IV 5.7	p. 28
Sunburst Peak	2820 m	NE Face/Ridge	II 5.5	p. 30

Mount Assiniboine Provincial Park is a small park surrounding Mt. Assiniboine. There are quite a number of other mountains within the Park boundary, but Assiniboine is the centrepiece and the main attraction to climbers.

The area is a very popular spot with climbers, backpackers and tourists alike, since the locale is extremely beautiful with many lakes and alpine meadows. Even if you don't end up climbing the mountain, for whatever reason, you'll enjoy just being there.

Access The Park cannot be accessed by motor vehicle. The usual methods of approach to Lake Magog at the base of the mountain are by helicopter, by mountain bike or on foot from the Spray Lakes Road via Bryant Creek. The helicopter is very quick and comfortable but costs money, whereas the trail is about a 20 km hike. A popular thing to do is have all your gear flown in via helicopter and then have a leisurely walk or ride into Lake Magog. Helicopters are only allowed to land at Assiniboine Lodge on certain days of the week. For schedule information contact either Canmore Helicopters or Canadian Helicopters in Canmore.

If walking or biking, drive the Spray Lakes Road from Canmore to a junction after 38 km signed Mount Engadine Lodge and Mt. Shark. (A few kilometres before the turn off you'll have passed a small tarn called Buller Pond on the west side of the road. From here you will be able to see the east side of Assiniboine and check out conditions on the mountain.) Turn right at the junction and follow the road to its end at the Mt. Shark parking lot. You'll pass a heli-pad on the left about 2 km before the parking lot. From the trailhead, follow the signed trail past Karst Spring and Watridge Lake to the Spray River bridge, then turn right to reach the Bryant Creek trail at the Trail Centre junction. Head up Bryant Creek past Bryant Creek Shelter and the Bryant Creek Warden Cabin to Assiniboine Pass and Lake Magog. At this point Mt. Assiniboine should be self-evident! 6 hours on foot — 3 hours by bike.

Facilities The nearest town is Canmore. For other amenities within Kananaskis Country look at the information in the Kananaskis Country introduction. For information about Mount Assiniboine Provincial Park you should contact East Kootenay District office in Wasa, B.C. A warden is stationed at the Lake Magog Warden Cabin from June 25 to mid-October and from December 15 to April 15. Once you are in the park, inquiries can be directed to the resident warden.

For accommodation in the provincial park itself, there are several overnight possibilities of varying degrees of comfort and cost at Lake Magog: Assiniboine Lodge, the Naiset Cabins, or several campgrounds. The Lodge is privately owned and is the expensive place to stay.

The Naiset Cabins, on the other hand, are similar to the ACC mountain huts and much cheaper than the Lodge. During the summer months the cabins are filled on a first come, first served basis. However, reservations are required between December 1st and May 31st. Contact B.C. Provincial Parks for further information. There are also a number of campgrounds on the west side of Lake Magog. Most climbers will choose to stay at the R.C. Hind Hut immediately below the N face of Mt. Assiniboine, 2 to 3 hours beyond the north end of Lake Magog. There is no booking required — first-come, first served.

Naiset Cabins

Map *82 J/13 Mount Assiniboine*
Location Above east end of Lake Magog on bench. GR 973402
Reservations First come, first served in summer. Booking required Dec 1 - May 31. Contact B.C. Provincial Parks
Capacity 28
Facilities Wood stoves, woodpile, axe
Water Magog Creek nearby

If you do not complete the walk-in in one day, there are two campgrounds and a hut in Bryant Creek. The campgrounds are located by the Warden Cabin and just before the junction with the Allenby Pass trail.

Bryant Creek Shelter

Map *82 J/13 Mount Assiniboine*
Location 600 m south-east of the Warden Cabin in the far corner of a meadow on the west side of the trail. GR 946373
Reservations Hut permit required from Canadian Park Service, Banff
Capacity 18
Facilities Wood stoves, woodpile, axe
Water Bryant Creek nearby

Officialese Unlike the National Parks, backcountry permits are not required within Mount Assiniboine Provincial Park. However, if you stay at the Naiset cabins or a campground there is an overnight fee, payable to the warden at Lake Magog — so take your wallet. A point about permits to bear in mind: on the approach up Bryant Creek you are in Banff National Park and you'll need a backcountry permit if you plan on spending a night in the Bryant Creek Shelter.

Also remember that mountain bikes are only allowed on the approach up Bryant Creek and over Assiniboine Pass to Lake Magog; they are not allowed on any of the other trails.

Helicopter access to Assiniboine Provincial Park is restricted to landing (only) at Assiniboine Lodge or Naiset Cabins on three days of the week, Wednesday, Friday and Sunday. On long weekends, flights are also allowed on Monday. Flights are limited to between 1100 and 1700 hours only.

In Emergency contact the warden at Lake Magog.

Mt. Assiniboine and approach route to R.C. Hind Hut (h)

Mount Assiniboine 3618 m

Mount Assiniboine is a most striking mountain with a certain resemblance to the more famous Matterhorn in Switzerland. Not surprisingly it is often referred to as the Matterhorn of the Rockies. However, it has one distinct advantage over the Matterhorn — you don't usually end up sharing the summit with 60 other people! Nevertheless, it is a popular summit by Rockies standards and it isn't uncommon to have three or four parties on the N Ridge on a summer weekend.

The R.C. Hind Hut is conveniently situated at the base of the N face and provides an excellent starting point for most routes on the mountain. *Map 82 J/ 13 Mount Assiniboine*

Access to Hut The gully in the middle of the headwall is a bad idea due to the threat of falling ice from the glacier under the NE face of Assiniboine and rockfall from the headwall itself. There have been many accidents in this gully.

The best approach is via "Gmoser's Highway", a trail that works its way through the headwall right of the gully. From the end of Lake Magog climb diagonally across talus slopes to meet the headwall well right of the central gully. Easy climbing and scrambling give access to a major ledge system that runs left across the headwall. Follow this until almost above the central gully before heading up to the snowfield above. The hut sits on top of a rock buttress about 500 m back from the headwall (GR 946373). 2-3 hours from Assiniboine Lodge.

R.C. Hind Hut

Map *82 J/13 Mount Assiniboine*
Location Above Lake Magog on rock outcrop at base of east snow arete of Mt. Strom. GR 946373
Reservations First come, first served
Capacity 12 - 16
Facilities Coleman stoves, oil-fired heater, foamies, dishes & utensils
Water Snowmelt. Do not drink water from the drainage leading to the headwall

Photo: Don Beers

North Ridge (Normal Route) II 5.5   photo →

FA. W. Douglas, C. Häsler and C. Kaufmann, July 1903. FWA. D. Gardner, C. Scott and E. Grassman, December 1967.
Not the original route up the mountain (it was used as a descent route by the first ascent party) but the most common ascent and descent route used today. A classic high mountain ridge. Mostly a scramble up boulder-covered bedrock with "red" and "grey" rock bands offering short sections of climbing interest. Very straightforward in dry conditions but much more difficult under snow cover. The route has been done up and down from the hut in 4 hours, but 6-7 hours is probably more usual. Snow cover could substantially lengthen your day.

From the hut gain the slopes at the base of the N Ridge and follow the ridge line up to the "red band". Break through this on the north side of the ridge and continue easily up the ridge to the "grey band" which is also bypassed to the right (5.5). Continue up the ridge to a small forepeak from which the summit is gained along a short section of usually corniced ridge.

Descent is via the same route. The two rock bands have rappel stations but can also be downclimbed without too much trouble. Beware of rolling rocks down on parties below.

North Face II 5.5   photo →

FA. Y. Chouinard, J. Faint and C. Jones, July 1967. FWA. R. Jotterand, 1977.
This is not the typically difficult N face route common to many Rockies peaks. In fact, it is little different in character and difficulty to the N Ridge route. Putting it a little more in perspective, Raymond Jotterand soloed the route in 3 hours in the winter of 1977!

From the hut go across the glacier towards the col between Assiniboine and Strom and then contour around to the prominent couloir in the middle of the base of the N face. Climb the wide couloir to its top (or climb rocks on its left side — much safer), then continue straight up through the "red" and "grey" bands to the N ridge, following the easiest line (at most 5.5). Follow the N Ridge to the summit.

Descend the Normal Route. 4-8 hours round trip.

Mt. Assiniboine from the Bob Hind Hut:
1. North Ridge (normal) 2. North Face
r. Red Band g. Grey Band

Photo: Leon Kubbernus

East Face, Cheesmond/Dick V 5.9 A2   photo →

FA. D. Cheesmond and T. Dick, September 1982. The hard route of the mountain and likely to be a Rockies grand-cours route. However, it is unrepeated as of September 1990. A member of the infamous "5.9 A2" class of alpine climbs, this route is subject to some intense rockfall and cold temperatures would, therefore, seem to be a prerequisite for an ascent. Also bear in mind that the first ascent team climbed two ice pitches that may not exist during the majority of the season. It is not known whether these can be bypassed on rock in the event that they are not there. Spring or Fall are likely the best times for an attempt. Two bivis were required on the first ascent.

Approach from the hut by traversing the N glacier below the N ridge and the triangular NE face of the mountain to the col between Mt. Assiniboine and Mt. Magog. From this point, climb or rappel down to the slope below the E face. Cross this in a downward traverse to the depression in the centre of the face. Start here, below the prominent gully system that leads through the lower bands.

Climb through the complex 'schrund and up the gully to where it opens out. Continue almost straight up, following the easiest line to the base of a 50 m rock band. The first ascent party bivied here. Two ice pitches (IV) lead to the base of the "grey band". To avoid the blank rock straight above, climb two pitches up a left-slanting gully/ramp and then traverse back right along an awkward ledge system for two pitches until below the lowest point in the wall above. You are directly below the upper couloir at this point.

The next bit is the crux. Climb a steep pitch on small incut holds and with the odd aid move (5.9 A2) to gain the upper couloir. Continue up the couloir past some short steep sections to the summit. The cornice at the top can be quite large. The first ascent party bivied on a rib to the right of the upper couloir.

Descend the Normal Route.

East Buttress IV 5.7   photo →

FA. B. Davidson and A. Simpson, September 1969. The first line on this side of the mountain and in its day the hardest route on the peak. It is likely that the route hasn't been repeated even though the climbing isn't too hard. The objective hazard is low, unlike the Cheesmond/Dick route, but access is a little longer. The first ascent party bivied once, though with an early start this shouldn't be necessary.

The original approach to this route was from Lake Gloria. However, the glacier is quite a mess and the quickest and safest approach is from the Hind Hut via the approach to the E Face route.

Keep contouring around the glacier below the E face until at the base of the E buttress.

From the base of the prominent buttress follow the easiest line upwards, typically left of the rib. The climbing is steepest in the middle section (5.7) but soon eases off again to scrambling.

Descend the Normal Route.

Mt. Assiniboine: 1. E Face
2. E Buttress (upper part)

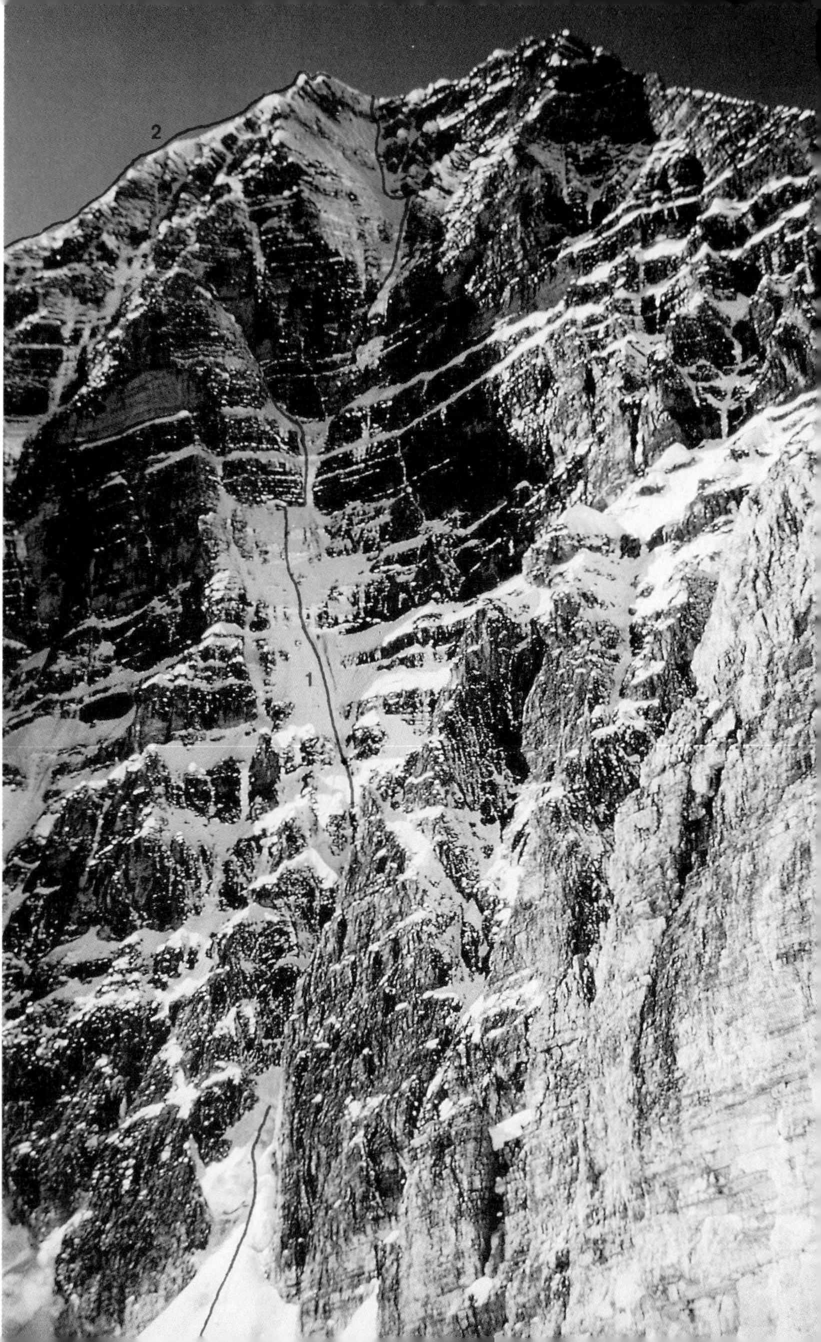

Photo: Dave Cheesmond Collection

Sunburst Peak 2820 m

Sunburst Peak is a subsidiary rock peak overlooking Sunburst Lake. It is actually the northern end of the ridge that extends from the col between Assiniboine and Strom, and then over Wedgewood. Few parties will come to Assiniboine to climb this route. However, it is included as either an alternative climb if you have made it all the way in to Lake Magog to discover that your choice of route on Assiniboine is out of condition or as a fun route to do before you leave the area. *Map 82 J/13 Mount Assiniboine*

North-East Face/Ridge II 5.5

FA. F. Dopf and H. Gmoser, August 1953. This is a short route though the face it climbs is quite impressive. Being quartzite, the rock is generally very good, giving excellent protection and solid belays. The climbing is typically 5.2 - 5.4. Numerous variations are possible, particularly at the bottom and top of the route.

From Lake Magog follow the pleasant trail to Sunburst Lake. The route starts up a crack 50 m to the left of the lowest point of the face overlooking Sunburst Lake. Follow the crack system for about 100 m, then continue over a rotten overhang and around a rib to a good belay on a small ledge.

Climb straight up to a narrow ledge which is followed to the right for 10 m. Continue straight up to the "black band", then traverse right to gain the NE ridge which is followed to a wide talus-covered terrace that crosses the ridge. 10 m to the right is a wide chimney that leads to a narrow chimney.

At the top of the narrow chimney traverse around to the left and move up to a grey slab. Cross the slab to the left and finish up a couloir that cuts between the N and NE faces. At most 5 hours.

To **descend**, scramble down the SE face.

Photo: Glen Boles

KANANASKIS COUNTRY

Mt. Fable	2702 m	S Ridge	II 5.4	p. 34
		SE Ridge	II 5.5	p. 34
Mt. Lorette	2487 m	S Ridge	II 5.6	p. 36
Mt. Kidd	2958 m	NE Buttress	III 5.7	p. 38
Mt. Blane	2993 m	NW Ridge	II 5.6	p. 40
Mt. Brock	2902 m	SE Pillar of W Rib	II 5.6	p. 42
Mt. Nestor	2970 m	E Ridge	II 5.5	p. 43
Mt. Lougheed	3125 m	Traverse	III 5.5	p. 44
Mt. Birdwood	3097 m	SSE (Lizzie's) Ridge	II 5.7	p. 46
Mt. Sir Douglas	3406 m	NW Face	III	p. 48
		NW Face Direct	IV	p. 50
		E Ridge	III 5.6	p. 50
		SE Face	IV 5.6/7	p. 50
Mt. Sarrail	3174 m	NE Buttress	III 5.10a	p. 52
Mt. Joffre	3449 m	N Face/NE Ridge	III	p. 54

Kananaskis Country Provincial Recreational Area is the first mountain area you come to when driving west along the Trans-Canada Highway from Calgary. It is some people's false impression that the mountains in this region of the Rockies are smaller than the mountains elsewhere. Granted, many of the faces do not have the relief gain or the grandeur of the mountains along the Icefields Parkway. But many of K Country's peaks are over 3,000 metres in height and some, like Sir Douglas or Lougheed, are just as impressive as their counterparts further north.

The routes are among the shortest in the book, the majority having the advantage of short approaches from a highway. Furthermore, when weather or snow conditions in the mountains farther north are poor, the weather in the Kananaskis is often better.

The mountains in the area offer predominantly alpine rock routes. Mount Joffre and Mt. Sir Douglas are the exceptions, with routes that require ice axe, crampons and other alpine climbing paraphernalia. These two peaks are also a little further from the road than the rest of the mountains described in this section and most parties will need overnight gear.

Access Kananaskis Country is usually accessed by two main routes. Highway 40 (Kananaskis Trail) branches off the Trans-Canada Highway 63 km west of Calgary and 28 km east of Canmore and heads south up the Kananaskis Valley to Kananaskis Lakes and then out of the area via Highwood Pass. The Spray Lakes Road connects Canmore to Kananaskis Lakes via the Smith-Dorrien valley. All the routes are accessed from these two highways, except for Mt. Fable which is reached from the hamlet of Exshaw on Highway 1A (Bow Valley Trail) 15 km east of Canmore.

Facilities The major townsite is Canmore, located on the Trans-Canada Highway immediately east of the entrance to Banff National Park. As in most small towns, you can find almost everything you'll need: groceries, camping supplies, motels, 24 hour gas stations, an excellent selection of restaurants and bars including a British-style pub. The one thing you won't find is climbing gear. Either pick up what you need in Calgary or go to Banff where there are two good climbing shops. If you are searching for gas and/or food at some bizarre hour of the day, the Husky gas station at Dead Man Flat 7 km east of Canmore on the Trans-Canada Highway is open 24 hours a day.

There are several other locations within Kananaskis where you can buy supplies. Exshaw on 1A Highway has a gas station with a small cafe and grocery store attached. On the east-bound lane of the Trans-Canada Highway, 2 km west of the Highway 40 junction, the Stoneys manage a gas station, restaurant and small store. On Highway 40 (Kananaskis Trail) Kananaskis Village at the base of Mt. Kidd is mostly a collection of hotels, restaurants and bars. You'll find the prices a little higher than in Canmore! However, you can purchase a limited range of groceries from the Village Centre as well as rent bikes for trips to Mt. Lorette. Farther south on the highway is Fortress Junction gas station opposite the access road for Fortress Mountain Ski Area. It's open for gas and a reasonable range of groceries all year round. At Kananaskis Lakes, a grocery store and cafe is located at Boulton Trading Post.

Canmore has numerous motels and guest houses for those who like a bit of comfort. Dead Man Flat has similar accommodation, only cheaper rates. If these forms of accommodation seem a little pricey, the ACC Clubhouse in Canmore may be more to your liking. You get all the comforts of a guest house at a more reasonable price. Enquire at the ACC offices in Banff or at the Clubhouse itself. At present, the only facility along Spray Lakes Road is Mount Engadine Lodge which offers meals, accommodation and guiding service. There is also a Youth Hostel at Ribbon Creek next door to Kananaskis Village.

Undoubtedly, many people will be interested in camping. There are numerous campgrounds and RV Parks spread throughout Kananaskis Country. Mount Kidd RV Park in the Kananaskis Valley has a snack bar, grocery store and whirlpools open to the public. All campgrounds are very popular with people from Calgary, especially on summer weekends and often get fully booked-up. Check first with the Kananaskis Country office in Canmore. General inquiries about accommodation and travel can be directed to the Alberta Tourism Information Centre in Canmore at the west end of the gas station strip.

For any other information go to one of five Kananaskis Country Information Centres: in Canmore opposite the Rose and Crown Pub, on the Trans-Canada Highway in Bow Valley Provincial Park, on Highway 40 near Barrier Lake, on the Spray Lakes Road near the Three Sisters Dam and in Peter Lougheed Provincial Park at the Kananaskis Visitor Centre. The ranger station at Ribbon Creek may also be able to provide assistance.

Officialese Kananaskis Country, which includes Peter Lougheed Provincial Park and Bow Valley Provincial park, does not require backcountry users to have backcountry permits. You can camp almost anywhere as long as you're 1 km from a road. However, there is a voluntary registration scheme in place. To register out just go to any of the ranger offices or visitor centres.

Regarding mountain biking, there are a few trails where mountain biking is restricted, namely heavy-use trails and interpretive trails. The only approach trail affected is the trail along the south shore of Upper Kananaskis Lake to Mt. Joffre.

The use of helicopters to approach routes is unlikely. However, for the record it is necessary to get permission from the Kananaskis Country office in Canmore to land a chopper within Kananaskis Country. If in any doubt phone the office for clarification.

In Emergency contact the nearest warden office or information centre or phone the Ribbon Creek Warden Office at 591-7767 (24 hours).

Rock Climbing There is lots of rock climbing in the immediate vicinity of Canmore and in Kananaskis Country as a whole. The type of climbing ranges from short, vicious sport climbs found in local canyons to more alpine-like routes on the many big limestone faces in the area. One of these, Yamnuska, is synonymous with the foundations of modern climbing in the Rockies. The climbing in the area is covered by the guides "Bow Valley Rock", "Bow Valley Update", and "Kananaskis Rock". You are referred to these books for all the information you'll need.

Mount Fable 2702 m

This is the prominent, monolithic rock peak seen to the north of Exshaw when driving along the Trans-Canada Highway or Highway 1A (Bow Valley Trail) near Lac des Arc. The south side of the peak is quite impressive, especially when viewed from the summit! *Map 82 O/3 Canmore*

South Ridge II 5.4   photo →

FA. D. Gardner, C. Locke and G. Walsh, June 1964. This a is good day out on a climb which isn't technically difficult. The rock is surprisingly good in places.

Start from Exshaw. Hike up Exshaw Creek for about an hour on a reasonable trail, then turn west into a major subsidiary valley that passes underneath the south side of the mountain. Follow this up to the base of the S ridge. A series of slabs present themselves. Pick the second to last slab and follow it on excellent water-worn limestone all the way to where the slabs end. Traverse left into an obvious gully and up to a horizontal ledge system. A 30 m diagonal crack (5.4) leads to the ridge just below the summit.

The **descent** follows the Normal Route on the mountain. Descend talus slopes to the col west of the peak, then romp down shale slopes into the approach drainage. 10-12 hours round trip.

South-East Ridge II 5.5   photo →

FA. G. Kinnear and P. Spear, June 1963 Another good day out on this peak. Though very similar in difficulty to the S Ridge, this climb is longer and thus offers a longer day on the mountain.

As for the approach to the S ridge, follow the trail up Exshaw Creek to where you turn west into the major subsidiary valley. Follow the subsidiary valley for only about 0.5 km before cutting up through timber to gain a well-defined ridge that leads up above treeline to the east side of the buttress at the base of the main ridge.

Climb the buttress, at first to the right, and then back left towards the crest of the ridge. The long continuation ridge is followed to the base of the main bulk of the mountain. In several spots the ridge is very sharp, offering exciting exposure. Stay on the ridge up to some steeper ground where a traverse onto the east (right) side of the ridge gains some slabs. Good climbing up these regains the ridge above, and eventually the summit.

Descend as for the South Ridge via the Normal Route.

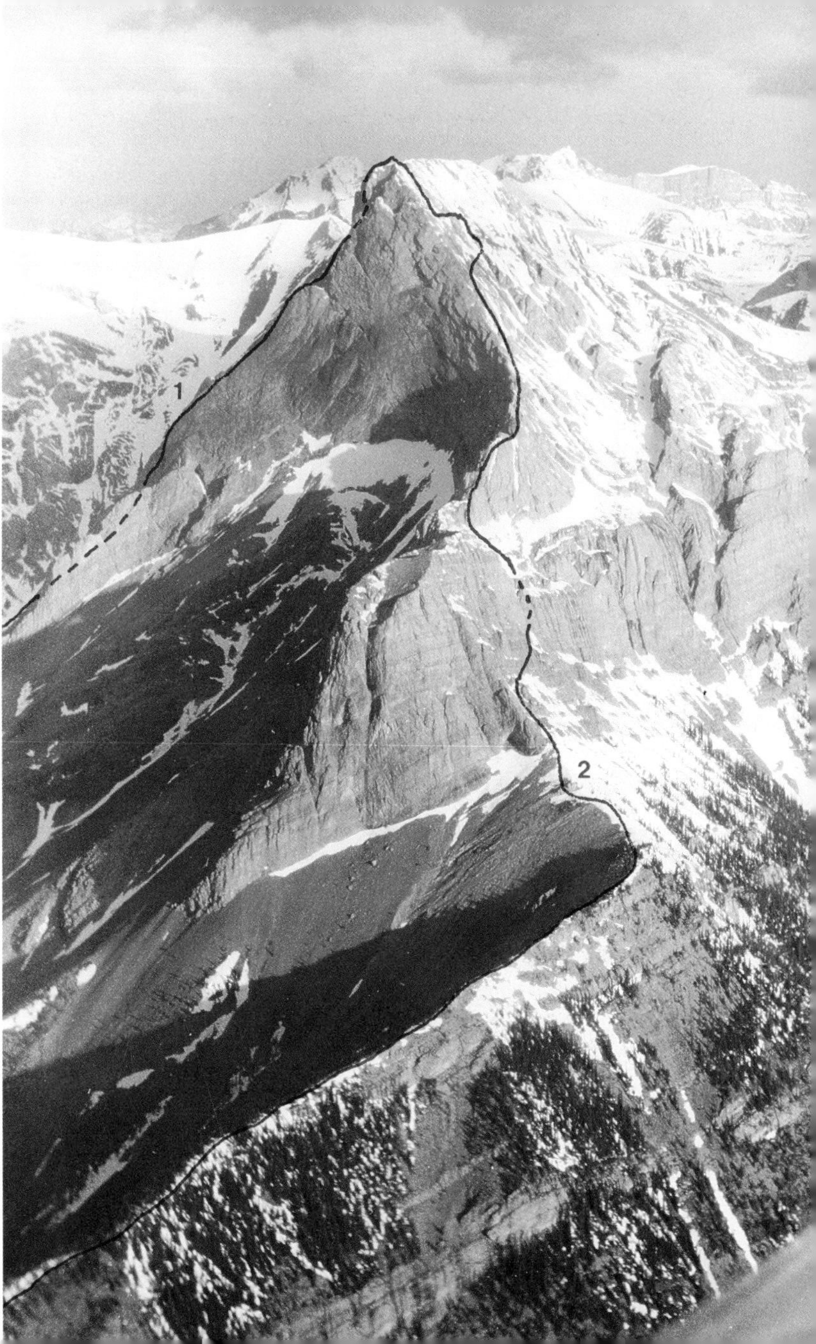

Photo: Glen Boles

Mount Lorette 2487 m

As you enter Kananaskis Country along Highway 40 (Kananaskis Trail), Mt. Lorette is the first peak of any note on the west side of the Kananaskis River. The rock peak is quite small by Rockies standards and an unlikely candidate for a recommended alpine route. However, the ease of access, the moderate route and the airy positions on the ridge make the S Ridge a very popular climb. *Map 82 J/14 Spray Lakes Reservoir*

South Ridge II 5.6   photo →

FA. R.C. Hind, B. Richardson, L. Keeling, J. Manry, J. Dodds and C. McAllister, May 1952. An excellent choice for a first rock route in the mountains. The ridge is quite narrow in many places and has quite an airy feel for such a small peak. The climbing is mostly scrambling up, over and around gendarmes of reasonable rock. The grade may seem quite high for such a route. Rest assured, the crux section is very short though a few medium-sized Friends and a few wires would come in handy. Don't take a lot of gear — there is quite a bit fixed along the route.

Park at the side of Highway 40 (Kananaskis Trail) opposite the peak and wade the Kananaskis River to its west bank. Waders or other means of keeping your toes warm and dry are very useful! The river is virtually unfordable at high water and it is then necessary to drive south to the Nakiska ski area access road, cross the bridge over the river and park at the end of the power line service road, signed as Stoney Trail. Hike or bike along Stoney trail to the base of the ridge.

From Stoney trail make your way easily through trees to grassy slopes leading up to the ridge. Flog up to the base of the rock. Gain the crest of the ridge and in general follow it all the way to the summit. At one point it is obvious you must traverse a ledge system on the east side of the ridge. Traverse about a ropelength from the ridge crest, then climb a short wall and a prominent corner (5.6) to regain the ridge.

From the summit **descend** the N ridge until it is possible to descend easy rocks and talus slopes into the prominent scree gully on the south-east side of the mountain. Follow this all the way back down to Stoney trail. About 6-8 hours round trip.

Mt. Lorette: S Ridge

Mount Kidd 2958 m

This large and bulky mountain is perhaps the most admired mountain in the Kananaskis Valley. And all by virtue of the world famous Kananaskis Country Golf Course that sits at the foot of the E face. The eastern side of the peak, a high, wide impressive rock face rising 1300 m from valley floor to summit, has as yet no recorded route. The NE Buttress route climbs the northern edge of this face and then for the adventurous, follows the ridge line all the way to the N summit. This is another route where you are going to have to carry water since there are no supplies other than the odd patch of snow once you leave the valley floor. *Map 82 J/14 Spray Lakes Reservoir*

North-East Buttress III 5.7   photo →

FA. G.W. Boles, H. Gude and B. Greenwood, June 1962. An enjoyable and straightforward rock climb to the top of the NE buttress. A basic rock rack is more than sufficient gear. A round trip to the top of the buttress can be completed comfortably in a day if you take the early descent option to Ribbon Creek. Most parties descend this way. However, for those who like to pack a lot into one day the N summit of Mount Kidd can be attained with a very early start.

Follow Highway 40 (Kananaskis Trail) south from the Trans-Canada Highway to Kananaskis Village and park in the most southerly parking lot behind the Kananaskis Inn. Head south on Terrace trail, bearing right in about 400 m onto Kovach Trail which is followed for about 2 km until you see an opportunity to strike upslope to the lookout. A trail to the lookout is planned but has not been built at the time of writing.

From the lookout amble along the grassy ridge to the base of the rock. Scramble up the ridge to the base of the first steep part which is bypassed on the left via a loose chimney. A further 50 m of scrambling brings you to the base of the second steep bit. Climb a groove to ledges below a prominent white spot. Traverse right and climb two short steep walls, then traverse back left until directly above the white spot on a grassy ledge.

Traverse up and right across the top of a slab into a scoop. Step around a pillar to easier ground. Follow the easiest line above, keeping to the right of the ridge crest to the top of the buttress. 3-5 hours from the base.

From this point either descend into Ribbon Creek via the easiest line down the west slopes or continue along the long ridge to the main summit. To do the latter, traverse mainly along the north side of the ridge past several pinnacles to the main summit block. A steep section is bypassed via some chimneys and obvious traverses to the summit ridge. 10-13 hours from the parking lot.

Descent from the summit is easily made down the large, slabby bowl to the southeast of the summit. Note: in winter this bowl is very prone to avalanche and undoubtedly a hazardous place to be. The parking lot at Galatea Creek can be reached in 2-3 hours or you can follow Terrace trail for 9 km back to Kananaskis Village.

Photo: Gillian Daffern

W

Mt. Kidd: NE Buttress   a. the "white spot"

Mount Blane 2993 m

This peak and its neighbour Mt. Brock are members of the Opal Range, a group of mountains characterized by rock peaks of good quality limestone (by Rockies standards) and very easy access from Highway 40 (Kananaskis Trail). Mt. Blane has an undeserved reputation for "horrible" and "horrendous" rock, no doubt due to three incidents involving falling rock early in its climbing history. Don't let any of the history or rumors deter you from climbing the mountain — the rock is no worse than most Rockies peaks and the mountain has had a larger number of ascents than some people care to think. *Map 82 J/11 Kananaskis Lakes*

North-West Ridge II 5.6   photo →

FA. G. Prinz, H. Jungnitch and L. Schmidt, 1962. A good, moderate ridge climb. The views from the summit of the Kananaskis Valley and Mts. Joffre, King George, Sir Douglas and Assiniboine are excellent.

Follow Highway 40 (Kananaskis Trail) south from the Trans-Canada Highway for 50 km to Kananaskis Lakes Trail. A few metres before the junction turn left into the King Creek picnic area. The approach to Mount Blane follows an interpretive trail through the narrow canyon of King Creek to a fork. Take the left (north) fork and follow the creek bed until below the third major gully on the east slope. Ascend the gully via grassy slopes until forced into the gully bed. Continue up rocks and talus until a final loose slope leads to the Brock-Blane col. 2-3 hours.

From the col scramble up the NW ridge, avoiding the first two steps by circling around to the right (west) side. After about 150-200 m of easy scrambling the ridge steepens, rising in three steps for several ropelengths. The ridge then narrows and presents some exposed climbing on slowly deteriorating rock. Stay on the ridge as much as possible, passing one minor step to the left (east). The summit ridge is quickly reached and presents no further problems. 2 hours from the col.

Descend the same route. 3-5 hours.

Mt. Blane: NW Ridge

Photo: Glen Boles

Mount Brock 2902 m

Mount Brock is immediately north of Mt. Blane. Like the majority of peaks in the Opal Range, the rock is by and large good. The route that is described has received very little attention, which is surprising given the short approach, an excellent line on reasonable rock leading directly to a summit and the short descent back to the highway. Furthermore, since the Opal Range is one of the last high ranges before the foothills begin, the weather here is often suitable for climbing when the rest of the Kananaskis Country peaks are being deluged. *Map 82 J/11 Kananaskis Lakes*

South-East Pillar of the West Rib II 5.6

FA. M. Toft and R. Mitchell, July 1976. An aesthetic line on generally good rock. It might be combined with an ascent of Blane to make for a very full day out. Quite a challenge!

As for Mount Blane. Follow King Creek up its north fork past five gully systems until below a prominent drainage that leads up to the base of the pillar. 3-4 hours.

Climb a prominent corner for two pitches (5.6) to a large ledge system that runs across the pillar. Follow this left-ward to the westernmost crest of the pillar. Continue up the ridge for four pitches (5.4 to 5.6) to easier ground. 3rd class climbing with the occasional steep bit leads to the W summit. Traverse the ridge to the main summit. 3-6 hours from base of climb.

Descend the S ridge to the Brock-Blane col (easy downclimbing), then plunge down the gully into King Creek.

Mt. Brock: SE Pillar of W Rib

Photo: Tony Daffern

Mount Nestor 2970 m

Mount Nestor is the southern peak of the Goat Range which forms a continuous ridge on the west side of Spray Lakes Reservoir. With its aesthetic E ridge, it is the most impressive peak of the group. *Map 82 J/14 Spray Lakes Reservoir*

East Ridge II 5.5

FA. M. Toft and J. Martin, 1975. Mostly a scramble with a short-lived crux. This summit affords excellent views of Mt. Assiniboine and makes for a pleasant day out on a straightforward rock route. A good route for a very late start after a night out in the Canmore bars!

Approach along the Spray Lakes Road from Canmore to the Three Sisters dam at the north end of Spray Lakes Reservoir. Cross the dam on a good dirt road and follow it past Spray Lakes West campsite until below the E face of Mt. Nestor.

Park at the side of the road below a prominent waterfall in the rock band 500 m above the road. About 100 m of thin bush leads to meadows which are ascended directly to the waterfall. Avoid the waterfall by scrambling up to the right and then climb back left over a rib to access the creek bed above the falls. Follow this creek to a steep meadow leading up and right to a col at the base of the E ridge. The ridge is followed in its entirety to the top.

Though the route is mostly scrambling up low-angled rock, there is an "interesting bit" (5.5) a few hundred feet from the summit where you traverse left underneath a roof.

To **descend** follow the summit ridge south, then race down talus slopes to meadows and back to the road approximately 1 km south of where your car is parked.

Photo: Tony Daffern   *a. "interesting bit"*

The 4 peaks of Mt. Lougheed from the north.   a. 4th peak   b. 3rd peak

Mount Lougheed   3125 m

At Dead Man Flat on the Trans-Canada Highway the most daunting skyline is that to the south of Mt. Lougheed. The whole of the NE face is an impressive rock wall, sadly composed of mostly rotten rock. Although this face has been recently climbed the first ascent team do not recommend it!

The mountain, which consists of four summits, was first named Wind Mountain by the botanist Eugene Bourgeau in 1858. In 1928 the name was changed to Mt. Lougheed in honour of Sir James Lougheed, a Calgary lawyer in practise with future Prime Minister R.B. Bennet. The name Wind Mountain is now applied to a subsidiary summit east of the fourth peak of Lougheed.

To the north of the NW summit is an impressive rock wall rising up from Wind Creek Valley. This is the Windtower, home of three long rock routes. *Map 82 J/14 Spray Lakes Reservoir*

c. main summit   d. NW summit   e. Windtower-Lougheed col

Traverse III 5.5

FA. (South-North) D. Gardner and N. Liske, July 1967. One of the most accessible traverses in the Rockies, offering excellent views of both the Spray Lakes Reservoir and the Bow Valley. The described route has been completed in a long day but most parties take a more leisurely two days. A winter traverse has yet to be completed.

From Canmore follow the Spray Lakes Road 4.8 km past the Spray District Office to Spurling Creek and park. Walk up the west bank of a dry creek bed a short distance (50 m) west of Spurling Creek on an indistinct trail. The trail soon improves, climbing up out of the creek and eventually leading to West Wind Pass. From the pass take the trail across the talus slopes of the west shoulder of Windtower to the Windtower-Lougheed col.

Continue up shale talus to the base of the rock bands on the NW peak of Lougheed. Start on the right side of the ridge and then work your way back to the ridge which is followed to the NW summit (5.5). Traverse left or right to avoid difficulties.

Descend easy talus to the first col and continue up the N ridge of the main peak via scrambling and a little climbing to its summit. Carry on down the S ridge over more easy talus to the second col in a few minutes! Wallow up more talus to the third peak. Descend the S ridge to a third col, staying close to the ridge and traversing sloping slabs to the base of the SE summit, the fourth and highest peak on the traverse.

From the col climb on the NW side of the ridge to meet the SW ridge about 50 m from the summit.

Descend the SW ridge and its lower slopes into the upper reaches of North Ribbon Creek. Follow the creek down on a reasonable trail to the main Ribbon Creek trail which leads to Ribbon Creek parking lot and Highway 40 (Kananaskis Trail). It may also be possible to descend into the drainage under the N face of Mt. Sparrowhawk and return to the Spray Lakes Road, but this is unconfirmed.

Mount Birdwood 3097 m

From the Spray Lakes Road Mt. Birdwood does not look particularly different from many of the surrounding mountains. However, seen from the south-west it appears a monolithic peak, a wedge of rock rising between Burstall Creek and Commonwealth Creek. The south side of the peak has several ribs, one of which, Lizzie's Ridge, offers the most continuous climbing on the best rock on the peak. The W face is made up of a series of large slabby faces that will undoubtedly be investigated by slab climbing fiends who frequent the nearby Burstall Slabs. *Map 82 J/14 Spray Lakes Reservoir*

South-South-East (Lizzie's) Ridge II 5.7　　　　photo →

FA. B. Deming, M. Brown, T. Colwell, D. Cobb, I. Carruthers, B. Seyferth and B. Schiesser, July 1972. This route takes the easternmost (right) of two prominent ridges on the south end of the mountain. Expect good climbing on excellent rock and sound belays. A good route for the grade and one of the best routes of its type in Kananaskis Country.

Approach Mt. Birdwood from the Burstall Pass parking lot on the Spray Lakes Road, 45 km from downtown Canmore. Cross the Mud Lake dam and hike along the signed trail (logging road) for Burstall Pass and the Robertson Glacier. The logging road degenerates into a narrow trail leading down to gravel flats. Cross the flats via the signed trail and switchback up the timbered headwall into Burstall Meadows below Burstall Pass. Leave the trail and wallow up talus to the base of the ridge.

Follow the ridge with occasional detours left and right for 300 m to a steeper 60 m section. At the top of this bit is a 6 m wall which is ascended to the right (5.7). Another 150 m of ridge lead to flatter ground and a junction with the SE face of the mountain. Follow a series of gullies and short ridges, working at first to the right (east) and then up to the summit.

To **descend**, start in a narrow gully in the SW face. This has a bit of tricky downclimbing (about 5.4). At the base of the gully work down some slabs and across a short ridge to the top of a little buttress. Continue down and left (south), taking the easiest line. A final pitch of moderate downclimbing gains the talus. Wander over to the left (south) and down into Burstall Meadows where you can pick up the trail.

Mt. Birdwood: 1. Lizzie's Ridge   2. descent   s. 60 m steep section   47

Mount Sir Douglas 3406 m

This mountain is the highest member of the British Military Group and presents an impressive sight from Spray Lakes Road and its neighbouring peaks; the E ridge leading from the col between the Haig and Robertson Glaciers directly to the summit is particularly aesthetic. The view from the top across the Haig Icefield towards Joffre is quite breathtaking.

Several routes are described, each different in character so there is likely something to suit most tastes. The NW Face route is a moderate snow/ice climb to the top of a high mountain whereas the SE face offers something a little more challenging, particularly in winter. Throw in the short approaches and it is easy to explain the relative popularity of the peak with a large number of climbers.

Access for all routes As for Mt. Birdwood to the gravel flats below Burstall Pass. For the E Ridge and SE Face routes follow the faint trail up the south fork of Burstall Creek to the Robertson Glacier which is climbed to the Haig-Robertson col (very straightforward but take crampons and ice axe). For the N face routes cross the flats via the signed trail and switchback up the timbered headwall into Burstall Meadows. Leave the Burstall Pass Trail where it turns right to climb up to Burstall Pass, and continue up the draw to South Burstall Pass (GR 155227). Most parties bivi near the pass. *Map 82 J/11 Kananaskis Lakes, (82 J/14 Spray Lakes Reservoir for approach)*

North-West Face III   photo →

FA. G. Boles, D. Forest and G. Scruggs, July 1971. FWA. D. Gardner, Winter 1987. In this day and age of following the "direct" line this route tends to play second fiddle to the Toft/Reasoner Direct route. However, it is a good route in itself and if the Direct is out of shape (rockfall etc.), it provides an excellent alternative up the face. The first winter ascent of the peak was via this route — an amazing solo tour-de-force by Don Gardner, completed in only 11 hours round trip!

From South Burstall Pass drop down into the Palliser drainage and contour around a spur of the NE ridge of Sir Douglas and down onto the moraines below the twin glaciers on the north side of the mountain. Climb the west edge of the easternmost (left) glacier to below a ramp that leads to a prominent couloir

ascending the west (right) side of the face directly to the summit (the line of the Direct). Follow the ramp to the prominent couloir but continue along a continuation of the ramp to the NE ridge. Take the ridge to the east summit. 5-7 hours from South Burstall Pass.

Descent is either back down the way you came or over the west summit and down the loose W ridge. From the top of the W ridge, descend a short couloir, then traverse left to the top of a large couloir that splits the SW face. Down climb the couloir, then traverse right to gain a prominent col on the W ridge. Drop down onto the W glacier on the north side of the mountain. Follow it down the moraines, then go around the spur of the NE ridge and climb back up to South Burstall Pass. 5-7 hours.

Photo: courtesy Kananaskis Country

Mt. Sir Douglas: 1. NW Face 2. Direct finish 3. part of descent n. notch on W Ridge

North-West Face Direct IV   photo p. 49

FA. M. Toft and M. Reasoner, August 1973. This route is somewhat harder than the original route and when icy it presents a sustained climb. Falling rock can be a problem but the original route offers an alternate way to the summit if the need arises. A straightforward couloir with modern alpine gear.

Follow the NW Face route to the prominent couloir and then climb the couloir directly to the summit. Expect ice up to 55°.

Descent is the same as the standard NW Face route. 9-14 hours round trip from South Burstall Pass.

East Ridge III 5.6   photo p. 49 & →

FA. A. Cole, D. Lampard and C. Locke, June 1970. A great line. The positions on the ridge are magnificent. The rock is pretty rank on the first few pitches but quickly improves to reasonable, and finally excellent quality.

From the Haig-Robertson col follow the easy lower ridge to the base of the rock. Start up a very loose, foul gully and escape as soon as possible to more pleasant ground on the left. Alternatively,

start up a crack to the left of the ridge and avoid the gully completely — probably a good thing for your continued good health! Continue up the ridge to a large step just below the NE ridge. Take a prominent crack (5.6) up the step onto the NE ridge and the summit. 3-5 hours from the col.

Descend the W ridge or down climb and rappel the E ridge.

South-East Face IV 5.6/7   photo →

FA. J. Elzinga and D. Renshaw, July 1977. This popular route takes the prominent couloir and ramp system on the south side of the peak. It has probably been attempted more times in winter than any other route in the book yet it is still awaiting a winter ascent! Rockfall can be a problem in the lower couloir so cold conditions are an asset.

From the Haig-Robertson col follow the lower, easy part of the E Ridge route a little way, then contour around onto the slopes below the couloir in the SE face. Winter climbers BEWARE: the slopes below the E ridge are prone to avalanche.

Once below the couloir, start up it and keep going until you reach the highest ramp system leading up to the right. At this point the couloir turns slightly left just below where it peters out. If you pick an earlier ramp you'll make things much harder for yourself — rest assured, a few people have done it. Follow the ramp for about three ropelengths to near its end. A prominent chimney/groove then leads straight up in three ropelengths to the summit (5.6). 5-8 hours round trip from the col.

Most parties **descend** the route since there is much fixed gear.

Mt. Sir Douglas: 1. SE Face   2. E Ridge

Photo: Glen Boles

Mount Sarrail 3174 m

The rock wall formed by Mt. Sarrail and its neighbour, Mt. Foch, gives a very impressive backdrop to the southern end of Upper Kananaskis Lake. The NE Buttress of Mt. Sarrail forms the most distinguishing feature of this rock wall, rising almost directly from Rawson Lake to the summit. Take water with you since there are no creeks between Rawson Lake and the Aster Lake trail on the descent. *Map 82 J/11 Kananaskis Lakes*

North-East Buttress III 5.10a   photo →

FA. S. Dougherty and J. Martin, August 1986. A surprisingly big route at 800 m that takes the prominent buttress on Sarrail facing towards Upper Kananaskis Lake. Typically the rock is reasonable by alpine standards though the crux area is a little loose. No need for big boots or ice axe — just rock shoes and a pair of light boots for the hike in and out. Expect a 12 hour day.

The trailhead is the parking lot at Upper Kananaskis Lake near the end of the Kananaskis Lakes Trail. From the parking lot follow the signed trail around the south shore of the lake. Cross one major creek (Sarrail Creek), then turn left onto the signed trail to Rawson Lake, a popular fishing spot at the foot of Mt. Sarrail.

From the far left end of the lake work your way up slopes towards the col at the base of the NE buttress, then scramble up rocks to the right of the col to gain grassy slopes on the buttress itself. 2 hours.

Amble pleasantly up grass and through a few rock bands until things get sufficiently interesting to warrant a rope. Two pitches up the crest of the buttress and two in shallow corners to the left lead to a large ledge system below a high, steep pillar. Traverse left along the ledge until it is possible to easily gain low-angled rock on the left side of the pillar.

Scramble straight up for about 100 m to a sharp ridge at the base of the upper headwall (bolt belay). Cross a small gully on the right and climb up rock to its right to an alcove below a roof. Continue up and left and then up a shallow groove to a roof where a traverse right (5.9) leads to another alcove belay. Go straight up to a talus-covered ledge with big blocks. Pass the blocks, taking care not to disturb them, and scramble up a low-angled corner to below a bulging wall (bolt belay).

Climb up and right for a few metres, then move up to a pedestal (bolt). A few steep moves (5.10a) lead to easier ground. 150 m of easier climbing up good rock tops out on the summit ridge. 7-9 hours from the col.

Descend easy slopes and glacier of the NW face to the Aster Lake trail. Follow the trail down past Hidden Lake back to the Upper Kananaskis Lake Trail and your car. 4 hours from the summit.

Photo: Gillean Daffern

Mt. Sarrail: NE Buttress   s. large ledge system

53

Mount Joffre 3449 m

Mount Joffre is the highest peak between the 49th parallel and Mt. Assiniboine 50 km to the north. It sits head and shoulders above the neighboring peaks, all members of the French Military Group of mountains, each named after high ranking French army officers from World War I. It is sufficiently high to retain a significant snow cover all year round. Its height, the pleasant walk-in to Aster Lake and the moderate snow/ice climbing one has to do to reach the summit make it a popular climb in the summer months. It is also climbed quite frequently in the winter months despite avalanche hazard on the approach. *Map 82 J/11 Kananaskis Lakes*

North Face/North-East Ridge (Normal Route) III   photo →

FA. J.W.A. Hickson and E. Feuz Jr, August 1919. FWA. E. Grassman, J. Jones and A. Simpson, March 1970. The original ascent party climbed the face to join the NE ridge at a col and the actual face was first climbed during the winter ascent in 1970. Technically there is little difference between the two routes. Usually a two-day outing from the car and back but occasionally a determined team does the round trip in a day.

The trailhead is the parking lot at Upper Kananaskis Lake near the end of Kananaskis Lakes Trail. Follow the signed trail around the south shore of the lake as far as Hidden Lake. Go around Hidden Lake on the east side and follow a trail up through trees to the talus slopes above. The trail works its way diagonally across these slopes and up through a rock band to gain the top of the headwall well to the east of Fossil Falls, the prominent waterfall down the headwall. In winter, these slopes are very prone to avalanche, particularly early in the season. Be wary! Follow the trail alongside Aster Creek to Aster Lake. Most parties bivi here. 3-5 hours.

From the lake head west and then south around the NNW spur of Mt. Marlborough, cross the gravel flats and hike up slopes to gain the snout of the Mangin Glacier which descends from the N face of Joffre. Continue up the glacier to the 'schrund. In winter it is possible to ski to this point. Once below the face take your pick of the following two lines. The original route bears left across the glacier to climb an obvious gully through the rock wall forming the north side of the NE ridge. After gaining the saddle on the NE ridge, continue without further difficulty to the summit. 4-6 hours from Aster Lake.

Alternatively, the N face can be climbed almost anywhere. Typically it is climbed either directly or on the right-hand side near the NW ridge.

The easiest **descent** is by the original NE Ridge route.

Photo: Glen Boles

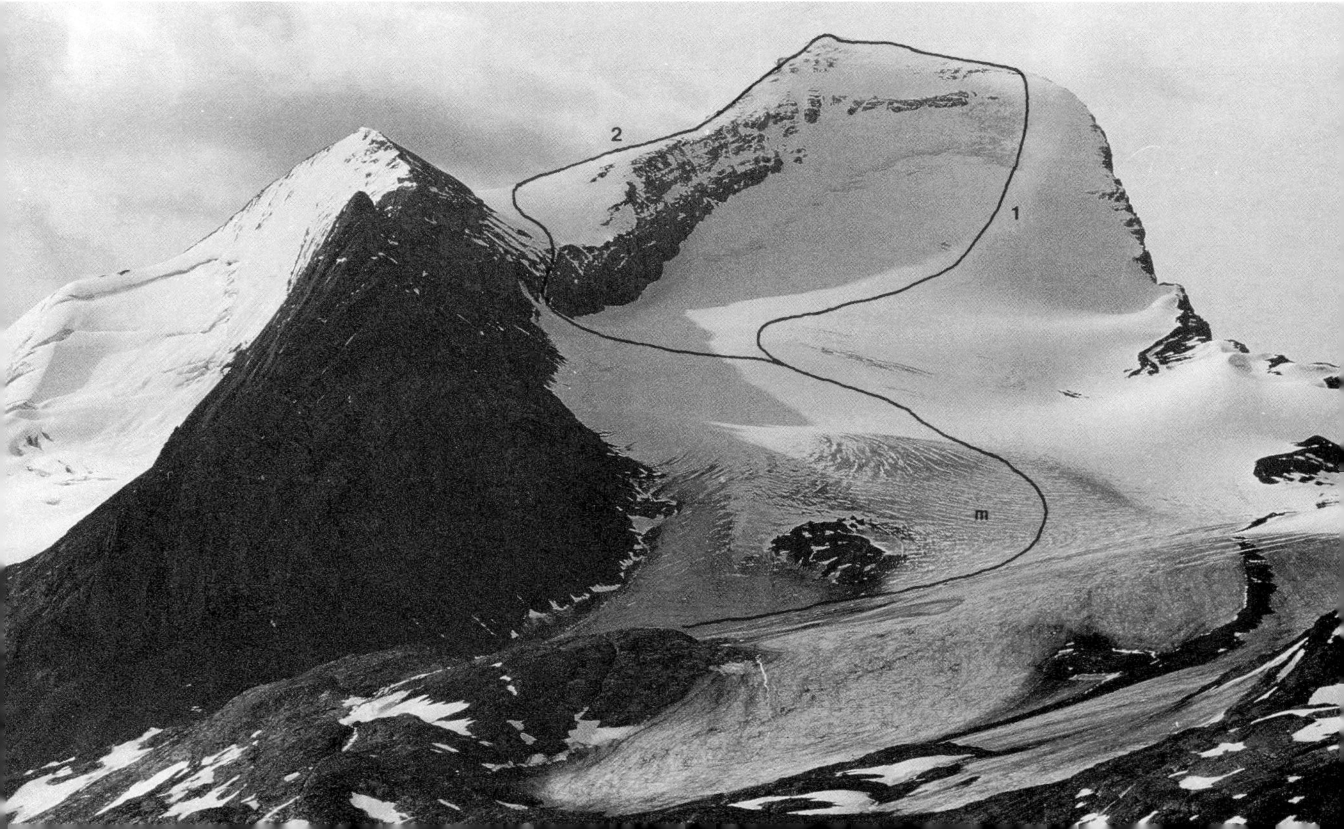

BANFF AREA

Mt. Edith	2554 m	S Ridge of S Peak	II 5.4	p. 58
		E Face of Central Peak	III 5.10b	p. 60
		Greenwood/Boles	III 5.8	p. 60
		The Kafir Strikes Back	III 5.10c	p. 62
Mt. Louis	2682 m	Kain Route (normal)	III 5.6/7	p. 64
		Homage to the Spider	III 5.8	p. 66
		Gmoser Route	III 5.8	p. 66
		Kor/Fuller	III 5.10d	p. 68
		Greenwood/MacKay	III 5.7	p. 68
The Finger	2545 m	Board Route	II 5.5	p. 70
Castle Mountain	2766 m	Bass Buttress	II 5.6	p. 73
		Brewer Buttress	II 5.6	p. 74
		Ultra-Brewers	III 5.9	p. 74
		Eisenhower Tower	II 5.4	p. 76
Storm Mountain	3161 m	E Ridge	III 5.6	p. 78
		NE Face	V 5.9 A3	p. 78
Stanley Peak	3155 m	N Face - Kahl Route	III	p. 80
		NE Face - Y Couloir	III	p. 80
Rockwall	3045 m	Grassman/Spohr	IV 5.7 A1	p. 82

This is the southernmost of four areas of climbing within the boundaries of Banff National Park. The climbing is very similar to that in Kananaskis Country: short approaches, good limestone (by Rockies standards) and mostly rock routes. For those folks on an alpine climbing trip, the rock routes in this area provide excellent days out when either the weather on the bigger peaks craps out or you feel like a break from the stress of alpine climbing. For locals, these routes offer alternatives to similar routes on the bigger limestone faces near Canmore. If you are looking for some climbing requiring crampons and ice axe in this area, Stanley Peak is the place to go. It should be noted that Stanley Peak and Floe Lake are both in Kootenay National Park, but since the nearest town is Banff they are included in this section.

The major townsite in Banff National Park is, not surprisingly, Banff. It is a real tourist trap at most times of the year, particularly during the summer months. You might find it all a little too much to handle and feel a lot happier heading off to Canmore which is, presently, somewhat more peaceful. Furthermore, if you are cash conscious the price of some things like eating out and accommodation are higher in Banff than in neighboring Canmore. However, an added bonus to being in Banff are the Hot Springs for relaxing weary muscles, though be wary of swallowing any of the hot pool water — you don't know what is in it but you can probably guess!

Access Banff townsite is located just off the Trans-Canada Highway 15 km west of the Canmore entrance to Banff National Park. All the routes described in this section are accessed from the Trans-Canada Highway, Highway 1A (Bow Valley Parkway) and Highway 93 south (Kootenay Parkway). Highway 1A is reached from Banff by following the Trans-Canada Highway west for 6 km to the turnoff. You can also reach the 1A from Castle Junction where Highway 93 takes off from the Trans-Canada Highway. This is especially convenient for reaching Castle Mountain. To reach Stanley Peak and Floe Lake follow Highway 93 South towards Radium.

Facilities In Banff you will be able to find everything you are ever likely to want on a climbing trip. There are a large number of groceries and shops with all manner of goods and goodies. There are also a number of gas stations, some of which remain open 24 hours. Catering to your possible needs for climbing gear are two large climbing stores, Mountain Magic and Monod's. In the unlikely event that they cannot help you, then Calgary is the next nearest place for gear. If you fancy eating out you'll find a good selection of restaurants and cafes with diverse cuisines and prices. Outside of Banff, there is also Castle Mountain Village below Castle Mountain at the junction of Highway 93 and Highway 1A which provides snack food, groceries and accommodation.

Being a tourist town, Banff has accommodation to suit all pocket books, from campgrounds to very expensive hotels. Most people are going to be interested in camping or Youth Hostels. For more information about campgrounds enquire at the Parks Information Office on Banff Avenue in Banff. There are two Youth Hostels in the immediate area: one in Banff on Tunnel Mountain and one at Castle Junction below Castle Mountain. These hostels are very busy in the summer season so you should book well ahead. For more information about accomodation visit the Alberta Tourism Information Centre in Banff.

For information about backcountry conditions, trail closures, weather, permits etc. the Park Information Centre is the place to go. The centre is open 0800-2200 in the summer months and 1000-1800 in the winter. For a more detailed weather report you could also call in at the Banff Weather office. If you feel like you need more information about specific climbs than is provided in this book you may wish to talk to a warden. You can either phone or drop into the office though it is a matter of luck whether one of the more experienced mountaineering wardens will be available.

Officialese All routes lie within Banff National Park and backcountry use comes under the regulations detailed on page 17.

In Emergency either contact the RCMP or the Banff Warden Office at 762-4506.

Rock Climbing Although the majority of the routes described in this section are rock routes, there are many more routes in the area that have not been included, particularly the short routes in the immediate vicinity of Banff. These provide a way of whiling away a few sunny hours. For information consult "Banff Rock Climbs".

Mount Edith 2554 m

Mount Edith is a rocky peak with three main parts: south, central and north summits. The proximity of the mountain to the highway and to Banff townsite make Edith, and nearby Mt. Louis, very popular peaks for one-day outings. The Normal Route to the S summit of Mt. Edith is little more than an interesting, yet in some ways novel scramble and attracts many hikers as well as climbers on an easy day out. It is left for all to discover for themselves — it is described here as a descent route. The register on the summit testifies to the very many ascents the route gets.

The rock on the mountain is quite shattered in places (but on well-travelled routes this presents little problem). On the east side of the peak, however, is a series of steep bedding planes where weathering has uncovered walls of surprisingly smooth and solid rock. The N face is the face of Mt. Edith that sits directly opposite Mt. Louis. The routes here are roughly 300 m long with typically good rock, although the ledges are covered in loose debris. All the routes on the mountain can be climbed comfortably in a day from the highway. Take water — there are no babbling brooks on this peak. *Map 82 O/4 Banff*

Access for all routes Park at Fireside picnic site near the junction of the Trans-Canada Highway and Highway 1A about 6 km west of Banff. Access the picnic area by a short 0.9 km road that leads off to the right 100 m along Highway 1A from the junction. Follow the signed Cory Pass/Edith Pass trail to where the trail splits at a junction for Cory Pass. For all the climbs continue along the right-hand trail to just before Edith Pass. A fainter trail breaks off left through the trees towards Mount Louis, contouring the hillside immediately below the east side of Edith.

South Ridge of the South Peak II 5.4   photo →

FA. M. Hicks, B. Hind and J. Tarrant, May 1951. One of the more frequently climbed of the easier routes in the Banff region. Very popular with beginners. The start of the route is notoriously difficult to find so make good use of the photograph!

When the approach trail crosses a small, two-log bridge continue along the trail for another 500 m, then go up left through timber to the first avalanche slope that can be seen from the trail. A faint trail switches back and forth up the slope avoiding small cliff bands and leads to the base of the S ridge. Scramble up to a prominent gully just to the right (east) of the ridge.

Climb the gully until it veers left. At this point take to the rock on the right and continue up to the crest of the ridge. Follow the ridge over broken rock to the summit.

To **descend** backtrack for about two ropelengths until it is possible to move down onto the W face. Follow cairns and scree ledges (almost a trail) until you reach the end of the ledges. Look for a hole in the ledge (yes, a hole!) and go down into the hole. This leads into an easy chimney that goes all the way down to the talus. Carry on down to the Cory Pass trail. This is the Normal Route in reverse.

Photo: Murray Toft

Mt. Edith: 1. S Ridge   2. E Face, S Peak   a. S Peak   b. C Peak   c. N Peak   d. Mt. Louis

East Face of the Central Peak III 5.10b photo p. 59

FA. B. Keller and B. Ehman, 1980. The east side of Edith consists of a series of steep, slabby faces. This route takes the largest and steepest face on the central peak of Edith via a very prominent water-worn groove that runs right down the middle of the face. The climbing is sustained and was a breakthrough in difficulty by local standards when it was originally climbed. Nowadays, it is rarely climbed, presumably since it is quite a serious "traditional" style route. Some climbers may find some of the run-outs a little disconcerting. More of a "big crag" climb than an alpine style rock route — for one thing it doesn't go to the summit!

Approach the east side of Edith as described above. The steep slabby E face with the prominent water-worn groove running the height of the face can be seen from the trail. Scramble up the hillside to the base of the groove.

At its base, the groove is about 1 m across. Climb the groove and the rock immediately to its right for about 80 m. Traverse right a little, then head up to the base of a left-leaning arch. Step over the arch (5.10b) and move left, back to the groove and a bolt belay. Finish up the widening groove. If you wish to go to the summit continue scrambling in the direction of the highest point! Most parties choose to forgo the summit.

Descend low-angled rock and talus ledges to the left (south) until it is possible to traverse back to the base of the route.

North Face of the North Peak, Greenwood/Boles III 5.8 photo →

FA. B. Greenwood and G. Boles, 1961. Certainly in its day this route was a pointer to future developments, treating a steep face as little more than a big crag. The majority of the climbing is very straightforward by modern standards. The original guides quote it as 5.7 — most parties would find it a little stiff at this grade. Well worth examining. Some wag soloed it in 1984!

Follow the trail all the way to the gap between Louis and Edith which is known as Gargoyle Valley. Scramble up the talus slopes/trail to the base of the very prominent corner system that runs up the centre of the N face. Follow the corner for a pitch to a ledge system that runs out left. The continuation of the corner is taken by The Kafir Strikes Back. Traverse along the ledge system, around the rib to the left into a series of corners. Follow the corners, stepping left each time the going gets harder than about 5.6. Eventually follow a corner up into a large alcove where there is often a small snow patch. Climb the corner above, over a small roof (crux 5.8) onto an easy gangway that leads left to a gully. Follow the gully to a shallow col in the crest of the N ridge of the N summit.

Descent For those who are so inclined, follow the loose summit ridge to the N summit. It's quite a way to the summit, over ground that requires care. Descend to Cory Pass via the W ridge. However, those of a crag climbing bent will probably be happy to drop straight down a gully directly on the other side of the N ridge from where you first gained the ridge crest. A few rappels (old slings) reach a ledge system leading out to the left side of the gully. Traverse along this a little way and drop down to another rap that reaches the talus-filled gully below. Romp down the talus back to the base of the route.

Mt. Edith N Face: 1. The Kafir Strikes Back   2. Greenwood/Boles

61

The Kafir Strikes Back III 5.10c

photo p. 61

FA. S. Dougherty and D. Cheesmond, July 1985. Takes the prominent corner line all the way up the centre of the face. Originally the majority of the line was climbed by A. Derbyshire and M. Toft in the fall of 1980 ("Black Rap Wall") but they avoided the corner when easier alternatives arose. Following the corner throughout is a climb very much in the modern alpine rock idiom. A sustained outing.

Start as for the Greenwood/Boles. From the ledge at the end of pitch one continue up the corner (5.10b/c) for one excellent pitch to another ledge system. Continue easily up the back of the corner and when things rear up take to the right-hand wall. Climb up and back left to the corner crack at the lip of a roof (poorly protected 5.10a/b). Belay in the crack a little higher up. Continue easily into a large talus-covered bowl below the upper corner. Grovel up loose rock (uugh) in a short chimney in the back corner of the bowl to a belay on top of a detached pillar. Climb the corner above for a few metres to a loose bulge. Traverse right (5.10b) and around the right end of the bulge into a crack system that leads back into the corner above. Continue up the crack (5.10b) to a hanging stance. The final hard pitch follows the corner above the belay until a step right is required to gain easier ground (5.10c). Climb the easy gully/crack system above past a loose, steep wall to the crest of the ridge, taking care not to drop anything on your beloved belayer. Follow the ridge for a short distance to reach the col at the top of the Greenwood/Boles and the descent gully.

Descend as described for the Greenwood/Boles.

Mount Louis 2682 m

Mount Louis is one of the few mountains described in this book that doesn't have at least one walk-up route. This is a peak you have to climb. And what a splendid summit to attain: a monolithic peak with steep faces on all sides, reminiscent of the peaks in the Dolomites. The upper E face is a huge diamond-shaped vertical wall that is an obvious yet unclimbed challenge. You can bet somebody is thinking about the possibility.... The rock is better than is typical of the mountains in the immediate vicinity. In fact, some of it is immaculate. As a result of the good rock and the fact that it is a "real" summit, Louis is a favorite peak amongst climbers. The summit register reads like a who's who of North American climbers. Regardless of your tastes, one of the described routes will appeal.

All the routes can be climbed in a day trip from the road. However, that's not to say you can be laid back about it considering the approach is two hours and the descent requires some care. One thing you should bear in mind is that the summit of Louis is not a good spot to get caught out in a lightning storm. Besides being reasonably pointed, there is a metal cross on the top. Lightning is most common in the afternoon, so bear this in mind when planning your climb. Having said all this, you will undoubtedly have a good day out on this mountain. Remember to take water — there are no creeks at the base of the routes and the peak rarely holds snow into the summer months. Enjoy yourself! *Map 82 O/4 Banff*

Access for all routes Approach Edith Pass as described under Mount Edith and continue along the faint trail below the east side of Edith. Eventually the trail descends a steep hill before climbing up again into Gargoyle Valley, the gap between the N face of Edith and the S face of Louis. All the routes are reached from this point. About 1.5 hours from the parking lot.

Descent The descent for all routes is a fairly complex affair so pay attention! From the summit scramble down the first gully immediately west of the cross You should come across rappel anchors a little way down. Rappel down around a right-hand corner in the gully and then down another 30 m rappel to a scree bowl above a steep wall. It is CRITICAL to go the correct way down from this point. DON'T go down the wall or the gully to the left (facing out). Instead, climb UP to the right (facing out) for 10 m into a notch and make a 50 m rappel down a slabby corner on the other side of the notch to a ledge in a large gully leading down towards the ridge between Cory and Louis. A 25 m rappel leads to some easy ground. The next rappel anchor is fixed in the left wall of the gully near a steep drop-off. A final 50 m rappel lands you on the ridge at the base of the W face, from where talus slopes to the south lead back to the bottom of the S face. See photo page 69.
Note: There are enough rappel points to permit half-rope rappels all the way down. Remember, the intermediate anchors don't get as much use as the 50 m ones and therefore the slings may not be upgraded as often. Take care.

Kain Route (Normal Route) III 5.6/7

photos p. 67, 69, →

FA. C.Kain and A.H.MacCarthy, July 1916. A famous climb put up in a very casual manner while Kain was accompanying MacCarthy and some friends on a "day's picnic to view the scenery". A testimony to Kain's ability! It is now a very popular route to the top of one of the more striking mountains in the area. The hardest climbing is at the very end. If the weather breaks, downclimbing the route is reasonable for experienced parties. In fact, some parties actually use this as the descent route. It has been climbed in two hours but most parties take a little longer. The first ascent was done in 4 hours. However, don't underestimate this route: the number of bivi walls in the upper half of the climb attests to the number of parties who either overestimated their ability or underestimated the difficulty of the route.

Start to the right of the SE ridge. From the bottom of the ridge follow the base of the E face towards a large couloir on the east side of the peak. Scramble up to the highest island of trees. Some way above is a short, steep wall stretching across the slabs. Break through this via a shallow water washed groove (5.4) or at its narrowest point and continue up the easy-angled rock until a diagonal left traverse can be made toward the SE ridge. Climb over broken steps to a terrace at the base of the upper part of the ridge. At the left end of the terrace is a gully leading down onto the S face. Downclimb or rappel the gully for 25 m until it is possible to traverse left (facing in) across several ribs to a ledge on a clean rib of the S face.

Move up for about 20 m into a wide, shallow gully. Gain the rib on the left as soon as possible and follow this to a large platform at the base of the summit tower. The summit tower is split by a deep, ugly chimney which is a grunt with a pack. Only climb it if you really, really have to! Thankfully, Walter Perren found a better way to finish the route. To the right of the chimney is a prominent crack, much more in keeping with the rest of the route. Climb this in one ropelength (5.6) to easy ground. Scramble up and left to the summit. 3-5 hours.

Photo: Don Beers

Mt. Louis E Face: 1. Kain Route   2. Homage to the Spider

Homage to the Spider III 5.8   photo p. 65

FA. T. Auger and R. Bunyan, August 1987.
This route is named in tribute to Walter
Perren, "the Spider of Zermatt", who pio-
neered the summit variation on the Kain
route by seeking out the best limestone.
There are about 8 pitches of steep climbing on some of the best rock found on the
mountain. It's an aesthetic line, well worth
the extra 20 minutes of approach. The
climb ascends the steep face on the east
side of NE ridge of the mountain.

Approach as for the Kain route and continue far to the right along the base of the
E face. From the highest steep meadow
near the right-hand (north) end of the E
face begin scrambling up ledges. Descend carefully to the right into and
across a gully to the base of a prominent
corner system. Follow this by alternately
climbing the face to the right or the crack
in the corner on beautiful rock for two
long pitches of strenuous 5.8. Pass an
overhang (5.8) and continue to a belay on
the first small pinnacle encountered. For
the fourth pitch cross over to the main
wall and climb up face holds to the base
of another obvious corner. (The first ascent party avoided this corner by traversing to a notch behind a pinnacle.) Belay.
Ascend the steep crack above where a
bolt protects a move around a block.
Belay at a ledge at the top of the crack.
Move right to the corner and climb up to
an alcove. Climb over a roof (5.7) and up
into a wonderful feature resembling an
alleyway in a medieval village. At the far
end of the alley, bridge up to big ledges
which signal the end of the steep climbing. Scramble up the ridge beyond, taking to ledges on the left when necessary.
The ridge ends right at the summit.

Gmoser Route III 5.8   photo p. 69, →

FA. H.Gmoser and party, October 1964. A
very impressive ascent for its day and one
of the best moderate alpine rock routes in
the Banff area. The rock is typically clean
and the standard is reasonably consistent
(5.5-5.6) except for a steep corner system
in the lower third. 5.7/8 climbers will find the
crux a good challenge. It combines with the
best climbing on the Kain Route and is a
fitting approach to the Perren variation. Go
do it — a very enjoyable day out.

The route climbs the S face via slabs just
to the west of the SE ridge of the peak.
Start at the base of the slabs, directly
below an obvious corner system break-
ing through the steep wall above the
slabs. Climb the slabs via a series of
shallow corners (5.5/5.6) to the base of
the steep wall. Move right into the base
of the corner system. Climb the wide
crack in the back until it is necessary to
take to small holds on the left face of the
corner to avoid a bulge. Move up the wall
until you can step back into the corner
above the bulge (5.8). Belay at a small
stance in the corner. A short bridging
exercise past another bulge (5.7) leads to
easier ground. Above is a "trough" which
is followed a short way and then left
around a rib to reach the gully one descends on the Normal Route. Follow the
Kain Route and the Perren variation to
the top of the peak.

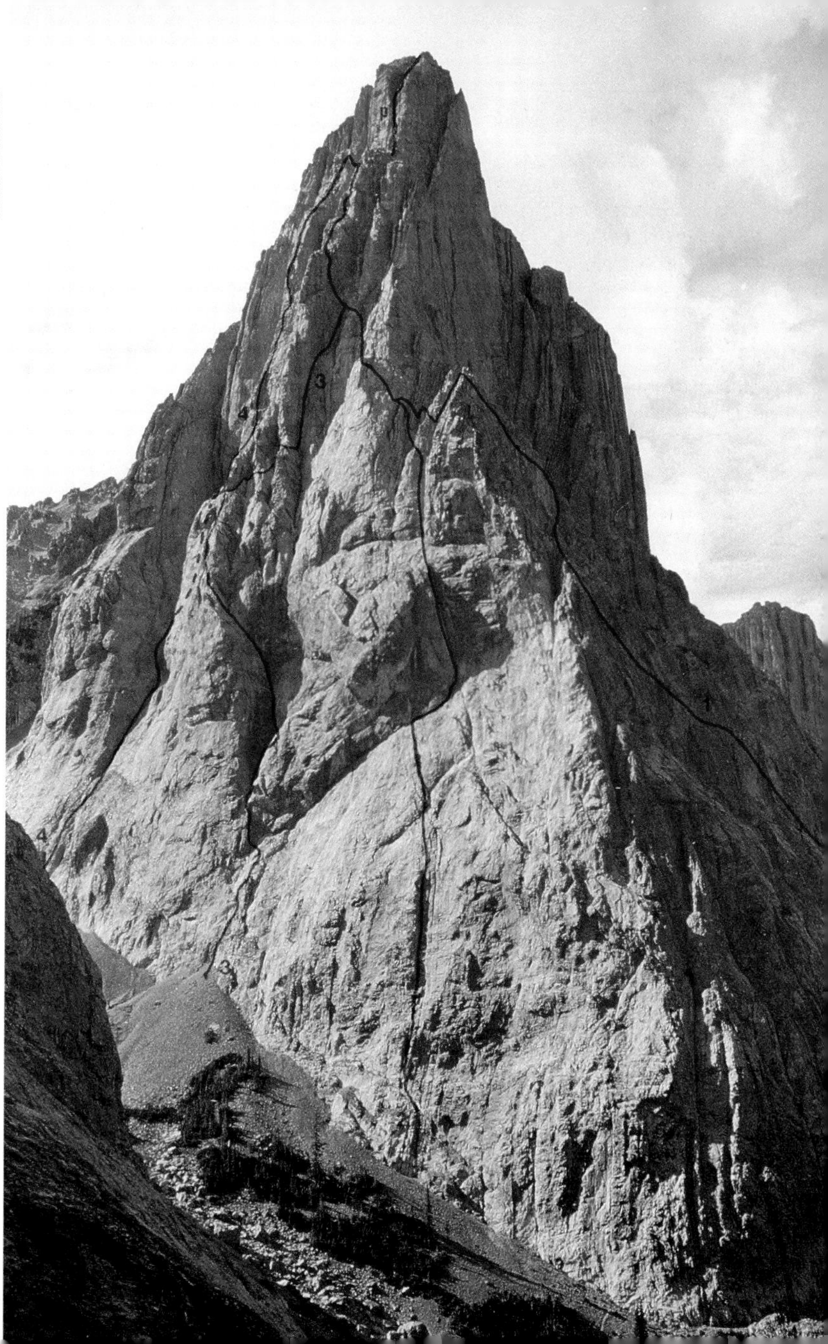

Photo: Don Beers

Kor/Fuller III 5.10d   photo p. 67, →

FA. L. Kor and J. Fuller, 1964. FFA. D. Cheesmond, S. Dougherty and C. Quinn, July 1985. Takes the big groove/gully in the centre of the S face. The crux pitch is sustained and tiring when done free. Undoubtedly much easier at 5.8 A1!

At the base of the middle of the S face, scramble up easy rock to the base of a short corner leading into a large gully-cum-alcove. Climb the corner (5.10a) into the base of the gully. Continue easily up to the upper part of the gully below a steep-looking exit. Climb the wall in the back of the groove to a bulge. Step right and up into the narrowest part of the gully below the exit bulge (difficulty with protection). After a few awkward moves over the bulge (5.10d), easy climbing up the continuation of the gully leads onto the rib to the left. At this point you are very close to the Greenwood/MacKay route and two alternatives come to hand. An excellent finish is to climb the upper part of the Greenwood/MacKay (highly recommended). Alternatively, work your way diagonally up and right. An awkward, steep corner crack (5.9) gives access to the ribs and gullies of the Normal Route. Follow this to the summit.

Greenwood/MacKay III 5.7   photo p. 67, →

FWA. B. Greenwood and L. MacKay, March 1965. Excellent for the grade; the position on the upper rib is superb. The lower gully section should be climbed as quickly as possible — it's a haven for falling rocks, though safer possibilities do exist.

Start up the large gully to the left of the Kor/Fuller. Climb the gully until it is possible to traverse easily to the right skyline over large, sloping ledges and a few ribs. It may be possible to reach this point by climbing diagonally up and right from the base of the gully. It would certainly be a way of minimizing rockfall hazard. Climb the skyline rib all the way to the large platform below the summit block (junction with the Kain Route). There is one fairly sustained pitch with little in the way of protection. However, the belays are good. From the platform, follow the Perren variation of the Kain route to the summit.

Mt. Louis S Face:
1. *Kain Route (upper part)*   2. *Gmoser Route*
3. *Kor/Fuller*   4. *Greenwood/McKay*
a. *Louis descent route*
b. *descent from N Face of N Peak of Edith*

Photo: Don Beers

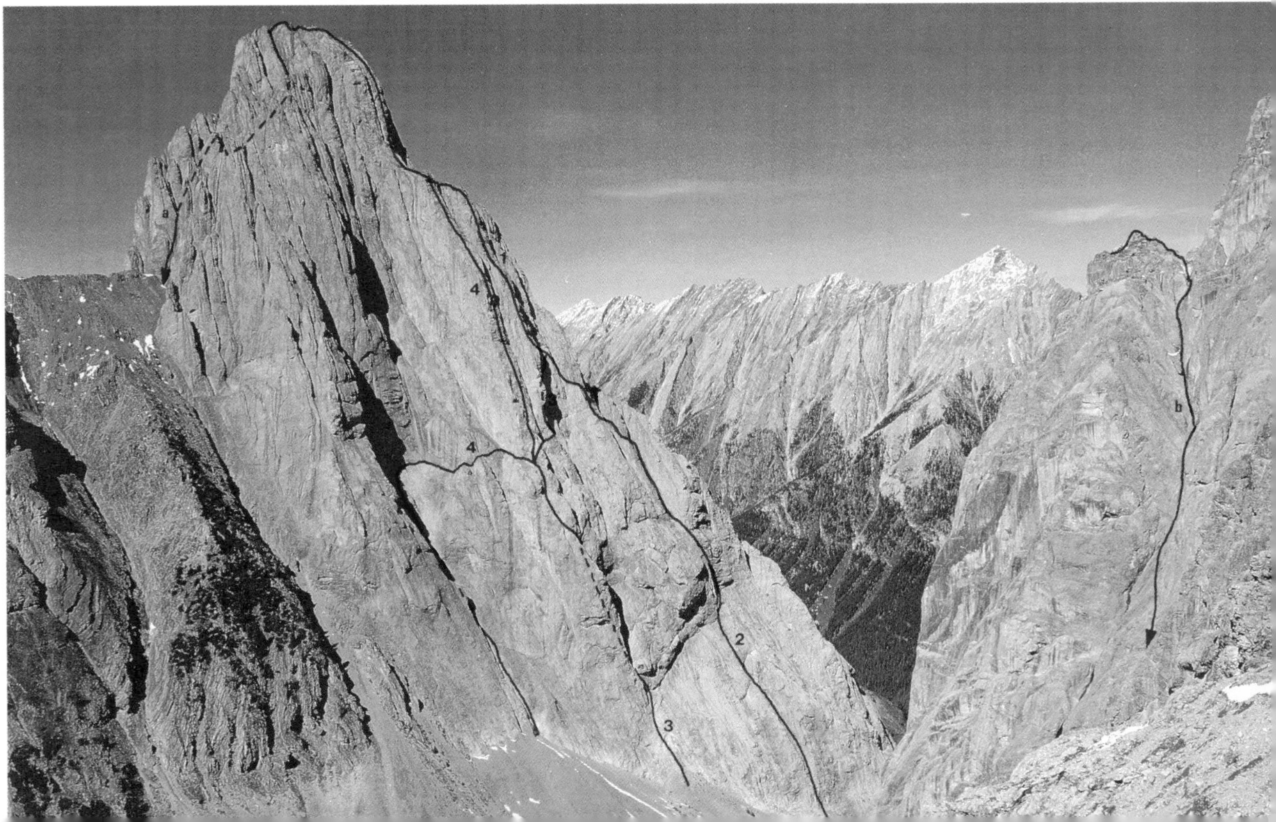

The Finger 2545 m

This is a prominent spire on the east side of the Bow Valley several kilometres to the north of Mt. Cory. It is a subsidiary spur of an unnamed peak (GR 895748) and is just one of several interesting mountain features in the immediate environs. *Map 82 O/4 Banff*

Board Route II 5.5   photo →

FA. J. Board and Ms. A. Morton, 1958. The best of a bunch of routes on the Finger. Not a difficult climb at 5.5 and a great day out for relative novices. A "nice" summit to attain with great situations on the summit ridge. The rock is reasonably solid except near the ridge where there are some loose bits. Start early because the best descent is over the far side of the mountain. Bear in mind that while the south side of the mountain is bone dry there will be snow on the base of the descent rappel early in the year.

Park at the side of Highway 1A about 17.5 km west of Banff. From Highway 1A follow the drainage immediately south of the Finger to a boulder field that leads up to the base of the SW face of the peak. Scramble up the talus beneath water marks on the main face until arriving at a large block that sprouts the only two trees in the immediate vicinity. A short distance up the talus is a large water-worn groove that marks the start of the Board route. The walk-in is a bit of a grunt. 2-4 hours from the highway. Some parties bivi at the base, though this means carrying your bivi gear over the climb.

The route follows the weaknesses in the face to the right of the large water-worn groove. Start off up the groove for 50 m and then move across ledges to the right for 170 m to the edge of a large flake and a squeeze chimney. Squirm up the squeeze, then continue with less effort up and left to the top of the large flake. Going straight up over more flakes leads to an obvious traverse line leading up to the skyline ridge. Scramble up the airy ridge, easy except for two 5.5 steps, to the top.

Descent is by downclimbing the N ridge for a short distance to the first obvious step. Find the rappel anchors and rappel down 25 m on the east side of the ridge to where easy downclimbing leads to the col at the base of the north side of the peak. Expect snow here in the early season. Work your way down into the drainage to the north, which takes you back to the highway approximately 1 km north of where you parked your vehicle.

Photo: Glen Boles

The Finger: Board Route

Castle Mountain 2766 m

A popular calendar peak that at one time was known as "Mount Eisenhower". From the Trans-Canada Highway it looks very impressive with its steep limestone walls. The routes described here are mostly on the walls above the large ledge system, called Goat Plateau, that traverses the mountain. Some activity on the lower walls has produced some excellent climbing and there is vast potential for many more routes. An attraction to climbing on Castle is the placement of a hut on Goat Plateau which provides an excellent base for several days of rock climbing. *Map 82 O/5 Castle Mountain*

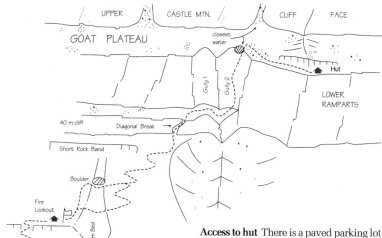

Topo courtesy Murray Toft

Castle Mtn. Bivouac Hut

Map *82 0/5 Castle Mountain*
Location On Goat Plateau below 3rd. buttress from SW end. GR 743836
Reservations Alpine Club of Canada
Capacity 6, 4 comfortably
Facilities Coleman stoves, water jugs, some cutlery and dishes, cooking pots, tick mattresses for six
Water Snowmelt from the first majorgully in upper cliffs immediately left of the hut

Access to hut There is a paved parking lot in the forest on the north side of Highway 1A (Bow Valley Parkway) 4.8 km west of the small grocery store at Castle Junction. This is the trailhead for the old fire lookout trail which is a narrow dirt road leading to tree line at the base of the mountain. The road is gated beyond the parking lot. A hike of nearly 4 km gains the lookout. The approach to the Calgary Mountain Club bivi hut (now looked after by the Alpine Club of Canada) from the lookout is another of those approaches best left to a topo! Eisenhower Tower is best approached from Rockbound Lake trail which leaves Highway 1A at Castle Junction (see under Eisenhower Tower description).

Castle Mtn: 1. Bass Buttress   d. Direct start   h. bivi hut   Photo: Gillean Daffern

Bass Buttress II 5.6

FA. B. Greenwood and J. Farrand, 1968. A good introduction to the steeper climbing on Castle Mountain.

Immediately above the hut is the left edge of a large square face. Bass Buttress follows this ridge. Where the buttress joins Goat Plateau, walk left a little to a deep chimney, topped by a chockstone. Start up the chimney on its outer right side and climb up behind the chockstone to a ledge below a pinnacle — the "Kraut Pinnacle". Just left of the crest of the buttress, follow an obvious weakness up to the left end of a large roof. Pass

the roof at a flake at its left end and follow the ledge above back to the crest of the buttress. The squeeze chimney above leads to a talus-covered alcove behind a pinnacle. Climb the steps above to the exit corner. 4 hours.

Descent is by traversing the summit plateau to the west, passing around a cairned peak to a wide talus-filled gully with a large cairn at its top. Follow the gully down to where it narrows and then either rappel or downclimb to Goat Plateau.

Brewer Buttress II 5.6   photo →

Photo: Glen Boles

FA. D. Brewer and L. Irwin, 1961. The classic route of the mountain and one of the classic lines in the Rockies. An excellent climb of moderate difficulty that leads to situations not typically associated with a climb of this grade. Should not be missed by anyone who visits Castle Mountain. When viewed from the bivi hut the route takes the first ridge line to the north (left) of Eisenhower Tower.

From the bivi hut follow faint trails along Goat Plateau to the south to the base of the ridge. Start 30 m right of the ridge crest in a bay of lower-angled rock to the left of a red arch. Climb up and left to gain the crest of the ridge in two leads. Climb some grey rock up and right to a belay behind a little pinnacle. Move right below a yellow wall and then climb a shallow chimney/groove and a grey wall on the right to another belay.

Continue straight up past a blocky ledge and a short groove to a big ledge. Traverse left around the crest of the buttress to belay a few metres from the crest. Climb directly above the belay and trend up and right around the ridge crest to gain a small belay at the bottom of a large corner. Climb the corner until 3 m from the large roof at its top where a short traverse right gains a ledge.

Follow the ledge to its end, then climb up and right to a second ledge at the base of a low-angled slab. Climb the slab to a shallow chimney (crux) and then follow the obvious line back left to the crest of the ridge. Follow the ridge for 15 m to a ledge below a roof. Climb through the roof on the right, following a crack to another ledge from where the last two pitches lead to the top.

Descend as for Bass Buttress.

Ultra-Brewers III 5.9   photo →

FA. T. Auger, P. Sheehan and C. White, 1987. One of the best routes yet climbed on Castle Mountain, it takes an aesthetic prow on the lower tier directly below Brewer Buttress in seven pitches. When done in combination with Brewers it gives about 16 pitches of by far the best climbing on the mountain, and is appropriately called "Super Brewers". Take the usual rock rack and include a 3.5 Friend.

From the bivi hut, traverse Goat Plateau and descend the gully north of Brewer Buttress. With a little judicious route finding it is possible to descend without rappeling. Traverse south along the base of the cliffs to a right-slanting crack system that leads up to a line of overhangs. Start here.

Climb the crack to a belay a few metres below the roof. Move a few metres right into the base of a big chimney to another belay.

Follow the obvious line above on solid rock to a large ledge system (which can also be accessed from the approach gully). The route continues up steep rock about 15 m left of the crest of the buttress. After 10 m move right over a loose block, then follow a shallow gully to a belay at the foot of some obvious face cracks. Climb the cracks and cross a bay to the right to a belay. Scramble up grassy corners to a classic ledge right on the prow of the buttress. Above are two very pretty pitches. Both consist of continuous steep climbing on perfect rock (5.9). Climb the right side of the detached pillar on sold, prickly rock. Continue up the steep face above to a piton, then trend slightly right into a shallow corner. Strenuous climbing (two fixed pins) leads to a tiny stance at 50 m. Belay. Continue up the corner. Before reaching a roof, swing left onto the crest of the prow and belay. Continue up the outside face to Goat Plateau.

Castle Mtn: 1. Ultra-Brewers 2. Brewer Buttress g. Goat Plateau a. approach gully   75

Eisenhower Tower II 5.4   photo →

FA. E. Feuz and J.W.A. Hickson, 1926.
FWA. B. Greenwood, A.Simpson, R.
Lofthouse and Jon Jones, 1968. In its day
this was a real tour-de-force and today it
still retains a reputation. The climb itself
isn't too much of a problem; rather it is the
descent that seems to get many people in
a mess. The descent rappels are set up
for a single rope. This route is done from
the road in a day using the Rockbound
Lake approach.

From the CMC Hut traverse across Goat
Plateau to the south end of Castle Mountain. At this point the tower is "towering" above you. If you are just doing a one
day trip to Castle to climb the Tower,
approach from Highway 1A via the
Rockbound Lake trail. The signed trail
leaves the parking lot 50 m east of Castle
Junction on Highway 1A. Just before the
trail flattens out towards the lake you
make a very muddy creek crossing. Continue a further 70 m or so, then cut up
through the timber on the left, working
your way up to the crest of the tree-
covered ridge that is aligned with the
Castle Mountain massif. Follow a trail
up to the base of the rock and continue
scrambling up steps until a ledge leads
left for 75 m to a deep gully system leading up to Goat Plateau and the foot of the
Tower. Memorize landmarks for the return
trip to the parking lot.

The first objective is to get on top of the
tongue of rock known as the "Dragon's
Back" that juts out from the base of the
Tower. Walk up to where the crest of the
talus meets the east end of the Dragon's
Back. 15 m to the left of the crest, climb up
a wide crack for 10 m and then up an easy
though exposed ridge to the flat top of the
Dragon's Back. Scramble along this to a
10 m-deep notch. Climb down into the
notch to the base of a crack in the opposite
wall. The crack is much harder than the
"harder-looking" wall to its immediate
left. Big holds (5.4) lead out of the notch
to a ledge at the base of the Tower.

Above is an obvious water course that
seeps for most of the season. Climb the
wall to its right on good rock (5.4) for 50 m
to a scree bowl (bolt belay). This line is
the safest of several alternatives. Cross
the bowl to a rib on its left-hand side and
climb the rib to the prow of the Tower.
Three pitches up the prow lead to the top.

To descend, make a 25 m rappel off the
top, then downclimb the ascent route to
the bolt belay at the base of the scree
bowl. Two short rappels lead back to the
Dragon's Back where more downclimbing regains Goat Plateau.

Eisenhower Tower   h. Castle Mtn. bivi hut

Storm Mountain 3161 m

The name dates from pack train days when packers used this peak to forecast the weather. When a storm was moving in over the Divide, Storm Mountain was usually covered in cloud. It is still true today. The normal route is a grovel up talus slopes on the north side of the peak. However, for the novice alpine climber the E Ridge is well worth a look and the NE Face will keep most experienced alpinists entertained. The rock on the whole is reasonable with some very compact sections, particularly on the NE Face. *Map 82 N/1 Mount Goodsir, 82 O/4 Banff*

East Ridge III 5.6   photo →

FA. G.W. Boles and B. Greenwood, June 1961. The most prominent line on the mountain, and apart from the stagger up the talus slopes on the N ridge, it is the most popular route on the mountain. The route is mostly a scramble though a few sections will keep most folks interested. There may be snow on the upper parts of the climb and an ice axe and crampons may be necessary. You'll be able to tell by examining the route from the highway. Be prepared for the descent — it's over large talus and is a knee-jarring affair.

Park at the side of the Trans-Canada Highway immediately east of Castle Junction. Follow the signed Twin Lakes trail to the lower lake in about 2 hours. Traverse the north and west sides of the lake until you can work your way up through rock bands into the cirque on the south side of the ridge. Climb up gullies and various weaknesses on the left of the ridge until about 150 m from the summit. At this point you'll be forced to climb on the ridge crest. Continue up the crest to the summit (at most 5.6).

To **descend** either hop over boulders to the south and descend south-west slopes to timber and the drainage leading to Highway 93 (Kootenay Parkway), or follow the N ridge, first to the north and then west down to tree line and, sometime later, Highway 93.

North-East Face V 5.9 A3   photo →

FA. K. Wallator and T. Thomas, March 1988. This was a fine first ascent of a difficult route in winter by two young alpinists over four days. Between the E ridge and the N ridge of the mountain lies the NE face with a prominent gully running up the lower half of it. The route follows the gully, then negotiates the rock band above via some difficult climbing. It is likely to be fairly hazardous in summer due to rockfall.

Approach via the signed Twin Lakes trail to the higher, northern Twin Lake and then walk up into the cirque between the N and E ridges. The route follows the left-hand of two gullies until things get very steep. At this point, move to the right and climb six difficult pitches (5.9 A3) up steep rock just to the right of the main corner. Once above the steep rock, lower-angled rock is followed to the summit. In winter, the final section consists of delicate mixed climbing up thin ice runnels.

To **descend** to the base of the face (where you will likely have left your skis), follow the N ridge until it is possible to follow its eastern spur down to the cirque.

Storm Mtn.: *1. E Ridge* *2. NE Face* *g. lower Twin L.* *h. upper Twin L.* *n. N Ridge descent*

Stanley Peak 3155 m

Stanley Peak is an attractive snow-covered peak quite close to Highway 93. The N and W faces have several alpine ice routes of a moderate standard. Combined with a relatively short approach from a highway, Stanley is an attractive outing for parties looking for alpine ice that isn't too difficult and doesn't require a large part of a day to reach. The number of parties that climb the Kahl Route are a testimony to the attraction of the mountain; it may actually be one of the most popular alpine ice routes in the Rockies south of the Columbia Icefields. Besides the Kahl Route there are two prominent couloirs in the NE face, the left-hand of which is known as the "Y" couloir. The obvious couloir in the centre of the face has most likely been climbed, but this is not known for certain. *Map 82 N/1 Mount Goodsir*

North Face, Kahl Route III   photo →

FA. H. Kahl and N. Ellena, July 1966. FWA. E. Grassman and U. Kallen, February 1969. A very popular route which is an excellent introduction to climbing ice faces. Not a technically demanding route except for a sometimes problematic 'schrund.

Turn off the Trans-Canada Highway at Castle Junction and follow Highway 93 (Kootenay Parkway) south, towards Radium. Park at the Stanley Glacier parking area, situated about 3 km beyond the summit of Vermilion Pass on the southeast side of the highway.

From the parking lot follow the signed Stanley Glacier trail to its end. Continue up the valley over old moraines and then talus slopes to the tongue of the glacier. Work your way up onto the upper flat part of the glacier below the N face of the mountain. Walk across the flat glacier to the west end of the N face until below an ice face that runs all the way to the summit. Cross the 'schrund (difficulty depending on the season) and ascend the snow/ice slope directly to the summit.

Descent is usually down the straightforward NW ridge and then down snow and rock to the glacier. Retrace your approach footsteps back to the trail.

North-East Face, The Y Couloir III   photo →

FA. M. Toft and G. Spohr, August 1975. This route takes the prominent Y-shaped couloir on the left side of the NE face of the mountain. A straightforward ice gully (at most 50 degrees) that has the usual objective hazards associated with couloirs. Nevertheless, it is a fun route in the right conditions. For those who can't see the Y, it is the second gully from the right end of the face.

Approach as for the Kahl route. Cross the 'schrund and climb the stem of the "Y". When it splits, follow the right-hand branch. The summit cornice can put up a bit of a battle.

Descent via the Kahl route implies that you are going to traverse the mountain. Most parties descend the east end of the face as shown in the photo.

Stanley Peak: 1. Kahl Route 2. Y Couloir

Floe Lake Rockwall

Floe Lake is one of the attractions of a very popular backpacking circuit in Kootenay National Park. The lake is situated in a high alpine meadow with the "Rockwall" forming a very impressive background to the scenery. This 1000 m-high wall has only one route on it to date but there is plenty of scope for further development. The rock is typically good and the climbing interesting. In addition, the scenery is astounding, especially late in the year. *Map 82 N/1 Mount Goodsir*

Grassman/Spohr IV 5.7 A1   photo →

FA. E. Grassman and G. Spohr, August 1976. The wall can be divided into four sections separated by three couloirs. The Grassman/Spohr takes the rib to the left of the left couloir, in the centre of the face. The climbing is hardest at the bottom of the climb, being quite steep and technical. However, it eases up on the main rib. It is advised that you bivi at Floe Lake and then climb the route the next day without carrying bivi gear. In this manner you will be more likely to make it back down to Floe Lake before the end of the day. An aesthetic climb!

Drive along Highway 93 (Kootenay Parkway) to the Hawk Creek highway maintenance depot. Opposite the depot is a signpost for the Floe Lake trail. Turn off the highway and follow a dirt road for about 400 m to a gate. From here the trail rises about 800 m over the next 10.5 km, the majority of the gradient being right at the end up a series of switchbacks leading to alpine meadows and a campsite. On the south side of the lake is the "Rockwall".

To gain the crest of the rib start about 200 m to the left of the base of the couloir, below a large snow patch on the face. Gaining the snow patch is the crux of the route. Four pitches culminating in a steep crack and an overhang (5.7 A1) gain ledges below the snow patch. Walk right along the ledges to gain the crest of the rib which is followed in its entirety to the summit. It has about ten pitches of 5.5-5.6 and a whole lot of 4th class climbing.

Descent The first ascent party bivied on the summit and then descended into Symond Creek the next day. This way down is not recommended since it is very, very long and involves intense bushwhacking. Only go this way as a last resort! Much more expedient and far less trying is to traverse the summit ridge to the west to the col between the westernmost summit of the Rockwall and Foster Peak, then rappel and downclimb the north side of the ridge to easy ground. A short downhill stroll returns you to Floe Lake.

Rockwall: Grassman/Spohr
f. Floe Lake

Photo: Glen Boles

LAKE LOUISE

Haddo Peak	3070 m	SW Ridge	II	p. 87
		NE Face	IV 5.8/9	p. 87
Mt. Aberdeen	3151 m	E Slope	II	p. 88
The Mitre	2089 m	Normal	II 5.5	p. 90
Mt. Lefroy	3423 m	W Face (normal)	II	p. 92
		SE Ridge	IV 5.7	p. 92
Mt. Victoria	3464 m	SE Ridge (normal)	II	p. 96
		NE Face	III	p. 98
		NE Ridge	II	p. 98
		N Face	III	p. 99
		SW Face	II	p. 99
		Traverse	IV	p. 100
Unamed Peak	3155 m	E Ridge	II 5.4	p. 100
Popes Peak	3162 m	N Face	III	p. 102
Mt. Whyte	2983 m	Perren Route	II 5.6	p. 104

The mountains around Lake Louise are perhaps the most well-known peaks in the Canadian Rockies. This is by virtue of the position of Chateau Lake Louise. The astounding beauty of the lake with Mt. Victoria as the background has been captured in countless calendars and photographic books of the Rockies. Naturally, the beauty and the ease of access have drawn alpinists since climbing first started in the area. To quote the local fitter and packer, Tom Wilson, as he discovered Lake Louise with his Indian guide Gold Seeker, "As God is my judge I never in all my explorations saw such a matchless scene".

The boom time was at the beginning of the century as the Canadian Pacific Railway progressed further into the mountains and brought climbers from far afield to challenge the as yet unclimbed peaks in the immediate area of Lake Louise. The peaks remain as popular with today's climbers as they were with the pioneers and for the same reasons. The ease of access means that most peaks can be climbed in a single day, though Mt. Victoria and Mt. Lefroy are usually climbed over a weekend with a night at the Abbot Pass Hut.

Access Lake Louise townsite is the next town west of Banff on the Trans-Canada Highway. To get to the lake and the trailhead for the majority of the routes, turn off the Trans-Canada Highway and drive into Lake Louise. Continue under the railroad tracks and up the road to the lake and Chateau Lake Louise. The road is well signed. The large parking lots just before the Chateau are your starting points.

Facilities Lake Louise is a tourist town and there are few facilities that are not geared towards tourism. You can find almost everything you need for a climbing trip: food, gas, information etc. Samson Mall in the centre of town is the place to buy groceries, maps, camping supplies and a limited amount of climbing gear (Wilson Mountain Sports). For the best selection of gear you'll have to go to Mountain Magic or Monod's in Banff. There are even showers at the laundramat, which is a good thing to know since the main campground in Lake Louise doesn't have any! Recommended for a quick snack is Laggan's Bakery which offers excellent food at a reasonable price. Note that none of the gas stations in Lake Louise are open 24 hours.

All types of accommodation needs are catered for in this town, from the expensive Chateau to the much more reasonable campground and Youth Hostel, a part of the Canadian Alpine Centre. The Canadian Alpine Centre is a joint venture between the Southern Alberta Hostelling Association and the Alpine Club of Canada. It offers low cost accommodation with 100 beds, and several support facilities for visitors and the general public, including equipment rooms, meeting rooms, library and lounges, cooking facilities and a public cafeteria. Wherever you choose to stay, book well beforehand because the summer months are very busy in this town and accommodation gets filled up quickly. For information about motels, hotels etc. contact Alberta Tourism.

For information about trails, weather, campgrounds, backcountry conditions and park permits go to the Parks Information Centre, a unique little building at the north-east corner of Samson Mall parking lot.

If you need specific climbing information or more detailed information on weather and conditions, head for the Lake Louise Warden Office located at the Park maintenance compound behind the gas station and restaurant complex immediately east of the mall. The office is regularly staffed only during business hours (0800-1630). At other times ring the warden office in Banff. If you are looking to local climbers for information then the Last Post Bar at the Post Hotel is a good place to start.

Lastly, there are two backcountry tea houses in this area, one at Lake Agnes en route to Mt. Whyte and another at the Plain of Six Glaciers under Victoria, which are open during the summer season. At these locations you can refresh yourself on the way back down from your day's outing, assuming you had a alpine start!

Abbot Pass Hut

Map 82 N/8 Lake Louise
Location Abbot pass, the col between Mts. Victoria and Lefroy. GR 553791
Reservations Alpine Club of Canada
Capacity 32
Facilities Coleman stove and lamps, some kitchen utensils, foamies
Water Seepages at base of Mt. Victoria or melt snow

Access to Hut
From Chateau Lake Louise follow the signed trail for the Plain of Six Glaciers past the Tea House to its end at a viewpoint. Take to the moraines until it is convenient to drop down onto the Victoria Glacier which leads up to Abbot Pass. Be wary of the seracs that overhang the right (west) side of the glacier. The name "Death Trap" was applied to the

final stretch of this approach by the early guides in recognition of the hazards posed by the crevasses on the glacier and the threat of icefall from the seracs. Although the hazard may have decreased over the years it is good policy to pass through this stretch quickly, though paying attention to crevasses, particularly on the final slopes to the hut. 4-5 hours from the parking lot.

From Lake O'Hara See access to Lake O'Hara on page 136. This approach to Abbot Pass is one of the more famous scree slogs in the Rockies. From Lake O'Hara follow the signed trail to Lake Oesa. A trail continues up and across the slopes on the left side of the lake into a gully. Climb the scree gully to Abbot Pass. Some snow will be present until mid-summer. Near the top either the left-hand or right-hand chutes can be taken.

Officialese All the routes are within Banff National Park and backcountry use comes under the regulations detailed on page 17.

Rock Climbing The Lake Louise area became quite the "hot spot" for rock climbing in the late 1980's, and is now widely regarded as one of the premier rock climbing areas in the Rockies. This is all because of the magnificent quartzite climbing at the west end of Lake Louise, known as the Back of the Lake. The quartzite strata outcrops in quite a few places though a lot of it looks dirty and scruffy and is largely unexplored. You are referred to the highly amusing topo guide "Back of the Lake" by Colin Zacharias and Bruce Howatt.

In addition to the Back of the Lake, the climbing at Saddleback is suggested as an alternative well worth examining. The routes are about four pitches long on excellent rock and range in difficulty from 5.8 to 5.10a. The potential for new routes is vast. Futhermore, the crag offers magnificent views of the N face of Mt. Temple. The best approach is to follow the signed Saddleback trail from the Lake Louise parking lot to the Saddleback. When you are one or two switchbacks from the "saddle", contour across steep grass slopes onto the east shoulder below the cliffs. Gear up here before descending a few metres to the base of the cliffs. About 1 hour from the car to the base of the crag.

Haddo Peak 3070 m

Haddo Peak, the immediate neighbour of Mt Aberdden, has a steep NE face overlooking Surprise Valley. These two peaks form the ridge on the north side of Paradise Valley. Though Mt. Aberdeen is the more popular outing, it is a simple addition to the day to ascend Haddo Peak as well via the SW ridge. The NE face is somewhat more extreme but hasn't seen much traffic, which is a little surprising given the face is in full view of the Trans-Canada Highway just east of Lake Louise. Undoubtedly, the presence nearby of the N face of Mt. Temple has something to do with this state of affairs. However, it is well worth someone's attention. *Map 82 N/8 Lake Louise*

South-West Ridge (Normal Route) II   photo p. 89

FA. E. Tewes and C. Bohren, 1903. Usually combined with an ascent of Aberdeen.

From Lake Louise parking lot, follow Saddleback trail to the Saddleback-Fairview col. Staying high, contour around the south slopes of Fairview Mtn. before dropping down into the upper end of a valley known as Surprise Valley. Climb up to the toe of the Aberdeen glacier. The glacier can also be approached from the west end of Lake Louise or Paradise Valley. However, the route described offers the most pleasant and time efficient approach.

Breach the steeper part of the glacier left to right in order to avoid the biggest crevasses. The 'schrund below the upper glacier is smallest on the left (east) side. Continue up to the Haddo-Aberdeen col.

5-8 hours from Lake Louise. This is where you get the great views of Paradise Valley and the N face of Temple. From the col, continue up easy slopes to the summit which is large and flat.

To **descend** from Haddo it is possible to get down into Paradise Valley from almost anywhere on the SW ridge by easy scrambling. Follow the Paradise Valley trail out to the Moraine Lake Road. About 2 hours.

For those bent on not descending into Paradise Valley, it is possible to scramble down the SE ridge of Haddo (requires judicious route finding in a few spots) to the Haddo-Sheol col. From there a low-angled snow/ice field on the north side of the col leads down to the approach trail in Surprise Valley.

North-East Face IV 5.8/9   photo p. 89

FA. M. Toft and M. Farrell, July 1972. Direct Finish: J. Elzinga and C. Miller, July 1977. This is an alpine rock route with some interesting climbing on typically good rock. The NE face sits in a bowl between two prominent ribs. The route takes a rib up the left-hand half of the NE face to a prominent ledge. The direct route climbs a distinctive corner system to the summit whereas the original route escapes up ramps to the left. The route is usually only in condition in the late summer when the upper corners will be dry. A round trip can be completed in a long day from Lake Louise.

Approach the base of the face as for the approach to the Aberdeen Glacier described under SW Ridge route. Start below and left of the prominent rib that has a large red "flat iron" at its base. Climb up through a tricky and loose rock band at the base of the face to gain 250 m of easy going. Climb up past the red "flat iron" on its left, then traverse around to the right-hand side of the rib above. Climb the rib and work your way up and left over several large flakes to gain the prominent ledge system.

Access to the wall above is barred by a series of roofs that extend above the ledge. The original route breaks through the overhangs (5.7) at a break that gives access to a steep ramp leading to the summit ridge.

The direct finish takes on the obvious break in the centre of the upper face. Walk right along the ledge system to below the break. A delicate pitch leads up into the base of the break. Continue up shallow gullies, chimneys and cracks that get increasingly difficult (5.8/9) until a final loose, overhanging crack can be avoided by traversing out left to the summit ridge.

Descend as for the SW Ridge route.

Mount Aberdeen 3151 m

This peak is mostly hidden from view by Fairview Mtn. or Haddo Peak unless you venture into Paradise Valley, Surprise Valley or up to the Plain of Six Glaciers. Its most impressive features are on the northern side, in particular the glacier that descends from the Aberdeen-Haddo col. This is the line of the Normal Route. The views of Paradise Valley and the N face of Temple from the ridge between Haddo and Aberdeen are superb. *Map 82 N/8 Lake Louise*

East Slope (Normal Route) II   photo →

FA. Miss W.E. Creech, A.A. McCoubrey and G. Feuz, July 1908. Gaining the Haddo-Aberdeen col up the Aberdeen Glacier provides the majority of the climbing. There is nothing too technical, making it a good introduction to this type of climbing which explains its popularity. A bonus — the approach is short, and the descent(s) are straightforward. Can easily be combined with an ascent of Haddo in a single day.

Gain the Haddo/Aberdeen col as described for SW Ridge route up Haddo Pk. Stroll easily up the east slopes to the summit.

Descent The easiest and quickest descent off Aberdeen is to head south-west from the summit into a wide gully that drops all the way into Paradise Valley. Once in the valley, pick up the main trail and follow it out to the Moraine Lake Road. About 2.5 hours from the summit to the road. The Lake Louise parking lot is about a 3 km walk down the Moraine Lake Road.

Haddo & Aberdeen: 1. SW Ridge Haddo 2. NE Face Haddo 2a. Elzinga/Miller finish 3. E Slope Aberdeen a. Haddo Peak b. Mt. Aberdeen c. Haddo/Aberdeen col d. Aberdeen Glacier e. Haddo/Sheol col

Photo: Gillean Daffern

89

The Mitre 2089 m

The "little" peak that sits between Mt. Lefroy and Mt. Aberdeen. Although this peak is rarely climbed in these modern times it is included for historic reasons. Actually, if the truth be told, it's because visitors ought to be given, at the very least, a chance to climb a route consisting of quintessential Rockies rock giving them a true Rockies climbing experience. This is the perfect candidate for such a climb. The standard route used to be a perennial favorite of the local guides when they used the relatively short approach from the Plain of Six Glaciers. However, the objective hazard of that approach has increased and it is no longer used by the guides. A longer approach up Paradise Valley is now used, though it is not as popular. *Map 82 N/8 Lake Louise*

Normal Route II 5.5   photo →

FA. C. Kaufmann and J. Pollinger, 1901. As a result of the reduced traffic the route has had in the last few years the amount of loose rock on the route has increased somewhat. In fact, the rock is pretty rank in many places — it always has been and always will be! However, don't let the state of the rock deter you in the slightest. The climbing is not difficult and in at least one place it is unusual. Furthermore, the situation on the summit is unique with the walls of Lefroy towering above you. It's quite "atmospheric". Go do the route — it's a fun day out, trust me (!).

The original approach was from the Plain of Six Glaciers but the retreat of the snow and ice just below Mitre col has exposed some very loose rock. Not that this approach is impassable, it just isn't recommended! The pleasant and safe approach used nowadays is from Paradise Valley. From the Moraine Lake Road hike up the signed Paradise Valley trail, but instead of turning off the main trail to go to Lake Annette as for the N face of Mt. Temple, continue along the trail to the Giant Steps (waterfalls). Pass the Giant Steps and follow the creek through meadows to moraines below the south side of the Mitre. Gain East Mitre col, the notch on the east side of the peak, over grassy slopes and talus.

From the notch, follow a rotten ledge system across the south side of The Mitre, crossing a short exposed bit (good rock, thankfully) to a slanting gully full of loose rock and blocked by a large chockstone about 30 m up. Scrabble up the gully and past the chockstone via a "key-hole" into another couloir. Follow this up to the summit ridge which leads to a solid! step. Climb a chimney on the right to regain the ridge below another step. 5.5 climbing leads to easier ground and the summit.

Descend by the same route. 9-12 hours round trip.

Photo: Bruno Engler

The Mitre. c. E Mitre col

91

Mount Lefroy 3423 m

This is the peak that "sits in front" of Mt. Victoria when viewed from Chateau Lake Louise. The E face is a very impressive sweep of rock, capped by seracs, that continues around the SE side of the mountain where the Lemire Route can be found. The most gentle aspect of the peak is the snow/ice slopes of the upper W face above Abbot Pass. The Normal Route ascends this slope. *Map 82 N/8 Lake Louise*

West Face (Normal Route) II   photo →

FA. H.B. Dixon, C.E. Fay, P. Sarbach, A. Michael, J.R. Vanderlip, C.L. Noyes, C.S. Thompson, H.C. Parker and J.N. Collie, August 1897. FWA. F. Becky, R. Burgener and J. Madsen, March 1966. A classic Rockies ascent; almost all Rockies habitues have climbed it at some time. Low-angled snow/ice slopes lead the whole way to the summit. Difficulty is determined by the amount, depth and solidity of the snow.

From the Abbot Pass Hut, go straight up the slopes towards the summit. Any one of the three gullies through the rock band will suffice — none are any harder than the others although pick the best one depending on conditions. 2-5 hours from the hut to the summit.

Descend the same way you came up.

South-East Ridge, Lemire Route IV 5.7   photo p. 94

FA. P. Lemire and A. Doherty, August 1971. This route takes a direct line up the east side of Lefroy from the moraines to the summit. Similar in difficulty to the Lowe route on the N face of Temple but without the objective hazards of that climb. The route was first climbed over two days but considering the approach is only 3 hours it may be possible to leave the parking lot in the early morning hours and complete the route in a day without the encumbrance of carrying bivi gear. Bear in mind that the route is east facing and so will be great for your tan. The snow on the final slopes is likely to be quite soft and wet. Probably best climbed in August when the rock will be driest.

Approach as for The Mitre on page 90. From the moraines below The Mitre, cross to the base of the ridge and follow it in the usual Rockies manner (ie. deke left or right to avoid any difficulties) until you run into a large vertical step near the top. Avoid this by traversing into a bowl on the left and climbing some slabs until it is possible to traverse back right to the ridge line. Once there, follow the crest all the way to the summit snowfields. Continue up to the top. 5-8 hours.

Descend via the Normal Route (W Face) to Abbot Pass, then descend the "Death Trap" to the Plain of Six Glaciers.

p

Mt. Lefroy W Face   p. Abbot Pass

Mt. Lefroy SE Face: Lemire Route

Mt. Victoria E Face 1. SE Ridge (normal) 2. S Summit, NE Face 3. NE Ridge 4 Traverse 5. upper part of N Face s. the "Sickle" m. S Summit n. N Summit

Photo: Glen Boles

Mount Victoria 3464 m

Victoria is the large mountain dominating the skyline from Chateau Lake Louise. There are two summits, North and South, with the South being the highest. The east side of the mountain is an eye-catching sweep of snow and ice dominated by the Upper Victoria Glacier and the seracs that overlook the walls of the "Death Trap". The north aspect of the mountain is another impressive sweep of ice, with a heavily crevassed glacier descending into Watch Tower Creek from almost the N summit. In contrast, the S and W faces of the mountain are predominantly rock, rising almost 1500 m above the Lake O'Hara valley.

The most popular route on the peak is the SE Ridge from Abbot Pass Hut, a climb that is often combined with an ascent of the W face of Lefroy to make a complete weekend of climbing. Depending on the route you choose to climb, your approach will be from either Lake Louise or Lake O'Hara (also see page 136). *Map 82 N/8 Lake Louise*

South Summit, South-East Ridge (Normal Route) II   photo p. 95, →

FA. J.N. Collie, C.E. Fay, A. Michael and P. Sarbach, August 1897. A typical Rockies scramble on loose rock leads to a magnificent ridge. It is unarguably one of the best of the classic alpine ridge routes in the Rockies. Alpine short-roping was invented for this type of climb. The views of both Lake O'Hara and Lake Louise areas are spectacular. In the early season the firm snow on your ascent may have turned to mush by the time you come back down. Take care.

From Abbot Pass, a short section of rock gains easier talus slopes on the east side of the ridge. Scramble up, avoiding going too far left by passing between two small rock towers and gaining the ridge about 200 m above the hut. Follow the ridge line, traversing on the east side at difficulties, to a false summit. To this point, finding the easiest route can be a little tricky. If there is a party ahead of you, keep an eye out for falling rock. Continue traversing the ridge past the "Sickle", a deep depression in the ridge, to a prominent rock step. Pass this on its right (east) side and then continue along the ridge to the S summit. 3-5 hours from the Pass.

To **descend**, retrace your steps back to the Pass. An **alternative descent** if you plan to go to Lake O'Hara is via the SW Face route. From the S summit follow the SE ridge for a few hundred metres back towards Abbot Pass to a prominent rock notch/gully that leads down the west side of the ridge. From here, descend into the notch/gully and down to a break on its left side. The break leads diagonally down to the left (south) to an open face that can be easily downclimbed to the Huber Glacier. It is possible to climb from the top of the notch/gully straight down to the glacier but this is only recommended if you are able to kick steps. By mid-to-late summer this will all be ice. If you want to bag Huber on the way down, traverse a little way south to the Huber-Victoria col and romp up the NE ridge.

Descent from the Huber-Victoria col entails descending the Huber Glacier to its south-west corner and then crossing the spectacular talus ledges on the W face of Huber to the Wiwaxy-Huber col (see NE Ridge of Huber on page 150). Allow 3-5 hours for a descent via the Huber Glacier route to Lake O'Hara.

Photo: Alan Kane

Abbot Pass and Hut. Start of SE Ridge of Victoria

South Summit, North-East Face III   photo p. 95

FA. V.A. Fynn and R. Aemmer, July 1922. FWA. D. Gardner, C. Locke, E. Grassman and B. Greenwood, February 1968 (This was the FWA of the mountain). The route ascends the vast snow/icefield that covers the upper E face of the mountain as seen from Chateau Lake Louise (a few big holes on the approach glacier provide a route-finding challenge). The final face to the summit ridge offers about six rope-lengths of good moderate snow/ice climbing. The route is not recommended in the early part of the summer since it is prone to avalanche. Best at the beginning of May or in August.

From Lake Louise follow the Plain of Six Glaciers trail to the Tea House. Continue past the Tea House a short distance, then leave the main trail and follow switchbacks up treed slopes on the right to the base of the unnamed peak between Mt. Collier and Popes Peak. Traverse west to the Upper Victoria Glacier. Walk across the glacier towards the N summit past some big holes (probably easiest left of centre). When you are on the highest bench of the glacier, traverse south to the end of the bench. Gain the ice/snow on the other side of the 'schrund , climb up to rocks, then tackle the ice face above to gain the summit ridge just north of the S summit. Turn left (south) to reach the summit. 6-9 hours from the Tea House.

Descent Parties have descended via the same route, especially if they have just kicked steps up it. However, later in the season most parties prefer to traverse the SE ridge to Abbot Pass.

North Summit, North-East Ridge (Normal Route) II   photo p. 95

FA. J.Outram, W.Outram, J.H.Scattergood, C.Clarke, H.Zurfluh, August 1900. FWA. E.Grassman and P.Zvengrowski, 1977. The Normal Route to the N summit ia an interesting day out for the novice alpinist since it involves a bit of glacier travel, a short face and then a final ridge climb to the summit. However, he/she should be well versed in glacier travel since there are some big holes on the approach to the slope up to the col. The route serves as a possible descent from the N face climb.

Follow the same approach as for the NE face until below the Victoria-Collier col. Cross the 'schrund and climb moderately-angled snow slopes and rock bands (often wet) to the col. In the winter of 1990 someone skied from the col down to the Tea House! From the col the snow-covered ridge is climbed past a short rock buttress at half height to the summit. 5-7 hours from the Tea House.

Descent is back down the way you came. Some parties may wish to also climb the rock ridge from the col to the summit of Mt. Collier.

North Summit, North Face III   photo p. 95

FA. U. Kallen, C. Locke, F. Roth and M. Toft, May 1969. The actual N face has little in the way of difficult climbing but the approach to the face through the glacier has become quite technical in recent years due to a lack of snow build-up. Be prepared for some interesting climbing getting around seracs and crevasses. A tricky, if not difficult, approach.

Start from the Lake O'Hara Road (see page 136). About 5 km from the gate is Watch Tower Creek, guarded by the impressive obelisk of rock known as the Watch Tower (see under Watch Tower on page 149). Follow this creek up to the glacier. Climb the glacier via the easiest route you can find to a bench below the upper ice face. In recent years

getting to this point has been the crux of the route! The upper face consists of a large ice bulge. Cross the 'schrund and ascend the face to the west (right) of the bulge to gain easier ground close to the N summit.

Descent is via the NE ridge to the Victoria/Collier Col. At this point you can either descend the north side of the col onto the glacier you just ascended a few hours ago or drop down the south side onto the Upper Victoria glacier and eventually emerge at the Plain of Six Glaciers (NE Ridge route). It all depends on whether you left your bivi gear down in Watch Tower Creek, carried it with you, or did without it. 3-6 hours from the base of the glacier to the summit.

South-West Face II   photo p. 151

FA. J.P. Forde, M. Goddard, A.M. Gordon, Mrs A.H. MacCarthy, Aug 1909. This route offers "the best day out" on Victoria available. You can easily combine it with an ascent of Huber and a descent via the SE ridge of Victoria to make for a very full day. However, if you run out of daylight the Abbot Pass Hut offers a great bivi! This route can also be done in the other direction (see alternative descent for SE Ridge route).

From Lake O'Hara, follow the route for the NE ridge of Mt. Huber to the Huber-Victoria col (See pages 150 and 151 for descriptions). If you feel keen, the summit of Huber is not too far away (1 hour return). From the col contour across the

glacier to the highest snow/ice of the glacier. This brings you to the base of a wide gully that ascends to the SE ridge of Victoria. Scramble up easy rocks on the right side of the gully to a break going up to the left and back into the top of the gully to the SE ridge. The gully can be climbed directly but it isn't as straightforward and you are more likely to be clobbered by a rock. The ridge is followed to the north for a few hundred metres to reach the S summit.

Descent can be by the same route, but for a round trip descend via the SE ridge to Abbot Pass.

Traverse of Victoria IV   photo p. 95

*FA. G.W.Culver, E.Feuz Jr. and R.Aem—
mer, September 1909.* A long day out in
the mountains but worth every minute.
Be prepared to deal with lots of loose
rock on easy 5th class climbing. It is
described for a north to south traverse,
since this leaves you at the Abbot Pass
Hut towards the end of the day, but it can
be traversed in either direction.

Follow the NE Ridge route (page 98) to
the N summit. Traverse the ridge toward
the S summit past numerous gendarmes
and gaps. The easiest and quickest route
is to traverse on the Lake Louise side of
the ridge, below the crest. However, the
purist will want to follow the crest, up,
down and around the gendarmes. Once
past the S summit follow the SE Ridge
route to Abbot Pass. 2-5 hours between N
and S summits.

Unnamed Peak 3155 m

Between Popes Peak and Mt. Collier is a
summit that is unnamed. The approach
to Upper Victoria Glacier on the Mt.
Victoria NE Face and NE Ridge routes
passes immediately below the mountain. In the pioneer days this mountain

saw quite a lot of traffic on its E ridge.
Since the 1940's, though, the route has
seen few climbers, mostly a few guided
parties. I have included it in the guide so
you can enjoy this unjustly neglected
outing. *Map 82 N/8 Lake Louise*

East Ridge II 5.4   photo →

FA. unknown. This is an "old" climb that
used to be popular way back in the pre-
war years. Nowadays, there are few
people around who even know of its existence, let alone know that it is a gem of a
climb. It offers a straightforward ascent to
a summit from which there is an unbeat-
able view of Abbot Pass, Lefroy and the
east side of Victoria. Furthermore, it is a
great outing for novices.

Approach from Chateau Lake Louise to
the Plain of Six Glaciers Tea House. Just
west of the Tea House gain the huge open
talus slope leading up towards Popes
Peak. Wander up this to the right-hand
end of a ledge that passes directly under

the seracs of a small glacier that descends from the Unnamed-Popes col.
Cross the ledge (it is easy, which makes
for a quick crossing) to the left-hand end.
Scramble up to gain the crest of the ridge
which is followed throughout (at most
5.4) to the summit. Great views.

To **descend**, you can either downclimb
the way you came up or traverse along
the ridge to just before the summit block
of Mt. Collier. Here you have two
choices. Either continue over Collier
and descend the approach to the NE
Ridge of Victoria (p 98), or descend the
Collier N glacier and its drainage to
reach the Lake O'Hara Road.

p

Photo: Glen Boles   *Unnamed: E Ridge   p. Popes Peak*

Popes Peak 3162 m

From the Lake Louise side this peak doesn't have any particularly compelling features. However, the north side of the mountain, framed in the hanging valley above Ross Lake, is sufficiently striking to make many people new to the Rockies stop and stare. As seen from the Trans-Canada Highway just east of Wapta Lodge the N face has an obvious line right up the centre, the line of the N Face route. *Map 82 N/8 Lake Louise*

North Face III   photo →

FA. M. Toft, M. Reasoner and E. Sanford, August 1974 FWA. J. Lauchlan and J. Tanner, March 1976. The route is the obvious gully in the N face, which is as straightforward as it looks. Beware of some small seracs that look down on the gully. In the early summer the couloir is névé and offers no difficulties; however, later in the season expect it to be ice and accordingly somewhat more involved. Usually by mid-summer the couloir is a torrent of water and rocks and not recommended. In recent years the amount of ice has decreased noticeably and in some seasons the ice may be completely gone in certain sections of the couloir. The exit through the serac(s) provides the most entertainment on the route.

Park on the Lake Louise-Lake O'Hara "back road" (Highway 1A) at the Ross Lake trailhead. Once you are at Ross Lake, walk round the west shore and bushwhack up slopes at the south end of the lake to gain a prominent ledge that allows access to the hanging valley below the N face. About 2 hours. It is advised that you walk in one evening, bivi in the hanging valley and climb the route early the next day.

Continue up the valley over moraines and glacier to the base of the gully. Cross the avalanche cone and the 'schrund and continue upward through the narrow entrance to the couloir. At the serac two possibilities should present themselves: a snow-covered ledge system going out left through the seracs and the obvious direct line. The ledge system used to be the easiest way to go but this is, unfortunately, subject to change. The direct finish offers some quite steep climbing (bring your ice screws) for about 30 m. Once you're above the serac barrier easy snow slopes lead to the summit pimple. The route has been climbed in 2 hours from the 'schrund, but most parties will require a little more time.

To **descend** walk down the north-east slopes of the summit block and over a large, low profile bump in the ridge to the top of a large rock step in the NE ridge. Two rappels down the north side of the step reach easy snow slopes leading down into the hanging valley and back to your bivi site. 2-3 hours from the summit.

Photo: Sean Dougherty

Mount Whyte 2983 m

Mount Whyte sits high above the east end of Lake Louise and affords tremendous views of the Lake Louise area. The SW ridge of the mountain, the Perren Route, has become a favorite for guided parties because of the short approach, straightforward climbing and the views — everything many clients desire. *Map 82 N/8 Lake Louise*

Perren Route II 5.6   photo →

FA. W. Perren, 1951. A good choice for an easy day out in the Lake Louise area. The views and the position on the ridge are worth all the effort. The route is mostly a scramble with a very short section of harder climbing near the top. Finding the easiest way up the ridge is an interesting challenge. The rock is quite loose in places, typical of the area.

From Chateau Lake Louise take the signed trail to Lake Agnes Teahouse, then continue up to the Beehive. Scramble west towards the Devil's Thumb and contour around the south side of the Thumb via game trails until below the Whyte-Devil's Thumb col. Scramble up talus to the left of the col into a small basin providing access to the ridge. Follow the ridge to the summit. Just before the summit there is a short, steep wall (sometimes wet) that can be climbed directly (5.6).

Descend the N ridge to the Whyte-Niblock col then work your way down through cliff bands back to Lake Agnes. 5-6 hours round trip from Lake Agnes.

Photo: Bruno Engler

Mt. Whyte: Perren Route   d. descent   t. Devils Thumb

VALLEY OF THE TEN PEAKS

Mt. Babel	3101 m	E Face	IV 5.10 A1	p. 111
Mt. Quadra	3173 m	N Face	II	p. 113
Mt. Fay	3234 m	SW Face (normal)	I	p. 115
		W Ridge	II 5.3	p. 116
		Roth/Kallen	II	p. 116
		Centre Ice Bulge	III	p. 116
		Chouinard Route	II	p. 116
		Berle/Kallen	II	p. 116
		NE Ridge	II 5.4	p. 118
		E Face	V/VI 5.8 W5	p. 118
Mt. Little	3140 m	NW Ridge	I	p. 118
Mt. Bowlen	3072 m	S Ridge	I	p. 120
Peak 4	3054 m		I	p. 120
Mt. Perren	3351 m	S Ridge	I	p. 120
Mt. Allen	3301 m	W Slopes	I	p. 120
Mt. Tuzo	3245 m	S Ridge/S Glacier	I	p. 120
Mt. Deltaform	3424 m	NW Ridge (normal)	II 5.5	p. 122
		The Supercouloir	IV 5.8	p. 122
Traverse of the Ten Peaks			III 5.5	p. 124
Grand Sentinel		S Face	II 5.8	p. 125
Pinnacle Mtn.	3067 m	SW Ridge	II 5.5	p. 126
Mt. Temple	3543 m	SW Ridge (normal)	I	p. 129
		E Ridge	IV 5.7	p. 130
		Greenwood/Locke	IV 5.8 A2	p. 132
		N (Lowe) Ridge	IV 5.6/7	p. 134
		Elzinga/Miller	IV 5.7	p. 134
		NE Buttress	IV 5.8/A1	p. 135
		NE Face	IV 5.9 A2	p. 135

The Valley of the Ten Peaks is a world famous beauty spot as well as a well-known mountaineering area. It is, in fact, depicted on the back of the Canadian $20 bill.

On the south side of the valley are the Ten Peaks themselves, beginning with Mt. Fay and ending with Wenkchemna Peak on the north side of Wenkchemna Pass, the latter mountain an uninspiring subsidiary summit of Mt. Hungabee. On the north side of the valley is Mt. Temple, the "Eiger of the Rockies", with its big N face visible from Lake Louise townsite.

The normal routes to the summits of the Ten Peaks are generally non-technical and make for pleasant and easy days out in the mountains. Let's face it, the majority of these routes should not be in a recommended route book — the rock is typically atrocious and many routes are little more than hikes up talus and snow slopes. However, the Colgan Hut provides the perfect starting point to bag a bunch of these peaks during a two or three day trip. It is not unlikely that a strong party on a good weekend can climb five or six. So in that sense they are worthy of inclusion. Mt. Fay is very much the exception, with several short, pleasant climbs on its N face ice slopes which are some of the most popular routes in the area. Its difficult E Face route is, without doubt, the hardest outing in the Ten Peaks. However, the Super Couloir on Deltaform is the big attraction for most visiting "hard" alpinists.

Mount Temple is also one of the major attractions of the Canadian Rockies, being the most popular summit over 11,000 feet. The SW Ridge route is a talus scramble that a large number of people are capable of doing. At the other extreme, the routes of the N face will keep most seasoned alpinists amused, all being of a technical nature and often on rock that is not above reproach. The rock on the face is highly fractured and belays and protection can be a problem. However, having said this, the two routes by Brian Greenwood have some rock that is amongst the best limestone you'll find in the Rockies.

Access For routes on the Ten Peaks the parking lot at Moraine Lake is the main starting point. This is reached by driving out of Lake Louise townsite up the hill towards Lake Louise. 2.1 km from the railroad tracks in Lake Louise turn left along the Moraine Lake Road and follow it for 13 km to the parking lot at Moraine Lake. The Moraine Lake Road is closed in the winter months and access to Moraine Lake is then by ski.

The starting point for routes on the N face of Temple is Lake Annette which requires an hour's approach walk from the Moraine Lake Road. Park at the Paradise Valley parking lot. From here, follow the excellent trail up Paradise Valley until you reach a trail junction about 1 km past the second of two bridges over Paradise Creek. Take the trail marked Lake Annette over the creek and up a short hill. There are bivi sites at the south end of the lake on a flat though rocky piece of ground, and under an overhang in some cliffs just a little further left (east).

Facilities Moraine Lake Lodge has a restaurant and small cafeteria which opens from late May to late September — a good place for a well deserved bite to eat when you get back down off your route. You will most likely be purchasing general groceries and supplies in Lake Louise townsite where you can also get information regarding other facilities in the area (see under the Lake Louise section on page 85).

Neil Colgan Hut

Map 82 N/8 Lake Louise
Location On the col between Mts. Little and Bowlen. W ridge of Mt. Little GR 568830
Reservations Alpine Club of Canada
Capacity 24 comfortably
Facilities Rucksack storage shelves, long cooking counter, table and bench, large water buckets, foamies
Water Mainly snowmelt but in late summer a large pool often forms in the depression east of Little-Bowlen col

Access to Hut

The Colgan Hut is a popular base for mountaineering on the Ten Peaks. From Moraine Lake there are two main approaches to the hut: the Schiesser Ledges and the Perren Route. Another approach used in the past is the 3-3.5 couloir. However, this latter choice should be treated as a climb, and one with all the objective hazards common to couloirs. It has a track record of being one of the worst spots in the Rockies for fatalities, most likely because people don't take climbing the couloir seriously enough. It is NOT recommended as a hut approach and is not described.

Perren Route (recommended). This approach used to require some climbing skill with two 5th class pitches at the top. These are now equipped with chains where the climbing gets tricky, significantly reducing the difficulty to easy 5th class. This approach is relatively free from objective hazard, making it possible either in ascent or descent at all times of the day, which makes it more useful than the Schiesser Ledges.

From the parking lot follow the trail around the north shore of Moraine Lake to the inlet creek. Cross to the far side and work your way over to the left to the

quartzite wall below and left of the drainage from the glacier just east of Mt. Bowlen. Hike up the talus alongside the quartzite wall to where it pinches out and then work your way up ledges above, following cairns through weaknesses to gain a small snow patch immediately below the final rock step. The first 25 m pitch (5.6) takes an obvious line a few metres right of the steep left skyline. Traverse right 30 m and climb lower-angled rock (5.4) to gain easy ground and the glacier (GR 573838).

If **descending** via this route you need a bit of info to find the rappel anchors. From the hut drop down into the bowl between Mts. Little and Bowlen and continue out onto the glacier until directly north of the Little-Fay col. Go north, down through crevasses and out onto the prominent rock spur that sticks out of the edge of the Fay Glacier (cairns). Down to the left are the rappel slings. One 20 m rappel off bolts leads to a further 25 m rappel. Yes, a 50 m rope is advised though it is possible with a stretched 45 m one! This is all dependent on how deep the snow is at the base of the step. Work your way down to the first rock bands where you'll pick up cairns that indicate the way back to the talus at the base.

Schiesser Ledges. Considering the low technical difficulty (easy 5th class) the popularity of this approach is not surprising. The ledges present little more than scrambling and when the going gets difficult chains are present to help you along. However, there is some objective hazard from falling rock.

From the parking lot hike around the lake and cross the inlet creek to the south side. Continue around the base of what is known as Peak 3.5 to the moraines of the Wenkchemna Glacier. Keeping to the left (south) side of the moraines, you will eventually pick up a prominent lateral moraine with a trail along its ridge. At its far end you will be below a low-angled snow couloir leading up to the col between Peaks 4 and 3.5, the 3-4 couloir. To the left of the couloir is a series of ledges reaching up to the col known as the Schiesser Ledges. The start of the trail is indicated by a big, ugly red paint mark on the rock. Just follow the trail of red marks and the odd cairn to the top. At one point a short length of chain makes things a little easier. Once on the glacier contour around Bowlen to the Colgan Hut.

Photo: Tony Daffern

Neil Colgan Hut access: 1. Perren Route   2. Schiesser Ledges

Tower of Babel
1. McKay Route
2. Greenwood Route
3. Fuhrmann Route

Photo: Glen Boles

Officialese All the routes are within Banff National Park and backcountry use comes under the regulations detailed on page 17.

In Emergency the nearest public phone is at Moraine Lake parking lot.

Rock Climbing In the Valley of the Ten Peaks the "traditional" cragging site for many years has been the Tower of Babel, the large obelisk of quartzite that sits above the parking lot at Moraine Lake. In its day it was the only quartzite outcrop to have been developed and was a popular spot for a day of rock climbing. With the discovery of other quartzite crags at Lake Louise, and the development of the limestone canyons and crag climbing in general, climbing on the Tower has fallen out of favour. The routes aren't sufficiently difficult for most crag-rats and the rock is quite scruffy. However, if doing routes about six pitches long at a moderate standard (at most 5.7) appeals to you then the Tower of Babel is well worth a visit. Presently, only the north side of the Tower has any routes but there is potential for more modern routes, especially on the east side. A fun way to spend a few hours.

To **descend** walk over the top of the Tower to the talus gully on the west side and make your way down, at first a little awkwardly, back to the base of the Tower. 20 minutes.

The Grand Sentinel is another rock climbing spot, though it is a long walk-in for many crag-rats (see page 125).

For those looking for something more modern the crags at Lake Louise are not far away.

Mount Babel 3101 m

The western side of this peak isn't anything spectacular and given the beauty of neighbouring Mt. Fay, it may go unnoticed altogether. However, the east side of the peak is a different kettle of fish, being a very steep and impressive rock face. It dominates the west side of Consolation Valley when looking south from the Moraine Lake Road. This was the location of one of the hardest routes from the '60's in the Rockies. *Map 82 N/ 8 Lake Louise*

East Face IV 5.10 A1

photo p. 112

FA. B. Greenwood and J. Moss, August 1969. An impressive rock route. Maybe it cannot be called a classic (having only been climbed twice) but it certainly offers an exciting day's climbing. An amazing effort for the time when it was first climbed. The majority of the route is now free, with a few points of aid that keep the grade reasonably sensible (5.10). The climbing and the rock are both very reminiscent of the longer limestone rock routes on Yamnuska and Chinaman's Peak. The route follows a line of cracks and chimneys to a ramp line that ascends right to left across the face. Above the ramp the right-hand of two prominent chimneys is followed to the summit. The second ascent was completed in a day but the party ended up spending a night out on the descent because of a wrong turn! If you don't get lost then this route can be a one day affair car-to-car.

From the Moraine Lake parking lot take the signed trail to Consolation Lakes. From the north end of the S lake climb talus slopes towards two gullies at the base of the E face of Babel. Pass the first gully and climb the next one, moving out to the left on broken rock near the base of the face. From the base of the face, climb a short ramp slanting from right to left into a chimney. At the top of the chimney traverse left along a ledge and climb up to the top of a small buttress (5.5). Continue up over broken rock for a few metres to a steep corner. Climb this and the steep wall above to the base of a chimney (5.7). Climb the chimney, then move left to gain another chimney (5.7). Continue up a steep, wide crack (5.8) to a small ledge. A short chimney followed by easier climbing leads to the base of a large slab. Climb a corner, then cross the slab (5.6) to reach a talus-covered ledge that runs across the width of the face.

The steep wall above is climbed via a crack (5.8, some aid). Easier climbing leads for two ropelengths to a good ledge on the right, below a steep corner crack. Climb the crack (5.8) and then traverse left to a chimney which is followed to a small cave (5.7). Traverse out left again over loose blocks to a crack that leads to a ledge (5.7, some aid). Follow the ledge to the right, then climb up a gully for 3 m. Traverse right across a steep wall and continue up into a bay (5.7). Climb the steep corner above. Follow the diagonal crack right to a ledge where the first ascent party bivied.

The remaining 150 m of the climb constitutes the crux. From the left end of the ledge, climb diagonally right and up a wall (old bolt) past expanding flakes to a wide crack. This leads to a belay in the back of a chimney (5.10, some aid). Climb out of the chimney via a steep crack, then take a ramp out right to a small ledge (5.10, some aid). The steep wall above leads to the top (5.7).

Descend by downclimbing/rappelling the N ridge of Babel down to Moraine Lake. The easiest line is somewhat left (west) of the ridge. Don't be tempted to peel off to the east too soon — you'll end up climbing back up to the ridge line.

Mount Quadra 3173 m

This peak, with several prominent snow/ice slopes dividing its N face, sits on top of impressive cliffs at the south end of Consolation Valley along with its companion peak, Bident. Until recent years, approaching the peak has been either via Consolation Pass or the Fay-Quadra col. The former approach is over seemingly never-ending talus and crappy rock and isn't particularly pleasant, though it is the line of the original ascent. A newer approach from the Consolation Valley via a prominent break in the impressive cliffs is, unfortunately, threatened by serac fall from the glacier below the N face. The Colgan Hut approach is by far the safest and easiest but is fairly long. *Map 82 N/8 Lake Louise*

North Face II   photo p. 114

FA. G. Jennings, D. Jones and J. Martin, August 1974. A pleasant ice climb directly to the summit; similar in character to the routes on the N face of Fay.

The two most commonly used approaches are described. You choose the one that suits your needs the best.

Consolation Lakes approach From the parking lot at Moraine Lake hike the signed trail to Consolation Lakes. From the south end of the S lake cross moraines towards the prominent snow/ice gully that breaks through the impressive cliff band below the N face. This relatively straightforward gully leads straight to the glacier below the N face.

Colgan Hut approach From the hut traverse around the south side of Mts. Little and Fay (as for the SW face of Fay) to the Fay-Quadra col. Continue over the col and onto the glacier below the N face of Quadra. The right-hand couloir (40 degree) on the face is climbed to the summit.

The **descent** is via the NW ridge back to the Fay-Quadra col. Start off down the S ridge until it is possible to traverse easy ledges on the W face to the NW ridge. This avoids a steep 60 m-high tower at the top of the ridge. Continue down to the col. From this point return along your ascent route.

1. Mt. Quadra N Face   2. Mt. Fay E Face   Photo: Don Beers

Mount Fay - Peak 1 3234 m

Fay is a very aesthetic looking snow-covered mountain high above Moraine Lake. There are four snow/ice routes on the N face, all extremely popular, meaning they get climbed more than once a year!

The climbing is typically straightforward on snow/ice slopes of about 40-50 degrees. Around 1 to 3 hours is required 'schrund to summit depending on conditions. The Central Ice Bulge is the climb most subject to changes in angle, being a direct assault on the N face icefall. Sadly, it now bears little resemblance to the route climbed on its first ascent. Likewise, the Chouinard Route is also subject to change (compare the photograph on p. 117 with that on p. 258 in the AAC/ACC guide). Fortunately, the most popular route on the face, the Berle/Kallen, is little affected by the state of the N face icefalls.

Note that in the past the Berle/Kallen has been popularly misconceived to be the Chouinard Route.

Usually the peak is climbed as part of a trip to the Colgan Hut since all routes are within easy walking distance of the hut (assuming the snow on the glacier is firm!), though some parties climb the N face in one day from the parking lot at Moraine Lake. *Map 82 N/8 Lake Louise*

Descent for all routes The easiest descent is down the SW face though the route down is not quite the same as the Normal Route up. Walk west from the summit along the summit ridge until you can move down to the south (left) into a likely looking gully that leads down to the glacier. It gets a little steeper near the bottom but nothing too alarming. Traverse the glacier around the south end of Mt. Little back to the hut. Some parties descend the W Ridge (see page 116) which gives direct access to the Perren descent to Moraine Lake as well as to the hut. The W Ridge is not as straightforward as the SW face, requiring some careful downclimbing, but it shouldn't give you grey hair. Your choice.

South-West Face (Normal Route) I photo p. 121

FA. Ms. G.E.Benham and C.Kaufmann, 1904. There are two routes on this face: only the line of the first ascent is described. In the early season the snow slopes should be treated with some caution.

From the hut, contour around the south side of Mt. Little, then head east across the glacier and up to the base of the SW face. Follow easy snow slopes and easy rock (scrambling) to the summit ridge. Traverse along the snow-covered ridge eastward to the summit.

West Ridge II 5.3   photo →

FA. L.Q.Coleman, W.J.Haggith, G.R. Kinney, J.A. Reid and G. Feuz, July 1907. FWA. D.Crosby, R.C.Hind and E.R. Gibson, December 1937. Maybe more "normal" than the Normal Route! The rock on the ridge is quite typical of the peaks in this group — not so good.

Approach to below the right (west) end of the N face of the mountain, at a small subsidiary rock peak on the W ridge. Climb a snow slope to the left (east) of this small peak to the ridge. Continue up the ridge over loose rock to the summit. A few hours from the 'schrund, or 7-10 hours return from Moraine Lake.

North Face, Roth/Kallen II   photo →

FA. F. Roth and U. Kallen, July 1968. The right-hand snow slope of the face. A straightforward snow/ice slope with a crux crossing the 'schrund or getting through the cornice.

Approach directly across the glacier from the hut or from the top of the Perren Route, depending on where you started your day. Climb right up the middle of the slope/couloir to the summit ridge.

North Face, Centre Ice Bulge Direct III   photo →

FA. L. Skreslet and L. Johnson, July 1976. In the eight years since the first ascent on the N face, attitudes and gear had changed sufficiently to make the Bulge itself look feasible. Made popular by a spectacular photo in "Climbing Ice" by Yvon Chouinard, but sadly the majority of the bulge has fallen off and little now remains.

Climb straight up the Centre Ice Bulge at its snout. It used to offer very steep, and sometimes overhanging, ice climbing. In the photograph opposite it looks like a pleasant, easy snow slope!

North Face, Chouinard Route II   photo →

FA. Y.Chouinard, P.Carman and D.Eberl, 1970. Takes the ice bulges at the left end of the face. Like the Central Ice Bulge this route is subject to large, dramatic changes due to changes in the amount of ice on the face.

Climb up snow/ice bulges immediately to the right (west) of the rocks at the left (east) end of the face. The last part is often very steep so avoid it by traversing left (east).

North Face, Berle/Kallen II   photo →

FA. Ø. Berle and U. Kallen, August 1968. Another straightforward snow/ice slope with a little mixed climbing. Crux is either the 'schrund or the cornice. In the recent past this route has often been climbed under the auspice of the Chouinard Route.

Climb up rock and snow next to the rock rib at the left (east) end of the face. At the top the original ascent line goes straight to the summit ridge, though many parties traverse left and finish easily up the N Ridge route.

Mt. Fay: 1. W Ridge 2. Roth/Kallen 3. Centre Ice Bulge Direct! 4. Chouinard Route 5. Berle/Kallen 6. NE Ridge

Photo: Glen Boles

North-East Ridge II 5.4 photo p. 117

FA. C.A. Fay and R. Kruzyna, 1961. A good introduction to ridge climbing in the Rockies and similar to the N ridge on Athabasca with stretches of both rock and some snow. A good place for honing your short-roping technique.

While the route can be approached via Fay's N glacier from Moraine Lake (the "old fashioned" method), the Perren Route is the usual approach used nowadays. From the Fay Glacier, gain the ridge just above the Fay-Babel col by scrambling up easy rocks and snow on the west side of the ridge. Follow the ridge throughout to the summit. If it gets tricky, traverse either left or right to find the easy way.

East Face V/VI 5.8 W5 photo →

FA. B. Blanchard, D. Cheesemond and K. Tobin, March 1984. This route takes the huge face overlooking the south end of S Consolation Lake. The long ski approach from Lake Louise and difficult ice climbing through the lower rock bands combined to make the first ascent somewhat more involved than anticipated. In the face of bad weather, the first ascent party had to forego the huge pillar-like headwall and "escape" to the NE ridge. Due to the nature of the face (loose rock etc.) this route is perhaps best left for the winter. It is definitely a modern, hard alpine route and should not be taken lightly!

The face consists of alternating rock-bands and snowfields in the lower third. On the first ascent a ribbon of ice breached these lower bands, offering very steep climbing. The angle of the face is a little less in the middle part of the route and the climbing eases somewhat. The upper third of the face is a vertical pillar of rock leading from the last snowfield directly to the summit. On the first ascent two days were required to reach the base of the pillar. From this point onward the first ascent party traversed right to an "escape ledge" system, and after a third bivi escaped to the ridge between Fay and Babel. The direct pillar awaits a first ascent.

Descend either the N glacier of Mt. Fay or the Perren Route to Moraine Lake.

Mount Little - Peak 2 3140 m photo p. 121

FA. J. Lisoway and G. Boles, July 1966. The NW ridge offers an easy scramble. *Map 82 N/8 Lake Louise*

From the Colgan Hut, step round the back and aim upward! Keeping to the snow/ice on the north side is the easiest way to go. Probably the second shortest route in the book!

Descend the way you came up.

Photo: Dave Cheesmond collection

Mt. Fay: E Face

119

Mount Bowlen - Peak 3 3072 m

FA. G. T. Little, C.S. Thompson, G.M. Weed and H. Kaufmann, July 1901. Another easy ridge hike. Takes about an hour to the summit from the hut. *Map 82 N/8 Lake Louise*

Walk down into the col and up the S ridge and/or S face to the summit. The shortest route in the book!

Descend the same route.

Peak 4 3054 m

FA. unknown. No technical difficulties. Easily climbed from the Colgan Hut. *Map 82 N/8 Lake Louise*

Cross the glacier from the hut aiming straight for the summit. Couldn't be simpler!

Descend the same way.

Mount Perren - Peak 5 3351 m

FA. H.F. Ulrichs and party, 1927. This is the lowest of the Ten Peaks and is often fobbed off as a subsidiary summit of Mt. Allen. A summit worth bagging the day you do Tuzo and Allen. *Map 82 N/8 Lake Louise*

From the Colgan Hut cross the glacier to the slopes on the east side of the peak. Climb these slopes or the E ridge directly to the summit.

Descend the same route.

Mount Allen - Peak 6 3301 m

FA. Ms. G.E. Benham and C. Kaufmann, July 1904. Most often combined with an ascent of Mt. Tuzo. The quintessential "Rockies Slag Heap". *Map 82 N/8 Lake Louise*

From the Neil Colgan Hut, traverse the glacier to the south of Bowlen and Peak 4, then climb up the east side of Perren and contour around to the Perren-Allen col. Either contour around to the south of Allen as far as the west slopes and scramble up loose rock to the summit or (a more pleasant alternative) scramble up the NE ridge. Your choice.

Descend the same route.

Mount Tuzo - Peak 7 3245 m

FA. Ms. H. Tuzo and C. Kaufmann, 1902. Usually climbed via the S glacier and S ridge. The longest approach from the Colgan Hut. *Map 82 N/8 Lake Louise*

Approach as for Mt. Allen to the Perren-Allan col. Either climb Allen or traverse around the south side of the mountain to its western slopes. Keep contouring around onto the glacier on the south side of Tuzo. Once on the glacier, climb easily to the summit. 7-10 hours from the hut.

Descend the same route.

120

Photo: Bruno Engler

Ten Peaks from the south-west 1. Fay 2. Little 3. Bowlen 4. Peak 4. 5. Perren 6. Allen h. Neil Colgen Hut

Mount Deltaform - Peak 8 3424 m

Rising nearly 1000 m above Eiffel Lake, the N face of Deltaform is easily the most impressive of the north faces in the Ten Peaks group. Three routes have been climbed: the Super Couloir, its direct variant and the North Glacier. The N Glacier was climbed in June 1968 but the glacier has changed dramatically since then and has recently been in an active state of decay. Objective hazard from serac collapse and rockfall is high and, needless to say, the route is not recommended and hence not described. Likewise, the Direct Finish to the Supercouloir is out of character with the rest of the route. It remains unrepeated and is not described either. *Map 82 N/8 Lake Louise*

North-West Ridge (Normal Route) II 5.5 photo →

FA. G. Boles and B. Greenwood, August 1961. This is the most technical of the normal routes described in the Ten Peaks group. The bulk of the route is a scramble but the final portion of ridge to the summit is quite steep and interesting. Overall, the rock is reasonable but still below average. Start early. This is a long route requiring a scramble over the top of Neptuak en route.

From Moraine Lake parking lot, follow the signed trail to Eiffel Lake and Wenkchemna Pass, a pleasant approach hike through woods and alpine meadows. At the pass turn left (south) and scramble up the NW ridge of Neptuak (Peak 9). Bypass a steep step near the base of the ridge by moving to the south and climbing moderate rock. 3-5 hours. Continue over the summit and down to the Neptuak-Deltaform col. There is some tricky scrambling leading down to the col.

From the col continue up through rock steps towards the summit of Deltaform. The last step to the N summit is about 150 m high, and is negotiated up easier rocks on the south side. The S summit lies across a gap 15 m deep, into which you rappel or downclimb before climbing back out. An alternative to climbing to the N summit and crossing the gap to the S summit is to traverse an airy ledge system below the last step on the NW Ridge, moving around the south side of the summit area to the SW ridge, then scrambling up to the S summit. Anywhere from 6-9 hours from the car to the summit depending on how much of an animal you are!

To **descend**, return the way you came.

North Face, The Supercouloir IV 5.8 photo →

FA. G. Lowe and C. Jones, July 1973. FWA. C. Buhler and M. Whalen, February 1976. One of the more popular of the harder climbs described in this book. It follows a relatively straight forward couloir for most of its length but has a sting in its tail. The rock on this face of the mountain is gross in places and rockfall is quite a hazard so pick a cold night and an early start for an ascent. The climb is typically managed in a day from Eiffel Lake but the walk-out could take you into the next day! Popular as a first "hard" route.

Mt. Deltaform: 1. Supercouloir   a. Alternate finish   2. NW Ridge

From Moraine Lake parking lot follow the signed trail to Eiffel Lake. It is usual to bivi at the lake where there is a good supply of water. The route is 20-30 minutes across the talus. After negotiating the 'schrund (often huge late in the season), climb up the lower couloir, staying to the right side to minimize exposure to objective hazards. At the top of the lower couloir, cross a rib into another couloir on the left and work your way up this past a bulge to the ugliest looking exit chimney (far right) which can be identified by a snow mushroom at about half height. Other exits to the left have been done but the described line is the original and, until recently, the most commonly used exit. Interesting and well protected steep climbing up the chimney leads to a snug belay behind the mushroom (5.8). This is a bombproof belay which is what is required. Continue up onto less steep but very shattered rock. After some difficult and poorly protected climbing, the top provides welcome relief! The last pitch has gained quite a reputation and many parties now opt for one of the left-hand exits. A pity since the chimney pitch offers great climbing.

Two **descents** are available. Although it is possible to traverse across the top of Deltaform and Neptuak to the west (the NW Ridge route in reverse), most parties descend to Kaufmann Lake and Tokumm Creek since it gets you down to treeline and a trail relatively quickly. To reach Kaufmann Lake descend talus and snow on the south side of the E ridge to the large snowfield between Deltaform and Tuzo. Wander down to the south to a gully leading to easy ground and the lake. With some judicious route finding it is possible to get down the gully without rappelling. At Tokumm Creek either head out to Highway 93 (22 km of good trail), or wander up the creek (9 km of poor or no trail) to Wenkchemna Pass and the Valley of the Ten Peaks. Take your pick. Bear in mind that if you walk out down Tokumm Creek you'll either have to carry your bivi gear or return sometime later to fetch it.

The Traverse of the Ten Peaks III 5.5   photo p. 121

FA. D. Gardner and C. Locke, August 1965. One of the best traverses in the Rockies and an excellent proposition if you fancy a weekend of summit bagging. The first traverse of the Ten Peaks was only a portion of an amazing traverse of the Moraine Lake-Lake Louise mountains. Starting over Babel and Fay, the first ascent party traversed the Ten Peaks to Wenkchemna Pass. After summiting on Wenkchemna Peak, they continued over Hungabee, Ringrose and Lefroy to Abbot Pass. Still not content, they continued over Victoria, Collier and Popes Peak. These days most people are happy to complete the Ten Peaks and call it quits.

Not that there is much difference in terms of climbing, the traverse is usually traversed west to east from Wenkchemna Pass. No cheating though — you should include Wenkchemna Peak via its S ridge for the full traverse. I hasten to add that almost all parties cheat and miss out on both Wenkchemna Peak and Mt. Fay. This, the usual traverse, was first done by T.B. Mason and G. Prinz in 1963. It has been done in a day from Moraine Lake to the Colgan Hut but most parties will be content with at least one bivi somewhere along the route. There are plenty of good sites in the cols between the peaks. Pick your weather carefully since the ridge is a lightning attractor.

Grand Sentinel

On the north side of Pinnacle Mountain are several large rock obelisks. The Grand Sentinel is the largest and has several excellent routes to its summit. These routes have gone through a recent revival with the modern development of quartzite climbing in the area. I only describe one route here and leave the rest for your own discovery. The rock is quartzite which is typically excellent and willingly takes good protection.

Highly recommended for a rock climbing day in the mountains.

From Moraine Lake follow the signed Larch Valley trail to Sentinel Pass. From a short distance down the Paradise Valley side contour across the northern slopes of Pinnacle Mountain and hike up a wide talus slope to the base of the Grand Sentinel. The south side faces towards Sentinel Pass. The route follows a beautiful corner system from the notch on the uphill side of the tower. *Map 82 N/8 Lake Louise*

Photo: Glen Boles

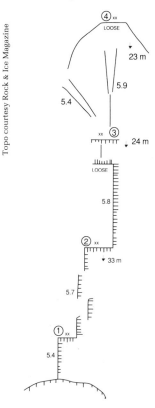

Topo courtesy Rock & Ice Magazine

Pinnacle Mountain 3067 m

Pinnacle Mtn. is the rocky summit immediately to the west of Sentinel Pass. The first ascent of this peak was quite a prize and succumbed only after a number of attempts by several of the leading guides of the day. The route was also the scene of some of the earliest "drilling" in the Rockies when during the third ascent the guides attempted to drill a hole for a long spike. They failed with the spike so "chiselled out the grooves round the sides and back of the rock" for a wire cable to which they attached a large rope intended as a permanent feature so "that in future it would be less dangerous". Great stuff for the early history of the Rockies. There is another route on the peak but it doesn't compete with the original when it comes to history. *Map 82 N/8 Lake Louise*

South-West Ridge II 5.5

FA. J.W.A. Hickson, E. Feuz Jr., R. Aemmer, 1909. Contrary to what it says in the most recent Rockies guide book ("Not recommended, rotten rock") this outing is recommended as an enjoyable, easy day in a spectacular situation on good rock (for the Rockies). The crux climbing is usually avoided by shinning up an old hemp rope — bags of fun. A comfortable day from Moraine Lake.

From the parking lot at Moraine Lake take the Larch Valley trail up the switchbacks into Larch Valley. Leave the trail to gain talus slopes below the south slopes of the peak which lead to the Eiffel-Pinnacle col. 1.5-2 hours. From the col traverse to the right (Moraine Lake side) on an obvious talus-covered ledge for 90 m to the base of an obvious weakness up the left side of a gully. An old, huge rappel anchor rope can be seen from below. A short pitch of easy 5th class brings one up to the rappel station and the bottom of a talus-filled gully. The gully is followed over short, easy rock steps to the base of a steep chimney and on old, fixed, fat hemp rope. In keeping with tradition, batman up the rope to a small ledge. Alternatively, 5.5 rock climbing attains the same ledge — boo! Traverse right from the ledge, around a corner and pass through a notch to reach another small ledge. Easy slopes above lead to the summit. 2-3 hours from the col.

Descend the same route. One rappel rope is sufficient.

Mount Temple 3543 m

This was the first mountain in the Rockies over 11,000 feet to be climbed. It is often referred to as the "Eiger of the Canadian Rockies", on account of its impressive N face, one of the few mile-high faces in the Rockies that can be seen from a highway. In common with the more famous Eiger, its routes are blessed with very short approach walks. In addition, all the routes with the exception of the NE Face have been climbed in a day, making them popular objectives for "Weekend Warriors".

The mountain is quite massive and bulky, and as a result it dominates the skyline from Lake Louise townsite. Though mainly a rock peak, it has several ice features. In particular, the N face is capped by a glacier whose seracs threaten the lower slopes in the region of the "Dolphin", the prominent dolphin-shaped icefield in the centre of the face.

The Normal Route up the SW ridge is one of the most travelled routes in the Rockies. Many people get to experience the feeling of topping out on an 11,000 foot peak via this climb. The fact that it is almost possible to just walk up a big mountain makes it a unique climb in the Rockies. The E Ridge is a classic outing climbed by many aspiring alpinists and could be considered the quintessential moderate ridge route in the book. Its "Big Step" start is a real Rockies treat with the hardest climbing on a wall of excellent quartzite. However, we cannot escape the fact that the N face routes are the big prizes on Mount Temple. Unfortunately, several of them are exposed to high objective hazards posed by collapsing seracs of the N glacier and rockfall from the upper face. The N ridge and the "Dolphin", in particular, are threatened and there have been several fatalities in recent years on routes in this part of the face. Furthermore, a lot of rock on the N face, particularly in the region of the "Dolphin" and Sphinx Face, is very shattered and pretty rank. Protection is often illusory at best! For your continued good health, pick a cold night, make an early start and climb quickly though safely through the hazard zones. *Map 82 N/8 Lake Louise*

Descent for all routes is by the SW Ridge (Normal Route) to Sentinel Pass. In cloudy conditions the cairns are a great help, though the trail is so well trodden that it is difficult to lose it!

DON'T try to descend the north side of the ridge — you'll most likely end up above some big cliffs. If you lose the trail for some reason, descend the slopes on the south side of the ridge which lead down into Larch valley, though care is needed to get through some small cliff bands.

From Sentinel Pass, you have the choice of descending either to Moraine Lake via Larch Valley or into Paradise Valley and picking up a trail that contours under the north side of the mountain all the way back to Lake Annette.

South-West Ridge (Normal Route) I   photo p. 129

FA. S.E.S. Allen, L.F. Frissel, and W.D. Wilcox, August 1894. A deservedly very popular scramble to the top of one of the highest mountains in the Rockies. It has a very short approach on a highway of a trail, the ridge is non-technical, and the view from the summit is stupendous. An ice axe could be really useful since the upper slopes are often covered in hard snow. Early in the season, beware of cornices along the final section of ridge and at the summit; several fatalities have occurred because of carelessness on the upper slopes, so take care. One of the easiest routes in the book.

From Moraine Lake follow the infamous "switchbacks" up to Larch Valley and eventually Sentinel Pass. The trail up to this point is certainly a highway amongst trails!

From Sentinel Pass a trail climbs up a long, laborious talus slope on the south side of the ridge, then traverses around a small rib to the right, below some big cliffs. Contour across talus-covered ledges (some cairns) and up to a break in the rock band above. Scramble up the break to more open talus slopes. Continue up these, and through another small rock band to the ridge line on the left. Follow the trail up the ridge to the top. The route is marked by small cairns most of the way. 4-6 hours from the parking lot.

Photo: Tony Daffern

E Ridge: "Big Step" start a. Big Step b. Black Towers c. top of Aemmer Couloir   Photo: Glen Bole

East Ridge IV 5.7

photo →

FA. O. Stegmaier and H. Wittich, August 1931. FWA. T. Auger and U. Pfaeffli, February 1977. At the time of the first ascent this was a major undertaking and a very impressive ascent. Only in the late '70's did it lose its reputation. Having said this, it is not a trivial route by any stretch of the imagination. For comparison, it is longer, more difficult and hence more serious than the E Ridge of Mt. Edith Cavell. Certainly it is an excellent candidate for those climbers looking for a challenging one-day alpine route. No doubt its modern popularity is in part due to its inclusion in the book "Fifty Classic Climbs of North America". The original line of ascent followed the ridge throughout, including the ridge through the "Black Towers". However, it is now common practise to forsake the intricacy of the ridge in the Black Towers area for a straight–tforward gully system that breaks through the Towers on the south side of the ridge.

Crampons and an ice axe are needed for the final section. The route has been soloed in a few hours but most parties will take a major part of a day for a round trip.

Two starts to the route are possible. The original start climbs an initial rock buttress known as the "Big Step" from the Moraine Lake Road; the second, more recent start, is up the "Aemmer Couloir" on the north side of the ridge and is approached from Lake Annette.

Big Step start Park on the Moraine Lake Road at a pull out about 2 km before Moraine Lake. Walk west for 50 m to an obvious avalanche slope which is followed to its top to the left of a prominent 90 m-high pinnacle. Climb an easy gully to the left of the pinnacle and at its top traverse right a short distance into a second, slightly steeper one. From the top of this couloir, another rightward traverse takes you to a third couloir. Climb a short, steep wall to enter the couloir and follow it up to an easy ridge which, in turn, leads to the base of the "Big Step", a steep 90 m buttress of good rock that looks a lot harder than it really is. Start off left of the ridge crest up a steep wall via the easiest line to a large ledge (5.6/7). Move left and up easier ground to broken ledges and good belays (5.5). Continue up into a gully system and trend either left and up a steep chimney or right to a broken face to reach the top of the step. Scramble up the long ridge above to where it steepens just below the main crest of the E ridge. The Aemmer Couloir start joins here.

Aemmer Couloir start From Lake Annette walk around the west end of the hillside immediately above the lake. Follow the talus slopes in an easterly direction towards the col below the east end of Temple. From the col, the Aemmer couloir is the obvious snow slope. The couloir is usually snow except for about 100 m at the top that is often blue ice (45 degrees). Take ice screws as you see fit. The cornice at the top is rarely very big. From the top of the Aemmer Couloir scramble up talus slopes on the south side of the ridge line to the base of a rock buttress on the ridge. Traverse left (junction with Big Step start) and into an amphitheatre on the south side of the E ridge.

Upper ridge A prominent ledge system running along the south side of the ridge line is followed until below the "Black Towers", a big black buttress that guards the summit snow slopes. Traverse left until below the first prominent wide gully that leads up through the Towers. Scramble up this large, easy-angled, open gully until it closes down a little towards the top (5.3/4). The top of the gully may be snowed up, making it a little tricky, but the face to the right can be climbed. Once on the snow at the top of the "Black Towers" amble up the ridge (watch for cornices) to the summit. There is sometimes a large crevasse to jump across immediately before the summit.

Photo: Greg Horne

Mt. Temple E Ridge. The Black Towers

North Face, Greenwood/Locke IV 5.8 A2   photo →

FA. B. Greenwood and C. Locke July 1966. A "must do" route. This route offers both the safest and the most technical climbing on the north side of the mountain. The majority of the climbing is on a rock spur and thus subject to little or no objective hazard. After a relatively tame start in the "Dolphin", the climbing on the spur becomes sustained, but is well protected and on good quality limestone. The crux is close to the top. Though predominantly a rock climb, crampons and ice axe are necessary to reach the start of the rock climbing. Rock shoes are an asset though not absolutely necessary. From a bivi at Lake Annette, the route can be climbed comfortably in a day with a pre-dawn start. It has actually been soloed in five hours! Best in August when it is usually driest.

Start up the right-hand tail fin of the "Dolphin", which is subject to far less objective hazard than the left fin. Climb this and easy rocks on the left to the junction with the left fin. Continue up the rock rib right of the "Dolphin" to a secondary icefield to the right. The technical climbing starts at the top of this icefield.

Climb a surprisingly awkward chimney (5.8) to some low-angled rock. Continue up and right to a prominent ledge that runs across the face. Traverse left along the ledge (very loose and poor protection, if any worth talking about!) to a rib which is climbed up the right side to a large ledge (5.6). Above is a steep peapod-shaped crack (5.8, maybe some aid) leading to small ledges. Continue up and right to belay behind a large flake. A corner crack on the left leads into a groove which is followed to a ledge on the rib (5.8). If the top of the groove is corniced, a thin crack leads straight up over the roof on the right (A2). Continue up the rib in a sensational position and up a shallow groove (5.7) to the crest of the rib.

Drop down the other side a few metres and work your way left to a ledge (possible bivi site) below a corner crack in a beautiful, clean-cut headwall. Follow the crack for a pitch, then move out right and up into a groove (crux, 5.8 or A1). Climb over a roof at the top of the groove to a loose ledge. Traverse the ledge to a small gully (great views down). Lower into the gully and climb easily out the other side to the top. The purist will then enjoy a talus slog to the summit. Everyone else will traverse the west side of the mountain to the SW ridge.

Mt. Temple N Face:
1. Greenwood/Locke 2. Elzinga/Miller
2a. exposed ledge variation 3. North (Lowe) Ridge
4. Greenwood/Jones 5. Robinson/Orvig
a. Aemmer Couloir b. descent (SW Ridge)
c. Sentinel Pass

133

North (Lowe) Ridge IV 5.6/7   photo p. 133

FA. G.Lowe and J.Lowe August 1970. Due to its position below the seracs of the N glacier, this route suffers from high objective hazard even though it follows a prominent rib. For some strange reason many people assume it is free of hazard. Check out the ice avalanche pictures in CAJ 1976 (p. 5) and judge for yourself! It is questionable whether this route should be included in a selected route book, but the few people I know who have done it say it is worthwhile. Probably the biggest gamble described in the book. The climbing is mostly easy 5th class with some short, harder sections.

Gain the rib from the right (west) and climb it, occasionally with interest, for one thousand metres until the seracs are reached. Expect to find some mixed climbing just after crossing the ledge system that runs across the whole face. The seracs can be tackled either directly, by traversing around to the right and via a number of crevasses, or to the far left where the barrier is much smaller. The latter choice is by far the easiest and least scary. Take your pick depending on how sane you feel. Whatever exit you choose, do it with haste! Once above this impasse, stagger up the snowfield to the E ridge and follow it up to the summit.

North Face, Elzinga/Miller IV 5.7   photo p. 133

FA. J.Elzinga & C.Miller, October 1974. FWA. C.Buhler & P.Hein, January 1976. Originally a variation to the N Ridge, this route has become the most popular route on the N Face. It is subject to some high objective hazards but it is possible to gain height much more quickly on this route than the Lowe Route and hence spend less time exposed to hazard. Furthermore, there are some route choices that dramatically minimize hazard. The route has been climbed in 6 hours though most parties will take longer.

Start up the right fin of the "Dolphin" (as for the Greenwood/Locke). Continue to its top left-hand corner (the "nose"). A very short, loose and surprisingly steep step gains the ledge that runs across the whole face. Two possibilities now come to hand. The original line of ascent was up low-angled slabs and corners above. For this route, go straight up, aiming for a prominent chimney on the left side of the N face headwall. Gain the N ridge about 100 m below the seracs via a short chimney (5.7) on the left. The alternative to this route is much easier: traverse east along the large ledge that runs across the face (one narrow and very exposed section) and join the N Ridge route (the most popular way). This ledge system is perhaps the safest spot on the route to bivi, if a biv is required. Follow one of the exits to the summit.

North-East Buttress, Greenwood/Jones IV 5.8 A1   photo p. 133

FA. B. Greenwood and Jim Jones, Summer 1969. This takes the rib that deliniates the boundary between the N and NE faces and provides the safest route on this side of the mountain. It has been climbed comfortably in a day. Rock shoes are useful but not absolutely necessary. Take your crampons and axe for the summit snowfield.

Approach from Lake Annette around the west end of a hill on the south side of the lake. Follow a prominent ridge of moraine up to the base of the route. Start directly below the rib at a break in a short, steep quartzite wall. After tackling the wall, scramble up rubble-covered ledges to the rib and continue up its right-hand side until steep rock is encountered on the crest. Climb the rib via several steep walls to a very loose and steep wall about two ropelengths below the final headwall. Traverse round the left side of the rib to a loose groove which can be climbed to a large ledge at the base of the main difficulties. Follow the obvious big groove in the wall above to a loose alcove. Exit the alcove up a steep corner on the left (interesting climbing on excellent rock) to a hanging stance in a big corner system (5.8). Tackle the corner until about 20 m below a big roof. A tension traverse to the right gains an arete. Make your way across a beautiful slab of boiler-plate limestone into a crack on the right. Climb this to easier ground above (5.8).

Note: Above the loose alcove several different exits of varying degrees of desperation have been climbed. The described line offers one exit. It is apparent that if you lower out from the alcove down to the right, a short pitch (5.5) gives access to the snow slopes. Once off the rock, walk up snow to the E ridge and hence the top.

North-East Face, The Sphinx Face IV 5.9 A2   photo p. 133

FA. W. Robinson and R. Orvig, October 1988. To the east of the Greenwood/Jones route is another face, dubbed the Sphinx Face by the late Bugs McKeith, which forms a subsidiary peak on the E ridge. In the middle of this face is an obvious snow/icefield. The route follows this up to steep, loose rock bands which guard the north side of the E ridge. Not a particularly great climb but certainly of interest to those keen on doing an alpine "5.9 A2". I've included it more for completeness than for aesthetic reasons. The nature of the rock is such that a summer ascent would be a lottery. The first ascent party required one bivi on the face and one on the descent.

Approach as for the Greenwood/Jones. Climb through the lower steep band and continue over rubbly ledges to the snow/icefield. Romp up this to the first steep band of rock close to the top of the face. Climb through the first rock band up a weakness left (east) of the top of the main ice slope and gain the prominent ledge system. This band has some atrocious rock which provides a supreme test of one's climbing "cool". Traverse to the right along a ledge for a ropelength to the base of a break in the upper wall. Climb the break in two excellent mixed pitches to the E ridge. Rappel to the prominent traverse ledge on the south side of the E Ridge route (see p 130). Either continue up the E Ridge route to the summit and down to Sentinel Pass or traverse east to the Aemmer Couloir and descend to Lake Annette.

135

LAKE O'HARA

Wiwaxy Peak	2703 m	Grassi Ridge	II 5.6/7	p. 139
Mt. Hungabee	3492 m	W Ridge (normal)	III 5.4	p. 140
Mt. Biddle	3319 m	W Ridge (normal)	II 5.4	p. 142
Mt. Schäffer	2692 m	N Ridge	II 5.4	p. 144
The McArthur Horseshoe			III 5.6	p. 144
Odaray Mtn.	3159 m	SE Ridge (normal)	II 5.4	p. 146
		NE Ridge, Tarrant	IV 5.7	p. 146
Watch Tower	2542 m	W Face	II 5.7	p. 149
Mt. Huber	3368 m	NE Ridge (normal)	II	p. 150

Lake O'Hara is synonymous with the foundation of alpinism in the Canadian Rockies. In 1906 the fledgling Alpine Club of Canada held a large mountaineering camp in the area with participants arriving on the recently completed CP railroad. Guides were hired from Europe where climbing was already an established pastime. All the peaks in the area had their first ascents during these times, perhaps the most notable achievement being the ascent of the W ridge of Hungabee.

The astounding beauty of the area plus the accessibility of a large number of varied climbs promoted its popularity which still continues today. In summer months the Elizabeth Parker Hut at Lake O'Hara is often full. Unfortunately, the immediate area around Lake O'Hara consists of delicate alpine meadows and the popularity of the area put the health of the meadows in jeopardy. As a result access to Lake O'Hara is now controlled. For example, you cannot drive up the road, you must take the bus instead or walk. Also the total number of campsites is restricted. This management scheme isn't a problem to deal with; it's just a matter of booking in advance to stay overnight, and then to book the bus. It may seem like a daunting amount of officialese, but it is all worth the time and trouble.

Access Lake O'Hara lies near the head of the Cataract Creek valley in Yoho National Park. Turn south off the Trans-Canada Highway 13 km west of Lake Louise townsite and 14 km east of Field onto Highway 1A, cross the railroad tracks, turn right and continue a short distance to the Lake O'Hara parking lot. Alternatively, take 1A Highway from Lake Louise. From here either hike up the 13 km Cataract Brook trail or, from mid-June to October, take the Lake O'Hara bus (see details under Officialese). You should know that mountain bikes are not allowed on the road.

Facilities Since Lake O'Hara is 13 km into the backcountry you are going to have to pack in everything you need. The nearest towns for groceries and supplies are Lake Louise and Field, though a limited range of goods can be bought at West Louise Lodge at Wapta Lake, 1.5 km west along the Trans-Canada Highway from the Highway 1A turnoff to the Lake O'Hara parking lot. There is also a restaurant, motel and gas station here.

Since Lake O'Hara lies within Yoho National Park, information concerning the area is available at the Park Information Centre in Field, as a second choice, the Information Centre in Lake Louise.

Many parties will only be interested in taking the bus to Lake O'Hara and then hiking up to Abbot Pass to stay at the Abbot Pass Hut (see page 85, 86). However, if you wish to stay at Lake O'Hara the most likely accommodation is the Elizabeth Parker Hut and the campground. There is also a lodge but I'll assume most parties will not be staying there. However, their afternoon teas are open to the public; a great treat after a good day on the hill! The Elizabeth Parker Hut requires reservations booked through the Alpine Club of Canada (see page 20 for details). The access trail leaves the road almost directly opposite the warden cabin and climbs over a small, low hill into the meadows, 0.7 km distant. The hut lies on the far side of the meadow and in daylight is obvious. At night time just follow the trail to the front door.

Thirty campsites are located downstream of the hut, with 20 reservable and

---

Elizabeth Parker Hut

Map 82 N/8 Lake Louise
Location Alpine meadow west of Lake O'Hara. GR 457893
Reservations Alpine Club of Canada
Capacity 24 in two huts
Facilities Fully equipped, custodian summer
Water Creek 30 m north of hut
Notes Locked when custodian is not present

---

10 available on a first-come, first-served basis. There are two kitchen shelters, water, chemical privies, fireboxes, firewood, axe, and a bear proof garbage storage building.

Officalese Since Lake O'Hara is within Yoho National Park, back country use comes under the regulations detailed on page 17. However, there are several regulations that apply only to Lake O'Hara regarding bus bookings and campground useage.

Reservations for campground and bus rides to Lake O'Hara are made by telephoning Lake O'Hara Reservations or writing to Yoho National Park, Box 99, Field, B.C., V0A 1G0. Reservations are accepted only within two months of the first day of your stay in the area. When making reservations for the bus and/or campground it is necessary to supply the following information:

1. Number of people in the party (maximum per group is 10)
2. Number of campsites required (maximum of 5 sites, 1 tent per site)
3. Dates required and length of stay (maximum stay is 4 nights)
4. Preference of ingoing bus times.

Buses run from mid-June to the beginning of October with three buses ingoing each day, two in the morning and one in the afternoon. On Fridays there is an additional one in the evenings. Outgoing, there are also three buses. You should ring Lake O'Hara Reservations to find out the schedule since it may change from year to year.

In the case of cancellation of bus seats or campsites or the possibility of a late arrival, notify Lake O'Hara Reservations as soon as possible. Failure to arrive or request to cancel the Thursday or Friday portion of a weekend booking results in cancellation of the entire booking.

Things you should also know about the bus are:

1. Ingoing passengers must be on board the bus fifteen minutes before departure or seats may be forfeited.
2. Luggage on the bus is limited to one piece per person which is strictly enforced. Coolers, boxes, etc. are not permitted. Dogs are also not allowed.

Rock Climbing Even though almost all parties are not going to Lake O'Hara to crag climb there are some small quartzite crags at the east end of Lake O'Hara that are similar in character to the quartzite crags at Lake Louise. Although they are not developed like the crags at Louise, they provide some possibilities when the weather/conditions are not conducive to going high or you just fancy a day goofing around on the rocks!

Wiwaxy Peak: Grassi Ridge

Photo: Glen Boles

Wiwaxy Peak 2703 m

Wiwaxy Peak consists of two quartzite towers at the west end of Lake O'Hara. The larger of the two has a big W face overlooking the O'Hara Road which has been climbed by several lines. The southern edge of this face is a classic climb that which has been popular ever since it was first climbed. *Map 82 N/8 Lake Louise*

Grassi Ridge II 5.6/7   photo p. 138

FA. B. Greenwood, Miss P. Johnson and D. Vockeroth, 1962. This classic climb takes the prominent ridge on Wiwaxy facing towards Lake O'Hara. It is about 300 m long, giving almost ten rope-lengths of mid-5th class climbing. The crux is 5.6/7. It has been many beginner's first climbing experience and is ideal for an "easy" day out with its numerous large ledges along the route and short approach and descent. A fun rock route on mainly good quality quartzite. Take along a small rack of gear.

From the warden cabin at the outlet of Lake O'Hara, cross Cataract Creek and follow a trail down the north side of creek for about 200 m to an avalanche clearing that leads up through the trees. Work your way up this and left towards the base of the prominent rib. Scramble up to the highest tree. Two pitches of moderate climbing up steep rock in a corner lead to the first large ledge. From here follow the rib to the top of Wiwaxy with the obligatory traverses, mostly to the right of the rib, when the going gets tough. About 200 m up is a steep buttress that provides the crux. The trick is to follow the crest of the rib. Start from a belay on a large block and climb directly up the steep crest on good holds (5.6/7) for 40 m. It is possible to bypass this pitch on the right, but it involves traversing across steep and loose rock and is quite unenjoyable, unlike the crest of the rib. From the top of the buttress, continue more easily to the summit.

Descend to the col at the head of the large gully just to the east of the route. DON'T descend this gully! Instead, contour around the south side of the other Wiwaxy Tower on talus-covered ledges and descend an easy, wide gully to gain the Wiwaxy Gap trail. Follow this the rest of the way down to the lake.

Mount Hungabee 3492 m

This very prominent mountain at the south end of the O'Hara Valley is the highest of all the peaks in O'Hara. Its normal route up the W ridge is more difficult than most "Normal Routes" on other mountains in the area. The E face which overlooks Paradise Valley is "one of the greatest single precipices in the Rockies", and as yet awaits a direct route. Unfortunately, the rock is not that good, just like the rock on many of the peaks in this neck of the woods! This is the major reason why the "obvious" line on the E face remains unclimbed. However, the rock on the W Ridge route is reasonable. *Map 82 N/8 Lake Louise*

West Ridge (Normal Route) III 5.4   photo →

FA. V.A. Fynn and E.O. Wheeler, 1909 FWA. B. Greenwood, C. Locke and C. Scott, December 1966. The W ridge is the prominent ridge that drops from the summit of Hungabee down to Opabin Pass. The rock is reasonable and the route finding a challenge. A popular route with aspirant guides. The route is not recommended in early summer because of avalanche hazard from snow slopes on the NW face.

From Lake O'Hara follow the signed Opabin Lake trail onto Opabin Plateau and work your way up the moraines and glacier to Opabin Pass. Follow the ridge crest over a small peak until the first band of cliffs bars easy progress. Diagonal upwards over easy ledges to the left and cross two shallow gullies (cairns) to a faint rib at the right-hand edge of the snow and ice of the NW face. Scramble up the rib to a small barrier of cliffs with an obvious weakness leading through to more scrambling and a much bigger barrier of cliffs. Traverse right (south) around a corner on an easy ledge along the base of the cliffs. Work your way up chimneys and ledges on the left side of the first gully you come across to access easier going in the gullies above. Scramble up tedious scree above to the summit ridge which is composed of the best (or worst?) example of the black shale band that outcrops on so many of the nearby peaks. Traverse onto the right (west) side of the summit ridge (snow/ice) to gullies and steps which lead back to the ridge a short distance from the summit. 6 hours from Opabin Pass.

Descent is back down the way you came.

Mt. Hungabee: W Ridge   p. Opabin Pass

Mount Biddle 3319 m

This peak sits on the opposite side of Opabin Pass from Mt. Hungabee. As seen from McArthur Pass, Biddle is an impressive mountain with a steep W face. As in most cases in this area the rock is not so good and the W Face route suffers as a consequence. However, the rock on the two main ridges above Lake McArthur is reasonable though the climbing is often little more than scrambling. *Map 82 N/8 Lake Louise*

West Ridge (Normal Route) II 5.4   photo →

FA. A. Carpe and R. Aemmer, August 1915. A pleasant scramble to the top of one of the more impressive looking peaks at Lake O'Hara. Not the original route on the mountain but it is certainly better than the original SW Face route and is the advised "Normal Route".

The first objective is to get to Biddle Pass between Mt. Biddle and Park Mtn. From Lake O'Hara take the signed trail to McArthur Pass and Lake McArthur. Traverse along the south side of the lake until almost below the pass which is gained via easy rocks and a short couloir. From the pass follow the W ridge to the summit over numerous small rock steps. When it gets difficult, traverse onto the south-west side of the mountain to find easy ways up.

The original **descent** off the mountain followed the S ridge a little way, then traverse the south-west slopes of the mountain back to Biddle Pass. However, the SW face is composed of down-sloping, undercut steps completely covered with ball-bearing talus. Death by cheese grater! It is much better to retrace your steps back down the W ridge to Biddle Pass. For a round trip from Lake O'Hara anticipate 10-14 hours.

Photo: Glen Boles

Mt. Biddle: 1. *W Ridge* 1+2. *McArthur Horseshoe* a. *Lake McArthur* b. *"cheaters start" to McArthur Horseshoe*

Mount Schäffer 2692 m

Mount Schäffer is the western end of the ridge extending westward from the NW ridge of Biddle. The ridge extending to the east of Schäffer is identified by a series of large gendarmes that prove to be a route finding challenge on the McArthur Horseshoe traverse. The N ridge of the peak is one of the traditional Rockies "first outing in the mountains" routes. *Map 82 N/8 Lake Louise*

North Ridge II 5.4   photo →

FA. Unknown. The N ridge of Schäffer is a popular climb for visitors staying in the Elizabeth Parker Hut. It offers a pleasant scramble requiring some simple rope work. A good introduction for beginners, with the standard no harder than 5.4

From the hut take the McArthur Pass trail to Schäffer Lake, then clamber up and left (east) to gain the ridge that leads directly to the summit.

The best **descent** is down the talus of the NW ridge.

The McArthur Horseshoe III 5.6   photo p. 143, →

FA. T. Auger and D. Whitburn, July 1968
For those who have a distinct dislike for descending their ascent route and enjoy long ridge traverses then this may be just the ticket — Mt. Schäffer, Mt. Biddle and Park Mtn — an interesting traverse of the "horseshoe" surrounding Lake McArthur. The first ascent party ascended the N ridge of Biddle and went down the W ridge. However, it could be completed in the other direction just as readily. Most parties forgo the joys(?) of the Schäffer gendarmes for either an easy ascent to or descent from (dependent on the direction of your traverse) the col between Schäffer and Biddle. Not many people will hold it against you. The first ascent party took 16 hours round trip. It has probably been done more quickly but still plan on a long day.

Gain the summit of Schäffer by either the N Ridge or the western talus slopes. Follow the ridge crest over some impressive gendarmes to the Schäffer-Biddle col below the N ridge of Biddle.

If the difficulty gets too much, just traverse to either side of the ridge to find an easier way ahead. You'll need to make some rappels. This initial section of the traverse is quite involved and many parties will avoid it by missing out Schäffer altogether and walking along the north shore of Lake McArthur and then up talus slopes to gain the col east of the gendarmes.

Follow Biddle's N ridge to a short section of flatter ground over a small double summit known as "the Gunsight". Continue up some final steps of the ridge to the summit of Biddle. There are some 5th class bits in the final section. Descend from the summit via the W Ridge route to reach Biddle Pass.

From Biddle Pass the summit of Park Mtn. is easily reached via talus slopes. To descend, work your way down rocks on the north-east side of the mountain until easier talus slopes lead down to Lake McArthur.

Photo: Don Beers

Mt. Schäffer: N Ridge   a. All Soul's Prospect   s. Schäffer Lake   145

Odaray Mountain 3159 m

Odaray Mtn. lies on the west side of Lake O'Hara valley to the north of McArthur Pass. The east side of the mountain is distinguished by a glacier that extends almost to tree-line. During the early days of Rockies climbing there were a large number of mountaineering camps at Lake O'Hara and Odaray was a popular

outing, presumably because it involved little difficulty. The normal route up the glacier remains popular today. The NE ridge forms a very appealing line when the mountain is viewed from the Elizabeth Parker Hut and it is not surprising that it has attracted modern-day alpinists. *Map 82 N/8 Lake Louise*

South-East Ridge (Normal Route) II 5.4   photo →

FA. J.J. McArthur, 1887 An impressive solo first ascent for its day. It has always been a very popular route: a little glacier, snow and easy rock, and a summit with impressive views.

From Elizabeth Parker Hut take the signed trail directly behind the hut up to Odaray Plateau. From here angle up

across the glacier below the SE peak (Little Odaray) to below the col between Odaray and Little Odaray. Scramble up some rock and snow to gain the col. Follow the SE ridge to the summit. There are two minor rock steps between the col and the summit. 3-6 hours from the hut.

The **descent** is back down the route.

North-East Ridge, Tarrant Buttress IV 5.7   photo p. 148

FA. D.K. Morrison and J.F. Tarrant, July 1955. This impressive and very aesthetic buttress of rock offers an excellent introduction to the longer and harder alpine rock routes. A bold undertaking in 1955. The rock is typically very good except for some rubble near the top and the climbing is always interesting, mostly easy 5th class with the crux right at the top. It is not really a ridge climb, rather a combination of ridge and face. One of the best routes in the Lake O'Hara area and highly recommended.

From Elizabeth Parker Hut, follow the signed Linda Lake trail to a tree-covered ridge about halfway between Morning Glory Lake and Linda Lake. Hike up the ridge to a large grassy scoop, on excellent bivi site. Start off by scrambling up steep grassy terrain for 50 m to where the rock steepens dramatically at a narrow grassy

ledge. Traverse right along the ledge to an obvious 7 m-high rock arch. Continue along the ledge for 30 m to the base of the first pitch. Climb up and slightly right to a small belay. After three more ropelengths (mid-5th class), trend left up to a very large shallow scoop in the face. Climb up the bowl, seemingly for ever, following the easiest line through occasional steeper sections towards a large rib on the left. Follow the rib to its end, past some large quartzite blocks. Move left to another rib and continue up in a similar vein to the base of an obvious black band of rock that forms the summit block. In this band are two foul-looking chimneys. Take the right-hand one (5.7) to an easy snow arete and the summit. 6-9 hours from the base of the ridge to the summit.

Descend the Normal Route.

Mt. Odaray: 1. SE Ridge   2. Tarrent Buttress

Mt. Odaray: 1. Tarrant Buttress   2. SE Ridge   Photo: Glen Boles

Watch Tower 2542 m

An impressive obelisk of rock overlooking Watch Tower Creek; you can't miss it from the Lake O'Hara Road. If you have a short day and are looking for something to do then the W Face climb is a good way of filling in time. *Map 82 N/8 Lake Louise*

West Face II 5.7

FA. B. Greenwood and G.W. Boles, July 1962. Takes a direct line up the centre of the West Face of the Tower. It looks a lot bigger from the road than it really is. This short (100 m), fun route makes an ideal outing for a short day. There is also a NE face route that is similar in character and difficulty. However, the approach to the W Face is shorter.

From the gate at the beginning of the Lake O'Hara Road, hike 5 km up the road to Watch Tower Creek, as for the approach to the N Face route on Victoria. Follow the edge of Watch Tower Creek to avoid the trees on the lower slopes. Scramble up some shale slopes and through small cliff bands to a shoulder below the W face. Scramble up to below a chimney in the centre of the face and climb it to a large ledge (20 m). Make a short traverse left to twin cracks and climb these until below the upper cracks which appear to be quite difficult. Step left and climb a pleasant wall to a large belay ledge (23 m). Above is a short wall, a chimney and a short, easy corner leading to a small ledge (20 m). Climb the steep corner above to a small slab which is climbed to its upper left corner. Traverse the steep wall on the left to a crack that leads to the top (35 m).

Descent Rappel the NE face, then drop down into the drainage to the north of the Watch Tower.

1. W Face d. descent 2. N Face Victoria

Mount Huber 3368 m

If Mt. Huber stood alone it would be a high, dominant summit. However, it is essentially a subsidiary snow-covered summit of Mt. Victoria, though a very prominent one at that. Some parties just rush past it in a mad dash up the SW Face of Victoria. Take the time to top out on this summit and then go on to Mt. Victoria, as many parties do. Map *82 N/8 Lake Louise*

North-East Ridge (Normal Route) II   photo →

FA. A cast of thousands from the ACC., 1907. FWA. C. Perry and P. Morrow, February 1973. This relatively easy ascent gains a superb vantage point from which to examine the Lake O'Hara area.

From the warden cabin, follow the trail clockwise around Lake O'Hara for 150 m to the Wiwaxy Gap trail (signed) which offers a steep climb up to the Wiwaxy-Huber col. Angle up and left across the W face of Huber along rubble-covered ledges (cairns) to gain the Huber Glacier on the north side of the mountain. Climb the glacier to the col between Huber and Victoria. An easy snow ridge leads to the summit. 5-7 hours.

Descent is exactly the same way you came up.

It is possible to continue to the summit of Victoria for more exercise (see the SW Face of Victoria on pages 96, 99).

Mt. Victoria: 1. SW Face
2. Wiwaxy Peak, Grassi Ridge
g. Huber Glacier   h. Huber Ledges
m. Mt. Huber   w. Wiwaxy Peaks

Photo: Bruno Engler

151

FIELD				
S Goodsir	3562 m	SW Ridge (normal)	III 5.4	p. 154
		N Face	VI 5.7	p. 158
N Goodsir	3524 m	S Face	III 5.4	p. 156
Mt. Stephen	3199 m	N Ridge	III 5.7	p. 160
The President	3138 m	E Ridge (normal)	II	p. 162
Vice President	3066 m	W Ridge (normal)	II	p. 162

The Town of Field is the major population centre in Yoho National Park. While the majority of popular routes within this park are at Lake O'Hara, this section includes a few other routes in Yoho National Park as well as the Goodsir Towers from Kootenay National Park. This may seem a little odd, yet geographically it makes good sense since the access to the Goodsirs is just down the road from Field. Hence the use of the name Field for this section of the book.

The routes described are all on high mountains, so you are going to have to anticipate dealing with snow and/or ice on your chosen outing. The N face of South Goodsir Tower is the extreme route in the area, a pointer to the extreme alpinism possibilities if one is willing to venture deeper into the back-country than normal. The most popular outing in the area is without doubt the President and Vice President, traditionally climbed over two days with a stay at the Stanley Mitchell Hut, but increasingly climbed in a single day from Emerald Lake. The N Ridge of Mt. Stephen is a big alpine rock route up one of the most aesthetic lines in the area.

Access The Town of Field lies 26 km west of Lake Louise along the Trans-Canada Highway. The principal access for all the routes in this section is from

the Trans-Canada, along a stretch of a road extending 6 km east of Field to Spiral Tunnels viewpoint, and 30 km west of Field to the Beaverfoot Lodge turnoff. The Yoho Valley Road, which leads to the famous Takakkaw Falls and the trailhead for Stanley Mitchell Hut leaves the Trans-Canada Highway 3.7 km east of Field. The Emerald Lake approach to the President and Vice President is accessed from the Emerald Lake Road, which starts 2.6 km west of the town.

Facilities Field is a small, quiet town quite unlike the bustling tourist centres of Lake Louise and Banff. There is only one general store, "The Siding" with in-store small restaurant. However, Lake Louise is not that far away and even Banff or Golden are within reasonable distance if you need something desperately. The nearest climbing stores are in Banff. Field has a gas station alongside the Trans-Canada Highway at the turnoff into Field. However, it isn't open 24 hours. The nearest 24-hour gas stops are in Golden or Banff.

Low-price accommodation possibilities are the drive-in campgrounds within the park, the nearest one to Field being the Kicking Horse campground 1 km along the Yoho Valley road. There is also a small store here. If you go 20 km west of Field along the Trans-Canada Highway you'll find the other drive-ins. At the end of the Yoho Valley road there is a walk-in campground close to the trailhead and also the Whiskey Jack Youth Hostel, 0.5 km south of the trailhead. The other Youth Hostel in the area, Amiskwi Hostel, is in Field.

In terms of more luxurious possibilities, there are no hotels or motels in town, only "private accommodations" (a room and kitchenette for self-catering). The nearest motel is West Louise Lodge, 9.4 km to the east on the Trans-Canada. For those with a fat wallet, Emerald Lodge at Emerald Lake may appeal. You may also consider Cathedral Mountain Chalets at the Kicking Horse camp-ground. For those folks off to climb the President and Vice

Stanley Mitchell Hut

Map 82 N/10 Blaeberry River
Location In Alpine meadow near head of Little Yoho Valley GR 303083
Reservations Alpine Club of Canada
Capacity 30
Facilities Fully equipped, custodian summer
Water River directly south of hut
Notes Locked when custodian is not present

President from the Little Yoho side the Stanley Mitchell Hut is the place to go. For information regarding weather, conditions, campsites, registration and the backcountry, visit Yoho National Park Information Centre on the Trans-Canada Highway across the town access road from the gas station. Contained in the same building is the Alberta Tourism office where enquires about motels, etc. can be directed.

Officialese All the routes are within Yoho National Park. Backcountry use comes under the regulations detailed on page 17.

Rock Climbing The nearest developed rock climbing is at Lake Louise and if you get the crag climbing urge that is where you should go (see page 86). However, there is some more adventurous climbing to be had at Takakkaw Falls. The wall to the left (north) of the falls has two routes on it (both at most 5.7), one that leads up to a cave close to the top of the falls. There is potential for more routes on the extensive cliffs in this locale.

South Goodsir 3562 m
North Goodsir 3525 m

The Goodsirs are two very impressive towers with N faces rising over 2000 m above Goodsir Creek. Regardless of your vantage point they are big mountains by Rockies standards. Access to both the north and south sides of the peaks is a long, long way even though it is possible to approach reasonably closely from the south by vehicle. This makes for long outings, particularly in the case of the N face of the S Tower where you approach from the north and descend to the south, given that you take the conservative descent. Throw in rock quality that is not far from the worst to be found in the Rockies and you complete the recipe for some serious climbing. Having said all this, the fact that they are so high makes them eternal favorites with summit baggers. On Goodsir North the S Face route is the best of the existing lines. The N face is still awaiting an ascent. *Map 82 N/1 Mount Goodsir*

South Tower, South-West Ridge (Normal Route) III 5.4   photo →

FA. C.E. Fay, H.C. Parker, C. Häsler and C. Kaufmann, July 1903. A long approach to a straightforward climb that consists mostly of steep hiking. The ridge is mostly a scramble with two sections of narrow ridge near the summit that make things entertaining. To complete the route in a long day car-to-car is quite a feat but it has been done. Most people will chose a more leisurely approach and bivi somewhere on the way in and complete the trip the following day.

Follow the Trans-Canada Highway west of Field towards Golden and turn off at the Beaverfoot Lodge Road. Stay on this road for about 25 km until it splits. Take the left-hand branch. In another 6 km turn left at another junction and follow the road over the Beaverfoot River. About 200 m after the bridge the road splits again. The left-hand road, buried in long grass, is the way you need to go. It is driveable but is greasy when wet and only recommended if your vehicle has good clearance. Follow this road in a north-westerly direction towards the Ice River. When the road peters out a short piece of bushwhacking leads down to the trail alongside the Ice River, which is followed to a warden cabin just north of the confluence of Shining Beauty Creek and the Ice River.

The trail continues a little way north of the cabin, then peters out at an avalanche slide area. If the logs are dry go straight across the slide area to a faint trail in the trees beyond. If not, drop down to river level, bypass the logs then head back up to the trail. You will likely get wet feet using this latter option. An indistinct trail continues north along the east side of the Ice River about 30 m above river level. Eventually, you'll reach a major avalanche slide area about 500 m south of Zinc Creek. A faint trail marked by a cairn leads up the avalanche slope, then turns left and angles up into the upper reaches of Zinc Creek. If you lose the trail at the avalanche slope just head into the trees on the north side of the open area and go straight uphill to intersect the trail. DO NOT stay in the valley bottom all the way to Zinc Creek;

The Goodsirs: 1. North Tower, S Face   2. South Tower, SW Ridge

155

it would be a horrendous piece of bush-whacking to get up Zinc Creek from its junction with the Ice River. You have been forewarned!

Follow Zinc Creek (a little bit of bush-whacking) until just downstream from a drainage (GR 412701) that descends from the summit. Head up the slopes just west of the gully line, first over pleasant grassy slopes and then through boulders and talus to a well-defined ridge line leading north-east towards the summit. After a short detour left, the remainder of the route takes the ridge line to the summit.

Just before the summit (3562 m) there is a narrow section of ridge that leads to the base of a surprisingly steep cliff band. Penetrate the cliff band near its left-hand end (easy 5th class climbing on fairly loose rock) to another narrow section of ridge. This spectacular finale leads to the summit. The two sections of narrow ridge would be quite exciting with snow cover. 6-10 hours from the Ice River Warden Cabin.

To **descend,** retrace your steps. 4-5 hours back to the warden cabin.

North Tower, South Face   III 5.4   photo p. 158, →

FA. G.W. Boles, R. Dawnay, C. Fay, and R. Kruzyna, July 1961. Like the South Tower, the approach is lengthy, the climbing is little more than scrambling and the rock is very rotten in places. Regardless, it will always be a well-travelled route. The route follows the prominent V-shaped snow ledges/gullies up the S face to the E ridge just below the summit. Most parties bivi somewhere in the upper reaches of Zinc Creek before an ascent.

Access is nearly the same as for the SW Ridge on the South Tower. Leave Zinc Gulch a little downstream of the drainage at GR 412701 and head-up slope, as for the SW Ridge route, but once on the grassy slopes begin contouring around the south side of the South Tower towards the North Tower.

After traversing the large amphitheatre that separates the two towers, head up over talus towards a spur just below the S face. Climb up towards the col just east of the North Tower, then move to the left to gain the right end of a horizontal ledge system running across the S face (the lower part of the V).

Traverse the ledge to the apex of the V, then scramble up rotten rock on the right-hand edge of the wide couloir that forms the upper part of the V. This avoids falling rock in the couloir and leads to a subsidiary pinnacle on the E ridge. Cross the head of the couloir that you have just been avoiding to the main summit block. Traverse left to easier ground and climb up to the summit (3525 m). 10 hours from Zinc Creek.

Descent is by the same route.

The Goodsirs: North Tower, S Face

South Tower, North Face VI 5.7   photo →

FA. D. Cheesmond and K. Doyle, April 1983. A very bold first ascent without bivi gear on a big and serious N face. The climbing is not technically desperate but the climb is very remote and long, and the rock leaves a lot to be desired. Not surprisingly, the face is prone to quite serious rockfall so choose a cold day for this climb, either in spring or fall. In summer, the face is usually falling apart. The unintentional descent by the first ascent party down the couloir to the east of the face in a raging storm was a "once-in-a-lifetime" experience for both of these very experienced alpinists. The Normal Route (page 154) provides a longer but more mellow descent, though the transportation logistics appear to be quite formidable. The climb is unrepeated as of October 1990.

Park at the Ottertail River Fire Road entrance, 8.4 km west of Field on the Trans-Canada Highway. Follow the access road for 14 km up the Ottertail River valley to the McArthur Creek Warden Cabin. A bicycle can be taken to this point. Pass the cabin, then branch off south along the Goodsir Pass trail. Where the trail splits, follow the horse trail (to the right) beside Goodsir Creek until it heads off up the hillside in a series of switchbacks. Continue along the creek to below the hanging glacier that lies at the base of the N face of the South Tower. The first ascent party bivied here.

The first problem is to get onto the hanging glacier below the face. The first ascent party followed a rib up to the base of the glacier where the seracs were smallest and did 15 m of 110° ice

climbing to gain the top of the glacier! If 110° glacier ice is not your forte, it is possible to gain the glacier up the slopes at its right edge. Traverse across the glacier until below the prominent rib in the centre of the N face of the South Tower.

Gain the rib from the right by climbing up snow/ice slopes to a left-trending snow ramp that leads back to the rib. A short section of interesting climbing gains mixed ground just to the left of the rib. Continue up this type of ground all the way to the top of the rib where a large snow ramp slants left up to the E ridge of the mountain. Follow the ramp to its end. The cornice could put up some stiff opposition.

Descent Two descents are possible: the one used on the first ascent, and the normal descent down the SW ridge. The latter is long and relatively easy but the other has the advantage of returning you to Goodsir Creek and gear that you may have left behind! Bear in mind, however, that the descent back to Goodsir Creek has a reputation for being quite scary. Don't say you weren't told!

The Cheesmond/Doyle descent follows the E ridge down towards the col between Goodsir South and Sentry Peak, but breaks off down slopes to the north just before the col is reached. Six rappels lead to the base of a couloir and easy snow slopes leading down to the Goodsir Glacier and more relaxing terrain! Descend from the north-east corner of the glacier into Goodsir Creek. 12 hours from the summit.

The Goodsirs: South Tower, N Face

Photo: Don Beers

Mount Stephen 3199 m

This is the impressive bulk dominating the skyline as you approach Field over the Kicking Horse Pass. Notice its large quartzite walls overlooking Monarch Creek and the very long N ridge descending from the summit almost to the CPR railroad tracks. The first ascent of this peak by the SW ridge by J.J McArthur and T. Riley in 1887 was the first time that a climb of over 10,000 feet had been done in the Canadian Rockies. *Map 82 N/8 Lake Louise*

North Ridge III 5.7   photo →

FA. C. Locke, C. Scott and G. Walsh, July 1966. FWA. *C. Locke, C. Scott and M. Toft,* 1972. This route offers a lot of mid-5th class climbing and is one of the longer routes (2000 m) in the book. It has a wonderfully short approach from the highway. The rock is typically good (lots of quartzite) and the situations on the ridge are superb. A party of two can complete this route comfortably in a day.

Park on the Trans-Canada Highway below the east end of the snow shed that lies directly below the ridge crest. This is just up the hill from the bridge across the Kicking Horse River and below a wide open avalanche slope. Hike up the avalanche slope, passing the tunnel on the left. Continue up talus slopes a little further before diagonalling up right along some ledges to the base of a wide crack. 15 minutes from the car!

Climb the crack (10 m) to a ledge, which is traversed to the left to a point close to the Monarch Mines. Belay at a spike driven into the rock. Head straight up the buttress above for five pitches (5.7 at most) to the top of the first steep section. 500 m of scrambling gains the large plateau in the ridge.

Alternatively, this point can be reached much more quickly by climbing the talus slopes directly below the N glacier and then climbing easy rock diagonally up and right to the plateau. Be aware of falling ice.

Above the plateau is the best part of the route. Start up the left side of the ridge for about six pitches. Regain the ridge below a steep step that is climbed directly. Traverse to the left side again and ascend snow and ice for some distance to get back to the ridge. Continue up the ridge until passage is blocked by some overhanging walls. Traverse onto the right (west) side of the ridge to a gully that leads back to the ridge just below the summit, which is just a short walk away. 5-7 hours.

Descent is down talus slopes on the west side, the Normal Route on the mountain. Follow the SW ridge down through a cliff band about 200 m from the summit, then head down talus slopes on the north side of the ridge in the general direction of Field. Eventually, you should pick up the "Fossil Bed" trail which leads steeply down into the townsite. 2-3 hours from the summit.

Mt. Stephen: 1. N Ridge
a. commonly used starts
g. N Glacier

The President 3138 m
Vice President 3066 m

These two snow summits dominate the view to the south from the Stanley Mitchell Hut. Their popularity can no doubt be attributed to both the location of the hut and the non-technical nature of the ascent routes. The views from the summit of the Yoho Valley, the Wapta Icefields and Emerald Lake are stunning.

One can approach from either the Little Yoho Valley or Emerald Lake. The latter approach has the advantage in that the climb can be done in a day trip. The northern approach is typically a weekend affair with a night spent at the Stanley Mitchell Hut. *Map 82 N/10 Blaeberry River*

President & Vice President II   photos →

FA. J, Outram, C. Kaufmann and J. Pollinger, July 1901. Both routes follow glaciers to President Pass, the col between the President and Vice-President. The summits are then easily gained along the skyline ridges.

Via Little Yoho Valley Follow the Yoho Valley Road for 13 km to the parking lot at Takakkaw Falls. The easiest approach from the Takakkaw parking lot is to pass through the campground and follow the signed trail up Yoho Valley to Laughing Falls (4.5 km). Turn left here and switchback up another trail to Little Yoho Valley and the Stanley Mitchell Hut. 3-4 hours.

To reach President Glacier, continue along the trail past the hut for a short distance until it crosses the Little Yoho River. From this point, work your way up slopes directly to the toe of the glacier which is followed to President Pass. 2-3 hours from the hut. The crux of the route is getting across the 'schrund at the base of the final slope up to the pass. From the pass the summit of The President is easily reached via the E ridge in half an hour. Likewise the W ridge of the Vice-President is very easily climbed.

Descend the way you came. For a little variety the parking lot at Takakkaw Falls can be reached via "Iceline" trail which intercepts the Yoho Valley Road a few hundred metres south of the parking lot.

Via Emerald Basin. Take the road to Emerald Lake. From the parking lot follow Emerald Lake trail around the west shore of the lake. The trail to Emerald Basin branches off at the north end of the lake just after you pass a horse gate where the lakeshore trail turns right. Follow this trail for 500 m to a junction. Take the left turn and climb up a steep trail into the basin. Cross the amphitheatre (sometimes a faint trail) towards the creek that runs down from the glacier. Work your way up beside the creek or up glaciated slabs to the snout of the glacier below the impressive walls of the S ridge of The President. Continue up the glacier directly to President Pass from where the two summits can be gained as described under Little Yoho Valley.

Descend the way you came up.

a. President b. Vice President

c. President Pass d. President Glacier

from Little Yoho Valley

from Emerald Lake

ICEFIELDS PARKWAY

Mt. Hector	3394 m	N Glacier (normal)	II	p. 166
Mt. Patterson	3197 m	Snowbird Gl. & E Face	IV 5.6	p. 168
Howse Peak	3290	NE Buttress	V 5.8 A0	p. 171
		N Face	VI 5.9 A3	p. 172
Mt. Chephren	3266 m	W Ridge (normal)	II	p. 174
		E Face	V 5.9 A1	p. 175
		The Wild Thing	VI 5.9 A3 W4	p. 176
White Pyramid	3275 m	E Ridge	II	p. 178
Mt. Forbes	3612 m	W Ridge (normal)	III	p. 180
		NW Face Variation	III	p. 180
		W Ridge of Rosita	III 5.3	p. 180

This is the northernmost of four areas in Banff National Park described in this book. It includes all routes accessed from the Icefields Parkway between Lake Louise and Sunwapta Pass where the Banff Park boundary butts up against Jasper National Park. The Icefields Parkway, known affectionately as the BJ (Banff-Jasper) Highway, is one of the most exciting roads in North America for alpinists to drive. Like many climbers before you on a first trip up to the Columbia Icefields, you will probably be stopping the car below many of the faces just to soak up the amazing scenery. Even if you don't climb any of the routes, do yourself a favour and take a drive along this road — it's a memorable trip, especially for newcomers to the Rockies.

Access As mentioned above, the routes are all accessed from the Icefields Parkway (Highway 93 north) which runs from Lake Louise to Jasper. This highway can also be reached from Red Deer, a town roughly halfway between Calgary and Edmonton, by taking the David Thomp-

son Highway (Highway 11) through Rocky Mountain House and Nordegg to Saskatchewan River Crossing.

Facilities There are no towns along the Icefields Parkway. However, at Sask-atchewan River Crossing there is a gas station, grocery store, restaurant and motel. Gas, food and lodging are also available at the Icefields Chalet on Sunwapta Pass (summer only). These places are both expensive and touristy: be advised to obtain gas and supplies in Banff, Lake Louise or Jasper. There are no 24-hour gas stations anywhere along the Icefields Parkway.

Beside the accommodations available at Lake Louise, there are campgrounds along the length of the highway and several excellent Youth Hostels. The saunas at some of the hostels are well worth investigating, particularly the "kennel" at Hilda Creek. You should be aware that the campgrounds and Youth Hostels are very busy in the summer season and fill up quickly. Consider booking ahead.

For information about campgrounds contact the Warden Office or the Park Information Centre in Lake Louise or Banff. There is also the Columbia Icefields Information Centre at the summit of Sunwapta Pass, which is open during summer months only.

Officialese All the routes are within Banff National Park and backcountry use comes under the regulations detailed on page 17.

Rock Climbing The nearest established rock climbing is in the Lake Louise area. For these crags, see under the Lake Louise area descriptions on page 86.

If you wish to climb on limestone then the vast potential of the walls of Mt. Wilson and the walls in the region of the Weeping Wall have yet to be tapped. The cliffs above the "Big Bend" at the base of Sunwapta Pass have, to a limited extent, been explored but essentially the sky is the limit in terms of doing new routes. If the weather is foul at these crags then there are endless crags along the north side of the David Thompson Highway to the east of Saskatchewan River Crossing.

Mount Hector 3394 m

Mount Hector is the first major peak you pass as you head north from Lake Louise on the Icefields Parkway. The south side of the peak presents an impressive precipice, quite a contrast to the relatively shallow-angled glacier on the north side which is where the normal route goes. The proximity of Hector to the road and the fact that it is the southernmost peak on the Icefields Parkway make it a popular winter summit for ski mountaineers from Calgary. *Map 82 N/9 Hector Lake*

North Glacier (Normal Route) II   photo →

FA. R.G. Cairns, A.A. McCoubrey Jr., R. Neave, July 1933. Perhaps one of the most popular ski ascents in the Rockies aside from those on the Wapta Icefield. In summer months it remains a popular ascent with no climbing difficulties except for an icy part at the end; crampons and an axe are necessary. The glacier has some big holes that you should avoid. In winter, there is some avalanche hazard on the approach up Hector Creek. Although it is a straightforward climb, a day trip will have you puffing with 1400 m of ascent.

Park at Hector Creek on the Icefields Parkway, 17 km north of the Trans-Canada Highway. Follow the creek – trail on the right (south) side – up through trees into a steep-sided bowl below a headwall. In winter months be wary of the possibility of avalanches here, particularly down the north side of the bowl. Continue up through the headwall via a gully on the left side and onto the flats below Hector Glacier. Gain the glacier and meander your way past some large crevasses to a col just below the summit. The summit is then reached up a short icy section. 5-6 hours.

Descent is via the same route. In winter, anticipate this being quite a quick return to the road!

Mount Patterson 3197 m

The view from Bow Summit Viewpoint on the Icefields Parkway is of Peyto Lake and the Mistaya River running north past the impressive pyramid shape of Mt. Chephren. It is most likely your eye will be drawn to this big peak. Just north of Bow Summit stands Mt. Patterson which may not look all that inspiring from this angle. However, on its east side is one of the more impressive sights along this stretch of road — the Snowbird Glacier (incorrectly called Bluebird Glacier in earlier climbing literature). During the summer season it is quite a popular ascent. In the winter season, the wall left of the glacier has several steep ice smears. One of these is "Riptide", presently the hardest ice route in the Rockies. *Maps 82 N/10 Blaeberry River, 82 N/15 Mistaya Lake*

Mt. Hector: N Glacier

The Snowbird Glacier and East Face IV 5.6   photo →

FA. K. Baker, C. Locke, L. MacKay, C. Scott and D. Vockeroth, July 1967. East Face: FA. J. Firth and U. Kallen, July 1973. FWA. D. Coombs and M. Paime, March 1980. The most prominent feature of this route is the Snowbird Glacier, the tongue of ice on the east side of Patterson. Technically, the climbing isn't too difficult but the objective hazard posed by two icefalls above the lower glacier tongue is considerable. Thankfully, the lower ice tongue has numerous holes and ice walls that provide shelter from any falling debris. It is advised to do the route quickly after an early start. It is usually climbed in a long day car to car. 10-14 hours.

Park at a pull-out on the Icefields Parkway immediately below the east side of Patterson, 7.2 km north of Bow Summit. Hike down through thin bush to the creek and cross it just downstream of a bog. Follow the drainage up to the base of the Snowbird Glacier. 2 hours.

Cross the glacier to the foot of the ice tongue and climb upwards, taking the line of least resistance to the bench in the glacier below the upper part of the route. Cross the bench to the base of a triangular face left of the second icefall. The original route scrambles up rocks just left of the icefall to gain access to the upper basin where straightforward climbing leads up to the summit ridge, well away from the summit.

The upper part of the mountain via this route is not very interesting, being much easier than the lower ice tongue, and is threatened by serac fall below the upper basin. A much more interesting, aesthetic and safer route is the E Face route as follows.

To avoid the serac hazard from just above the second icefall, start in the middle of the triangular face and move up to a ledge. Work your way up and right to the prominent ledge that runs across the whole of the triangular face. Towards its right-hand end, move up and gain the right-hand rib of the triangle. Follow this (or the ice just right of the rib) to its apex. Climb four pitches of snow and rock on a rib above to the base of the upper rock band. Continue up the rib through the rockband (5.6) until one pitch from the top where a short traverse left gives easier access to the summit. Many parties forsake climbing the final rock band and cross the snow/icefield to its left and exit up mixed ground in the obvious break at the top. It is likely that one way is as good as the other.

To **descend,** drop straight off the summit down the south slopes to the easy-angled glacier just west of the S ridge of Patterson. This leads all the way down into the upper reaches of Delta Creek, a miserable place to be hiking after a hard day on the mountain. Keeping your feet dry will require a Herculean effort. Most parties quit worrying about such luxuries after the first creek crossing! Follow the creek (many crossings) and then wade through a seemingly endless swamp (beautiful scenery) to the Mistaya River. Follow this downstream for about 1 km, cross and head back up to the highway.

Mt. Patterson: 1. Snowbird Glacier   2. E Face

Howse Peak 3290 m

Howse peak and its close companion Chephren are an awe-inspiring sight for climber and tourist alike. Once you walk in to the base of the mountain, the walls that look big from the highway become quite awe inspiring. The NE Buttress takes the obvious line on the mountain, staying close to the crest of the impressive buttress at the junction of E and N faces all the way to the summit. The N Face route follows the large and deep gully on the north side of the peak and can be clearly seen from the road. In winter the E face is adorned by ice smears and is a tantalizing proposition. It has been attempted but remains one of the unclimbed alpine prizes of the Canadian Rockies. *Map 82 N/15 Mistaya Lake*

Access From Waterfowl Lakes campground on the Icefields Parkway, 16.8 km north of Bow Summit and 17.6 km south of Saskatchewan River Crossing, follow the signed trail to Chephren Lake. Take a narrow trail, at times indistinct and tricky, along the east shoreline to the south end of the lake. 2-3 hours. In winter things are much simpler — just ski across the lake.

Descent for both routes can be achieved one of two ways. The quickest descent is over the summit of White Pyramid to the col between White Pyramid and Chephren. The alternative is a 25 km hike down the Howse River valley which is less appealing!

For both descents, walk directly west from the summit down snow and ice onto a glacier which is followed to its north end.

For those climbers who cannot stop themselves from the long hike down the Howse River, continue down low-angled slopes to the river and then head north until someday (usually the next) you will reach the highway. This is actually the Normal Route up the mountain!

For those who like a short descent (most of us) continue down from the north end of the glacier to tree line and traverse around a set of large cliffs that prevent direct access to White Pyramid. Once around these cliffs aim straight for the north end of the summit ridge of White Pyramid. After reaching the summit, descend the steep, icy E ridge to the Chephren col. This part of the descent is quite exhilarating, especially the drop on the north side, and requires careful downclimbing. Once at the col, contour right to reach the snow ramp leading down to the glacier below the north side of Howse Peak. Finish down easy moraines to Chephren Lake.

North-East Buttress V 5.8 A0 photo p. 173

FA. Lloyd MacKay, Don Vockeroth and Ken Baker, Summer 1967. One of the most aesthetic routes described in the book. It was the hardest route in the Rockies in its day; very impressive for 1967. Not only is the climb long, it is sustained throughout. The rock quality reaches both extremes; mostly it is good, though really shitty in a few spots. The situations on the buttress are superb and the technical climbing is excellent. The climb can be completed with a light pack with one bivi. Anticipate at least two days for a round trip. And don't forget crampons and axe: you'll need them on the way up as well as on the way down.

From the end of Chephren Lake gain the glacier below the E face by following the crest of a prominent moraine. A short jaunt across the glacier leads to a scramble up the initial grassy slopes and rock steps of the buttress to the base of the "Grey Bands".

Start up a crack system about 50 m east of the ridge — an interesting (5.7) start to the day. Bolt belay. Scramble up another 30 m to a ledge that leads round onto the north side of the ridge. DON'T go down it! Instead, continue up steeper ground (5.6) to a stance immediately below a white overhang. Bolt belay. Step around the arete and make an airy traverse down and right to a steep and awkward crack system that gives access (5.6) to a wide, scree-covered ledge system.

Above is a very prominent gully. Get into it by some steep climbing on excellent rock from the left (5.7) and then scramble up for a short distance to an obvious impasse. Escape to a ledge on the ridge to the left over slabby rock and a horribly loose ledge. Climb up the

ridge, avoiding difficulties by stepping to the left and climbing cracks and grooves to regain the ridge crest. After a flat section (three star bivi site) continue up grooves and a loose corner system until a loose crack leads to a wide, low-angled ledge at the base of the "Yellow Band". Gain the top of the band by following a loose corner system about 40 m to the right of the ugly gully dominating the upper E face.

Traverse easily about 100 m to the right along another wide ledge to below an obvious corner system leading up through the "Black Band". Climb the corner past a prominent roof (A0 or 5.9) to a sloping ledge on the left. Traverse back to the corner and move up a steep little wall to the base of a grim-looking chimney. Climb this (5.8) to a shattered ledge where the chimney splits. The right-hand exit is usually iced up so squeeze up the left-hand one until below a huge chockstone where a surprisingly straightforward exit to the left (or through the back) can be made. Continue up easy ground to the right to an airy ridge. Good rock leads to snow and ice after 70 m. Either step left up a short gully/ramp to gain the crest of a ridge leading to the summit (the best climbing) or climb up right towards a prominent gully (the original exit) and when convenient move back left to the ridge. Follow the ridge to the summit.

North Face VI 5.9 A3   photo →

FA. W. Robinson and B. Blanchard, March 1988. A serious, modern alpine route with sustained difficulties throughout. "The Gash" contains an awkward and difficult crux, while in the upper sections above the hanging glacier the belays and protection become "difficult" and provide a phenomenal cerebral exercise. There is, however, an escape from the trauma of the upper section if your brain can't take it.

From Chephren Lake, the first ascent party gained the glacial bowl below the N face and then climbed to the base of the NE buttress by way of a gully system. (You can also use this approach for the NE Buttress route.)

Follow the NE Buttress route until on the wide scree ledge system above the airy descending traverse. The first ascent party bivied here. Above this point there is a prominent gully called "The Gash" leading up to the hanging glacier on the N face. Follow this gully to the technical crux of the route at its top. In winter conditions with enough snow in "The Gash" it is possible to climb up under a prominent roof, and then move out round the roof (A3). The first ascent party bivied in the snow under the roof. A party in the spring found there wasn't enough snow and ice to reach the roof, and so bypassed this section altogether via a difficult ice smear on the right wall.

Once you've reached the hanging glacier, the upper section of the route follows the prominent corner system that extends from the highest point of the icefield. Sustained run-out climbing up the corner eventually leads to the top. On the first ascent one more bivi was required about two pitches from the top.

If the top corner doesn't appeal to you, for whatever reason, traverse to the far right (west) end of the hanging glacier and ascend a wide easy gully to the col between Howse and a subsidiary summit to the north-west.

Descend to the glacier on the west side of Howse, then follow the normal descent route described on page 170 .

Howse Peak: 1. NE Buttress
2. N Face   3. N Face escape   a. Grey Band
b. Yellow Band   c. Black Band   d. "The Gash"

173

Mount Chephren 3266 m

This majestic mountain is a prominent landmark between Bow Summit and Saskatchewan River Crossing. It sits close to the highway, making its 1600 m relief even more impressive. The pyramid-like shape of the peak led to it being named after the Black Pyramid of Ghiza, the spelling of which leads to quite a variety of pronunciations. To set the record straight it should sound like "Kefren".

The Normal Route, which ascends the slopes on the "back" of the peak, is one of the more popular scrambles along the Icefields Parkway. However, the E face is the big attraction for alpinists who can often be found parked on the highway gazing at the face through binoculars! The E face consists of several prominent ribs and gullies capped by a series of large rock bands that guard the summit.

The Wild Thing takes an audacious line up the gully left of the middle rib and is only really possible in winter. The rockfall down this gully during summer months dictates that keeping

it a winter ascent is a wise habit! The rock is typical Rockies fare, though in the rock bands it is quite solid, giving excellent difficult climbing. *Map 82 N/ 15 Mistaya Lake*

Descents for all routes You have two choices. The easiest, though longest route is to descend to the White Pyramid-Chephren col, then drop down the Normal Route to Chephren Lake.

Alternatively, one can scramble down the SE ridge to the north shore of Chephren Lake. It is sometimes necessary to traverse right (west) to bypass the odd cliff band. A quick hike around the lake shore soon gains the trail back to the campground. In winter, it's possible to descend a large diagonal couloir on the east side of this ridge (starts about halfway down the ridge to the lake). From the base of the couloir, grovelling through snow for a short distance leads back to the base of the E face. This descent has the advantage that it is expedient. 3-5 hours to the base of the face.

South Face/West Ridge (Normal Route) II   photo p. 178

FA. J.W.A. Hickson and E. Feuz Jr., August 1913. The Normal Route is a popular outing. No doubt the majestic nature of the mountain and the approach past the impressive walls of Howse Peak are part of the attraction. Expect a straightforward snow slope and some scrambling with nothing in the way of difficulty. Most parties take 6-8 hours for a round trip from the south end of Chephren Lake where most parties bivi. It has been completed in a day from the highway. Take your axe and crampons — the route may look snow free but don't be fooled.

Approach Chephren Lake as described under Howse Peak on page 170. Here you have a choice of routes to the White Pyramid-Chephren col. Most parties approach the W ridge from the south end of Chephren Lake via the snow slope leading to the col between White Pyramid and Chephren. From the lake head west up moraines onto the glacier below the N face of Howse. Cross the glacier towards an ice/snow slope that drops down from the White Pyramid-Chephren col, meeting the glacier at its north-west corner. Ascend this slope, keeping to the right when a large cliff band impedes progress. Once at the top of the snow slope, contour round to the left (north) to the col.

The original ascent party gained the prominent grassy slope on the south side of the mountain that leads up to several rock bands. If you choose this

ascent line aim for the White Pyramid-Chephren col and then take the easiest breach in the rock band. The rock band provides some easy 5th class climbing. Keep going up until you can contour around and eventually reach the col.

From the col, easy scrambling leads to the summit via the W ridge.

East Face V 5.9 A1   photo p. 177

FA. P.A. Geiser, A. Gran and J.R. Hudson, Summer 1965. A long alpine rock climb that required 27 hours on the first ascent. It has since been climbed in 12 hours. A similar challenge to the NE Buttress of Howse though not as aesthetic. The crux of the route occurs in the upper third of the climb where you work your way through the summit rock bands. The route finding here is a little complex so take your time to sort it out. If things don't pan out as wished, a relatively straightforward escape from the upper part of the face is possible. Rock shoes are an asset. The first ascent party bivied on the face. Nowadays, the route can be done in a single day return trip by a competent team.

Approach as for the Normal Route to the north end of Chephren Lake. From here, bushwhack through trees across slopes beneath the east side of the S ridge. The going is easier above treeline. Once out of the trees keep contouring until you can aim towards the small pocket glacier at the base of the left-hand side of the E face. In the event of a winter attempt, approach as for "The Wild Thing" (see page 176), then contour around to the pocket glacier.

From the top of the pocket glacier climb the middle one of three parallel ramps leading up to the right. If rock-fall is a problem, the slab can be gained from the right. Climb the slab to about 1/3 of its height, then take ledges on the left side of the slab to reach the left-hand and largest of the three ramps. Follow this slab up to where it turns into a prominent rib. Climb the rib to the wide ledge that runs right across the E face (possible escape).

The wall above is overhanging and provides an impasse. To break through, traverse left 75 m to the base of a weakness just right of a rib in the ledge and wall. Climb up the weakness (some aid) to another ledge system below a large roof. Traverse back right 30 m to a rib which leads up to another steep rock band. Go up and right to reach a ramp that leads back left to the top of the band. Continue up and left across a gully. Climb the left side of the gully and at its top move back across it to the right and aim for a ramp that leads up and right to the ledge system at the base of the summit rockband. Traverse right to the base of a gully that takes you to the summit in three ropelengths.

The Wild Thing VI 5.9 A3 W4   photo →

FA/FWA. B. Blanchard, W. Robinson and P. Arbic, March 1987. A very impressive modern climb. The first ascent of this route took many attempts before it succumbed, mostly because of the persistence of Barry Blanchard who was on the route four times before the successful ascent. Expect very varied, difficult climbing up a direct line. The lower part of the route isn't particularly inspiring or difficult but the major rockband offers hard mixed climbing and the final ice vein running up towards the summit for five ropelengths is the type of climbing one dreams of finding. Certainly, the route is a winter/spring climb since the lower gullies would be all-star rockfall chutes in the summer months. Beware of avalanches — there is no escape from them in the lower two gullies! In the event of adverse conditions/ weather near the top of the route it is possible to escape by traversing north along large snow ledges that separate the upper rock bands. These give access to a low-angled gully (it has been bum-slid!) at the north end of the face that leads almost back down to the bottom of the face. One rappel is needed to reach the ground. The first ascent required three nights out.

Park at the roadside pull-out at the northernmost Waterfowl Lake, 17.7 km north of Bow Summit and 16.7 km south of Saskatchewan Crossing. Drop down onto the lake and ski across to its north end. Follow the Mistaya River until under the route, then go easily up through timber to open slopes and eventually the snow cone at the base of the route. 2-3 hours from the highway.

A 5.7 mixed pitch gains 3rd class territory in the large gully above. Keep going up this gully a long way, looking for a traverse ledge leading out right after about 300m. Follow the ledge right, around the rib into the right-hand gully system. More 3rd class ground up the gully leads to a waterfall pitch (W3/4) followed by more easy going for another 100 m. A short rock band will succumb to either 5.8 or some more ice climbing (if it's there!).

Romp up the big snow band aiming for a prominent corner/chimney line that leads up through the first major rockband above. Snow hole possibilities are endless. Climb 3rd class as high as possible until a 5.8 mixed pitch brings you up to the base of the right-facing corner/chimney above. Squirm up the (tight) chimney for about 10 m, then pendulum/tension across the blank slab on the left into a right-facing corner/ chimney. Climb the chimney a little way, then aid up thin cracks (A3 at first) in the left wall. Eventually, squirm over a classic chockstone to a belay. Continue up the chimney above via some exposed bridging (wild climbing) until a struggle with an off-width section (5.9) leads to a snow band. Step left to belay. Snow holes. Break through the next rockband via a chimney (5.7 and loose) to another snow band. Trend up and left into the obvious line that splits the upper part of the E face. Classic alpine mixed climbing up the thin ice smear in the back of the prominent break leads up for four-five pitches to a chimney (W4). Continue up the chimney and over an awkward chockstone to the summit. The first ascent party spent a third night out here.

2

White Pyramid 3275 m

The poor neighbour to Chephren; unfortunately for this peak, Howse and Chephren steal all the limelight. However, the E Ridge route offers an exciting way of reaching its summit. The glacier on the north side of the peak leads down to the impressive N walls of White Pyramid and Chephren, home to one of the more radical ice climbs in the Rockies, the "Reality Bath". *Map 82 N/ 15 Mistaya Lake*

East Ridge II

FA. K. Hahn and M. Toft, August 1971. A straightforward exposed climb up a prominent snow/ice arete. The drop down the north side of the ridge makes the route quite exciting. Sometimes combined with an ascent of Chephren, depending on how much time you have after you return to the col. 6-7 hours round trip from the south end of Chephren Lake.

Approach the White Pyramid-Chephren col as described for the S Face/W Ridge route of Chephren on page 174.

From the col work your way up the E ridge, either keeping to the south side or cramponing up the north side over an impressive drop. Your choice.

Descent is exactly the above in reverse.

Mount Forbes 3612 m

A popular peak. Undoubtedly this is because it is the highest mountain within Banff National Park, and one of the few peaks that has a "remote" feel to it without being a week's hike from the road. Futhermore, the Normal Route is a classic high glacier ascent.

The mountain is infamous for the number of parties it repulses. Not that the described routes are difficult or have high objective hazard, but rather because the approach is long (21 km to the base of the N glacier) and the weather has a habit of changing before many parties get a chance to step on the snow. The recipe for a successful attempt is a minimum of two days of good weather. Some fast parties will complete the round trip in two days but most parties take three. The peak also makes an interesting winter ascent.

There are two variations to the standard W Ridge route that some people might be interested in trying. The direct route up the NW face of the mountain above the north glacier is an obvious challenge and the base of the W ridge provides an excellent rocky scramble over a small peak known as Rosita en route to the main summit of Forbes. *Map 82 N/15 Mistaya Lake*

Access For the walk-in to Forbes, park at the trailhead (old gravel pit) for Glacier Lake on the west side of the Icefields Parkway 1.1 km north of Saskatchewan River Crossing. Follow an excellent trail to the east end of Glacier Lake, then hike along the north shore of the lake to the Glacier River.

Continue up Glacier River on the rapidly dwindling trail up broad river flats to the canyon that leads to the Mons Glacier. Avoid fording Glacier River until close to this point since here the river is quite braided and relatively shallow (waist deep). Rest assured, the water is brutally cold. It may be possible to find other, shallower alternatives further upstream. In the past, parties have even gone as far as the SE Lyell Glacier and crossed without having to do any wading. However, this may no longer be possible. At the base of the Mons Glacier drainage is a huge boulder where parties have bivied. 5-7 hours from the highway.

To gain the Mons Glacier, follow a trail up through timber on the west side of the Mons drainage to an alpine basin below the toe of the Mons Glacier. Access to the Mons is barred by a headwall. The headwall can be negotiated 500 m right of the creek by easy, waterworn limestone ledges and an old fixed handline (check its condition before you heave on it!). Drop down onto the Mons Glacier just above the toe and cross to meadows and a small lake at the base of the N glacier. This is a great spot to bivi and is where most parties spend the night before an ascent. 3 to 4 hours from the valley floor.

Mt. Chephren: 1. W Ridge
d. S Ridge descent
2. White Pyramid, E Ridge
c. Chephren-White Pyramid col

Photo: Bruno Engler

West Ridge (Normal Route) III   photo →

FA. A.J. Ostheimer, M.M. Strumia, J.M. Thorington and E. Feuz Jr., July 1926. FWA. C. Locke, J. Tanner, D. Eastcott, 1972. This is the route that everybody staggers 21 km to do. No technical problems and very much a pleasant route up a big high mountain.

Work your way up the N glacier towards the col in the W ridge. From here, either follow the snow just north of the ridge line or stick to the rocks of the ridge. Both lead just as easily to the summit. 5-7 hours.

Descent Retrace your steps.

North-West Face Variation III   photo →

FA. Unknown. This is the face that the Normal Route avoids. Claimed as a first ascent in 1971 but probably climbed much sooner. If you'd like something a little more invigorating than the W ridge finish then this an ideal candidate.

Instead of working your way to the col on the W ridge, take the NW face up to the top. A natural line is to take the face to the W ridge, joining it close to the summit. Similar in standard to the Skyladder on Mt. Andromeda.

Descend via the W ridge.

West Ridge of Rosita III 5.3   photo →

FA. L.F. Andrew, H. Gilman, R. Kruszyna and R. Seale, July 1965. Rosita is the summit to the west of the col on the W ridge of Forbes. Though it is little more than a bump in the W ridge, the ridge that rises from the Mons Glacier up to the "summit", is an interesting scramble that provides an alternative way of gaining the upper W ridge.

From your bivi in the meadows gain the ridge line across moraine and low-angled slabs. Follow the ridge crest to the "summit" with little difficulty. Continue along the ridge to the col and then up to the summit of Forbes in the usual way.

Descend via the W ridge.

Photo: Bruno Engler

Mt. Forbes: 1. W Ridge   2. NW Face   3. W Ridge, Rosita

COLUMBIA ICEFIELD

Mt. Athabasca	3491 m	N Glacier (normal)	II	p. 186
		Silverhorn	II	p. 186
		Regular N Face	III 5.4	p. 186
		The Hourglass	III	p. 188
		N Ridge	III 5.5	p. 188
Mt. Andromeda	3450 m	Skyladder	II	p. 189
		NW Shoulder Direct	III	p. 189
		NW Bowl, Photo Finish	III	p. 190
		NW Bowl, N Face	III	p. 190
		Shooting Gallery	IV 5.9	p. 190
		Asteroid Alley	IV 5.9	p. 190
		Andromeda Strain	V 5.9 A2 W4	p. 192
		The Practise Gullies	III	p. 192
Mt. Kitchener	3480 m	SW Slopes (normal)	I	p. 193
		Grand Central Couloir	V 5.9 A2/W5	p. 193
	Ramp Route		V 5.8 A1	p. 194
Little Snow Dome	2672 m	Sidestreet	III 5.9 A1	p. 196
Mt. Bryce	3507 m	NE Ridge, Traverse	IV 5.6	p. 202
		N Face	IV 5.7	p. 202
Mt. Columbia	3747 m	E Face (normal)	II	p. 204
		N Ridge	V 5.7 W3	p. 204

The Columbia Icefield, situated immediately west of Sunwapta Pass on the Icefields Parkway, covers an area of 280 square kilometres and is the largest icefield in the Rockies. Furthermore, it is also the hydrographic apex of North America, draining into three different oceans: the Atlantic, Pacific and the Arctic. It contains a quarter of the fifty highest peaks in the Canadian Rockies, including four of the eight highest. There is no doubt that the discovery of the Icefield at the turn of the century was one of the great moments of North American alpinism.

The stretch of highway between the summit of Sunwapta Pass and the flats of Tangle Creek to the north allows access to some of the premier alpine climbing routes in the Canadian Rockies, and perhaps North America. Judging by the number of climbers of various nationalities occupying the Icefield campground during summer months, you'd be hard pressed not to think that the area had some special attraction. Climbers can find classic routes of all grades on both rock and snow/ice so there is something to please everybody. For the novice alpinist, Mts. Andromeda and Athabasca have some excellent routes, in particular Skyladder and the Silverhorn. At the other end of the spectrum of difficulty there are few challenges anywhere like the N Face of Mt. Alberta and the North Face of North Twin Tower, the king of Rockies Alpine Routes (see Mt. Alberta area page 207).

The rolling nature of the Columbia Icefield and the height of its peaks make it a popular ski mountaineering area. Mounts Columbia, North Twin, South Twin, Stutfield, Kitchener, and Snow Dome are most commonly climbed on skis in the Spring months of April and May via the "normal" routes. Knowledge of glacier travel is essential for these trips — you wouldn't wish to fall down a crevasse and not know how to get back out. The "mother of all ski trips" would be to knock off all these summits in a single push. Just so that you can appreciate the strength and fitness of some of the early pioneers, A.J. Ostheimer and H. Fuhrer set out one day in the Athabasca River valley below Mt. Columbia and climbed North Twin, Stutfield (West), Kitchener, Snow Dome and were

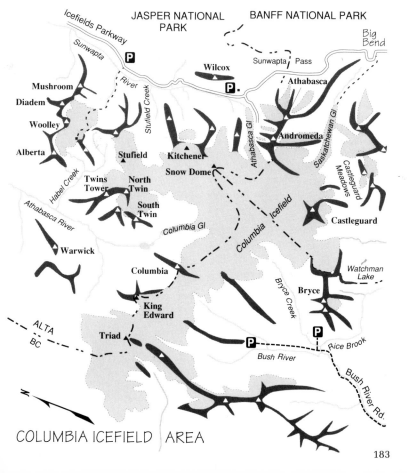

COLUMBIA ICEFIELD AREA

headed for Columbia when deteriorating weather forced a return to camp 36 hours after leaving! There are few climbers around today who would take on such an outing.

Lastly, if the weather is pretty grim at the Icefield and you are spending a lot of time holed up in your tent at the campground bear in mind the other areas described in this book. It is likely that in at least one of them the weather isn't too bad and you'll be able to do some climbing.

Access The Columbia Icefield is accessed via the Icefields Parkway, 113 km south of Jasper and 130 km north of Lake Louise. The normal method for accessing the Icefield itself is on foot or ski from Sunwapta Pass via the Athabasca Glacier as described for the E Face of Mt. Columbia on page 204. The far western part of the Icefield is now commonly accessed via the Bush River logging road — a very expedient way of reaching Bryce and the north side of Columbia (see page 200). It is possible to access the parts of the Icefield not within the boundaries of a National Park by air: either helicopter or ski-plane. However, this seems unnecessary considering the excellent access offered by the logging road. Winter is when it may be useful. Contact Amiskwi Air or one of the local helicopter charter companies for further information.

Facilities For a stay at the Icefield you are advised to buy groceries in either Banff or Jasper on your way out to the area. If you run out of goods, then Jasper is the nearest town, 113 km to the north, with numerous shops where you can purchase almost anything you require. (see Jasper Area section page 281). Right

at the top of Sunwapta Pass is the Icefield Chalet Restaurant which opens during summer months for tourists, but prices are high. You can also get a selection of snacks at the Icefield Bus Tours (Snocoach) station next to the Park Information Centre. There is also a gas station at the summit of the Pass but again the prices are higher than what you'll pay in Jasper. The nearest 24 hour gas is in Jasper. The organization of the buildings at Sunwapta Pass is subject to change in a dramatic way in the early '90's. However, the Information Centre and the Snocoach station will still be there, just in a different guise.

The preferred location for climbers staying in the area is the Icefield Campground located 1 km south of the Icefield Information Centre. There are cooking shelters (good rain shelters!), fire pits and food hangs. If you want a bit more luxury (relatively speaking!), the Youth Hostel at Hilda Creek lies about 8 km south of the Information Centre. There is also Wilcox Campground next door to the Icefield Campground, though this is not the usual hang-out for climbers.

For information on weather, campsites, backcountry conditions and permits, the Park Information Centre at the top of Sunwapta Pass is the place to go. The Icefield is within Jasper National Park, so the Information Centre in Jasper will also be able to provide the same information. The nearest warden office lies 32 km to the north along the Parkway at a place known as Mile 45, next to Poboktan Creek.

Officialese The routes are within either Banff or Jasper National Parks and backcountry use comes under the National Park regulations detailed on page 17.

Mount Athabasca 3491 m

Mount Athabasca is one of the most popular snow/ice outings described in this book. The Normal Route and the regular N Face Route see more ascents in one season than many other routes in the Rockies have ever had from day one! The mountain is a big favorite with photography buffs since the north side of the peak is in full view as you drive to the crest of Sunwapta Pass coming south from the Jasper direction.

The distinguishing features of the mountain as seen from the highway are the large glacier descending the N face, and the Silverhorn, a subsidiary summit immediately west of the main summit. The N face is easily identified as a sweep of ice topped by a narrow band of rock. The two routes on the face exit through two distinct weaknesses in this band: on the left the Normal Route and to the right the "Hourglass". All routes on the mountain have short approaches and are, at most, of moderate difficulty and, therefore, very suitable as a first ice experience for the novice alpinist.

Access For routes on Mts. Athabasca and Andromeda turn up the road opposite the Icefield Chalet at the top of Sunwapta Pass. This is the access road for the legendary Icefield tour buses called Snocoaches. This road is gated during daylight. However, at night the gate is left open and it is possible to drive about 2 km further up the road to another gate that is always locked to the likes of climbers. Just before this point is a bridge over a creek, and a pull-out at the side of the road. Park here. *Map 83 C/3 Columbia Icefield*

Descent for all routes is usually back down the N Glacier route. However, if the snow gets to be mush by the time you are descending, then the Athabasca-Andromeda (AA) glacier is perhaps a safer, though more technical descent. To reach the AA glacier continue down the W ridge until open snow or talus (dependant on season) lead down to the glacier. Once on the glacier aim for the bottom right corner where a prominent trail takes you down to the moraines and eventually the "Snocoach road".

North Glacier (Normal Route) II   photo →

FA. J.W.A. Hickson E.L. Redford and E. Feuz Jr., August 1920. A very popular climb and one of the classic ascents of the Rockies. It's a good choice for an outing with a novice since the technical nature of the route lies essentially in glacier travel rather than climbing. The seracs on the N glacier pose some objective hazard.

From the parking spot follow a well-worn trail up the moraines on the west side of the creek to the glacier. Cross the glacier towards the main bulk of the mountain until below the seracs of the Normal Route.

Starting below the left (east) end of the seracs, pick the line of least resistance up through the seracs to open slopes on the north-west side of the Silverhorn. Wander up these to the NW ridge which is easily followed over the Silverhorn onto the main summit. Be aware of the cornices.

Silverhorn II   photo →

FA. E.R.Gibson, G.G.Macphee, N.E. Odell, and F.S.Smythe, August 1947. Somewhat steeper than the Normal Route and hence a little more challenging. An aesthetic route which is deservedly popular.

The line of ascent follows the obvious steep shoulder immediately east of the N Glacier route and west of the N face. Once at the base of the shoulder, aim straight up the rib and keep going until the NW ridge is reached, and shortly thereafter, the summit.

Regular North Face III 5.4   photo →

FA. D. Rau and D. Soper, August 1971. A Rockies classic. It was one of the first of the "big" ice faces to be climbed when ice faces were the vogue of the day. Since then it has been the first N face route for many aspiring alpinists. On weekends, it is not uncommon to be on the route with another party. The face consists of 40-50 degree ice leading to a short crux through the rock band.

To reach the base of the face approach as for the N Glacier route and continue through the col at the base of the Silverhorn into the basin below the face. Start below the distinct weakness towards the east end of the rock band. After negotiating the 'schrund (usually not too difficult) head straight for the weakness. Once there, pick your way up a short section of moderate mixed ground (crux) to snow slopes and the summit.

Mt. Athabasca N Face: 1. N Glacier (normal)
2. Silverhorn   3. Regular N Face
4. The Hourglass   5. N Ridge
a. "Snocoach road"

The Hourglass III

photo p. 187

FA. Unknown. A variation to the popular N Face route. At the very right-hand end of the top rockband is a serac barrier. The climb sneaks up between the rock and the serac on a strip of ice which presumably looked like an "hourglass" in the early '70's! The crux is steeper and more technical than the Regular N Face route.

Approach the N face as for the Regular N Face route, then work your way up the ice to the base of the "Hourglass". Continue up a short but fairly steep pitch of glacier ice/snow to the summit slopes.

North Ridge III 5.5

photo p. 187

FA. J.N. Collie and H. Woolley, August 1898. A typical scrambling Rockies ridge climb with good position and a great variety of rock quality! A good place to practise your short roping technique.

The best way to approach this route is to follow the usual trail from the parking lot up the moraine for about 250 m to where a subsidiary trail breaks off to the left from the crest of the moraine. Follow it down to the creek and up to the toe of the glacier. Climb up the left side of the glacier directly to the A2/Athabasca col. Indifferent rock and one steep bit (crux) gains a snowy shoulder. Continue up to the summit ridge past a final loose rock band via a groove just to the left of the ridge crest.

Mount Andromeda 3450 m

Mount Andromeda, like Mt. Athabasca, is one of the more popular summits in the Rockies. The Skyladder is the classic moderate route on the peak and is the route of choice for most parties climbing the mountain. At the other end of the difficulty spectrum, the Andromeda Strain is also a popular route, perhaps the most often repeated of the harder routes in the book — it has had about a dozen ascents since it was first done!

Unfortunately, many routes on this mountain suffer from unusually high amounts of rockfall (as some of their names indicate), particularly routes on the NE face. One of the joys of climbing on this face is that the sun hits it in the early part of the day and keeps you nice and warm. However, the rockfall has to

be seen to be believed — just be in a safe place to watch it! Cold nights and very early starts are strongly recommended .

The routes in the N bowl are certainly more friendly and see much more traffic. The face at the back of the N bowl and the NW shoulder can be climbed in a multitude of ways, as demonstrated by the number of "new" routes climbed here every season. Claims and counter-claims of first ascents are perhaps more common on these two faces than any other face described in this book. However, only those reported as of 1985 are described here. If you don't like them, pick a line you like and climb it! These routes are straightforward in execution with low-to-moderate technical difficulty, the crux being either the approach across the glacier, the 'schrund, or the cornice. The faces are typically 40°-45°. The NW Shoulder Direct is technically the most interesting of the bunch.

The long spur of the N ridge drops down between the NE (Athabasca-Andromeda) glacier and the NW bowl. The lower end of the ridge forms a large, steep rock wall split by a prominent couloir, the Shooting Gallery, and a narrower tributary chimney taken by Asteroid Alley. *Map 83 C/3 Columbia Icefield*

Access Park as described for Mt. Athabasca. For all routes on Mt. Andromeda continue walking up the road to the Icefield Tour Bus parking lot. About 100 m before the lot there is an indistinct trail on the left-hand side of the road, sometimes marked by small cairns. Follow this up through moraines to the glaciers on the north and north-east sides of the mountain. For routes on the NE face pick up a well-worn trail leading up into the basin of the A/A glacier from the left. To reach routes in the N bowl contour across moraines to below the bowl. Take care on the glacier — there are some big holes. Not a place to be soloing about. Expect to take about 2 hours to reach the start of the described climbs.

Descent for most routes is commonly down the E ridge. Follow the summit ridge eastward until the ridge drops steeply down to the Andromeda-Athabasca (AA) col. Work your way down through small cliff bands and steep talus to the col. The easiest way down is close to the ridge itself. Descend the snow/ice slopes on the north side of the col towards the AA glacier. The slope gets steeper as you descend, eventually ending at a large 'schrund. By keeping to the rocks on the right (east) side you will find a rappel station just above the 'schrund. Once on the glacier aim for the bottom right-hand corner where a good trail leads to the "Snocoach road".

Skyladder II · photo p. 191

FA. J.Fairly & B. Parks July 1960. The most popular route to the summit of Andromeda and, for that matter, in the Columbia Icefields. It is very aesthetic and, as a bonus, the top affords great views across the Columbia Icefield region. In the early season one can kick steps all the way to the top. However, by August the route is mostly ice.

At the north end of the NW shoulder is a large curving snowfield that leads up to the summit ridge. After crossing the 'schrund assault the slope ahead. Initially, the ice is at its steepest (40-45 degrees), but the angle lessens towards the top.

North West Shoulder Direct III · photo p. 191

FA. J.Lowe, Summer 1973. To the left of Skyladder, the NW shoulder presents a face of mixed ice and rock. Technically, the most interesting route in the NW bowl.

Climb up a line approximately in the middle of the face. The rock bands offer short sections of steep climbing though these can easily be avoided by traversing to one side. In some years the cornice is so large that it provides an interesting exercise in aiding. Hanging from horizontal axe placements has scared more than one well known alpinist!

North Bowl, Photo Finish III   photo →

FA. G.Lowe, J.Glidden, D.Hamre and G. Lowe, August 1972. Very similar in difficulty to the N Face route but threatened by the serac-cum-cornice system at the top of the face.

Climb the ice slope immediately to the right of the seracs at the top of the face. (Be wary of the seracs, especially in the lower part of the route.) The ice steepens towards the top.

North Bowl, North Face III   photo →

FA. J.Gow and C. Raymond, August 1966. A straightforward snow/ice slope, very similar in difficulty and character to Skyladder, though not as aesthetic.

From the back of the N bowl aim for the saddle between the twin summits of Andromeda, taking a line midway between the rocks that extend to the N ridge and the seracs of the N bowl.

Shooting Gallery IV 5.9   photo →

FA. T.Sorenson & W.Strugatz, August 1975. A reasonably popular route by Rockies standards with a section in the middle providing the bulk of the interest. Its name says lots about rockfall hazard! In winter it is a good, though not easy, introduction to Rockies winter climbing.

Start up the prominent wide couloir. A steep section of rock is encountered at about half-height. Climb up this with some difficulty to gain the upper couloir. Some classic mixed climbing in the upper couloir leads to the N ridge.

To **descend** either continue up the N ridge to the summit ridge and then down the E ridge, or drop down the west side of the N ridge into the N bowl.

Asteroid Alley IV 5.9   photo →

FA J.Lowe, October 1981. An imposing chimney climb. The purity of line and excellent mixed climbing make a route that deserves to be more popular. The exposure is quite alarming! Though It has less objective hazard than Shooting Gallery, care is required not to dislodge too many rocks on your trusted belayer.

Just below the top of the ice slope that constitutes the start of Shooting Gallery, a prominent deep chimney can be seen aiming straight up towards the N ridge. Gain the base of the chimney over some mixed ground and then start up the slot in earnest. Climb the steep chimney almost in its entirety past two chockstones, making liberal use of a column of ice in the back. Above the second chockstone two alternatives present themselves: two steep cracks straight above the chimney or some slabs (often iced over) out to the left. Take your pick. Take care with loose rock in the chimney for the second's sake!

Descend as for the Shooting Gallery.

*Mt. Andromeda: 1. Skyladder   2. NW Shoulder Direct   3.Photo Finish
4. N Face   5. Shooting Gallery   6. Asteroid Alley   7. Andromeda Strain
8. Practice Gullies   a. N Bowl   b. AA col   c. "Snocoach" parking lot*

190

Photo: Bruno Engler

Andromeda Strain V 5.9 A2 W4   photo p. 191

FA. B.Blanchard, D.Cheesmond and T.Friesen, April 16-17, 1983. FWA. W.Robinson & I.Bolt, January 1987. Direct Route: G.Glovach and J.McKay, May 1989. This route takes the prominent gully system bisecting the NE face. One of the Rockies "grand cours" routes, it took six years of numerous attempts before it was eventually climbed. It is now the most popular of the hard routes in the Rockies. In difficulty it compares favourably with Grand Central Couloir on Mt. Kitchener. Although quite a bit shorter than the Grand Central it makes up for lack of size by having a sustained section of climbing near the middle. Rockfall is a major hazard in the summer months yet it has been climbed most often in August. If you decide to tackle it in summer there are two things to bear in mind: the exit ice pitch has been "missing" on several recent attempts and make sure you reach the rockbands in the middle of the route before the sun comes up — the rockfall can be watched quite safely from there!

Ascend the easy lower couloir until a wide, ugly chimney is reached. The original and most commonly ascended route is to traverse rightwards two ropelengths to the base of a short corner that leads up to a ledge that runs across the face. Traverse back left two ropelengths to a belay at the base of a left-facing corner with a perfect A1 crack in its right wall.

The direct route avoids the traverses by taking a direct line up the ugly chimney (difficult climbing) to the stance below the A1 crack. Climb up into the chimney to a roof near its top. A hard step (5.9) to the right past a smooth, blank wall gains easier moves and the stance. This single pitch offers the hardest climbing on the route. Some snow build-up may be very useful.

Ascend the corner to gain the A1 crack which leads to another corner. Continue up the corner above (bolt) to a narrow ledge leading off out of sight to the right. Either continue up the corner above (usually choked with snow) or follow the narrow ledge out right for 20 m to a decrepit bulge and crack (A2) that leads up into the upper couloir. Climb the upper couloir for about four ropelengths to a good belay at its top left corner. Gain the ice bulge on the opposite wall of the couloir (interesting mixed climbing) which is ascended (W4) to easy slopes and eventually the top.

North-East Face, The Practise Gullies III   photo p. 191

These three perhaps inappropriately named gullies are on the extreme left-hand part of the NE face. They are all similar in difficulty (45-55 degrees) and are often capped by large cornices that provide some fun. Rockfall is a hazard to take seriously on each of these routes. A summer ascent of any of these routes is not particularly recommended; there are far safer 45 degree couloirs to climb at this time of year.

Mount Kitchener 3480 m

The very impressive N face of this mountain dominates the skyline to the north of Sunwapta Pass. Unfortunately, the face consists of some of the worst rock that climbers will ever have the pleasure of touching. During an attempt at the first ascent of the Ramp Route, the frequency of the rockfall was so bad it reminded the climbers of a busy railway station. Cold nights are a useful ingredient for success and longevity of life, and so these routes are usually climbed in the spring or the fall, though both have had a number of winter and late summer ascents. A summer ascent can be a lottery. Bivi ledges are noticeably absent on both routes. The best method seems to be to climb with a light pack and get the routes over with as quickly as possible. 24-30 hours for a round trip from a bivi at the base.

The south side of the mountain is a complete contrast to the N face — a gentle slope of glacier ice used as an ascent route by skiers. *Map 83 C/3 Columbia Icefield*

South-West Slopes (Normal Route) I

FA. A.J. Ostheimer and H. Fuhrer, July 1927. An easy ski ascent usually combined with an ascent of Snow Dome.

Gain the Icefield plateau via the Athabasca Glacier as described for the E face of Columbia (page 204). From the head of Athabasca Glacier pass around the west side of a heavily crevassed area on the south end of Snow Dome, then ski north-north-west for 3 km to the top of Snow Dome.

From the summit of Snow Dome head north-west into the col between Snow Dome and Kitchener which is the top of the Dome Glacier. Watch for crevasses in the col area, particularly on the Snow Dome side. The summit of Kitchener is 2 km to the north-east from the col.

Return to the road by contouring across the western side of Snow Dome back to the head of the Athabasca Glacier.

Grand Central Couloir V 5.9 A2/W5   photo p. 195

FA. M.Weiss & J.Lowe 1975. FWA. T. Sorenson and J. Roberts, January 1978 The Grand Central Couloir is another of the Rockies "grand cours" routes and deservedly so. This climb usually puts up a good fight. Nevertheless, it should be on everybody's hit-list. A bit of a trade route. However, don't bother trying it unless you have cold temperatures — save yourself downclimbing the lower section of the couloir as you run from the rockfall!

From the Icefield Information Centre, drive north along the Parkway until the road begins a short climb just before it drops steeply down to Tangle Creek Flats. This point is the north end of the Sunwapta gravel flats. Park at the side of the Parkway and cross the gravel flats to large talus boulders. Pick your way diagonally rightward across the slope through all the ankle-wrenching boulders to more open terrain leading up to a ridge line. Follow the ridge for a few hundred metres, then contour across the slope on the right side of the ridge to the lateral moraines of the glacier below the north side of Kitchener. Bivi sites.

Start at the left side of the hanging glacier. Work your way up through seemingly interminable crevasses into the base of the main couloir. There are two large couloirs on this face. Make sure you don't end up in the right-hand one! (You'd have to make a long traverse right for this to happen). Having decided that you are on the right track, keep going for about 400 m at which point you should be at the "Narrows", the crux of the route. Two possibilities present themselves: the corner, or a narrow strip of ice on the right wall (the Doyle/Blanchard variation). Take your pick — one is probably just as evil as the other! The corner has a difficult section getting into the upper corner (5.8 A2); good protection seems scarce. The ice vein is very steep (W5) and narrow.

Once above the "Narrows", some sanity can be restored in the upper couloir. Instead of attempting a direct finish (which has been done in winter), aim off to the right up a narrow gully behind a prominent pinnacle known as the "Cheeseburger". At the top of the gully (note the impressive view of Ramp Route) is a short, steep wall that provides a sting-in-the-tail for an exit (5.9).

Once again, protection seems scarce. Wander up much easier ground above to the cornice. The cornice can be a little time-consuming. Plan on an hour of tunnelling. An easier alternative to the sting-in-the-tail wall behind the Cheeseburger is to climb up high in the upper couloir (the direct finish), then just below the very steep exit make a traverse right along a sloping snow ledge across the right wall of the couloir. The availability of this option is, however, dependent on conditions.

Descent is down the E ridge. Walk eastward along the edge of the mountain to the conspicuous notch in the E ridge (about twenty minutes from the top of the Grand Central). The rappel station is a few feet down into the notch. It is probably best to rappel into the notch (10 m) and then use the rappel rope as the belay while someone climbs out the other side onto the E ridge. Once on the ridge, stroll down to the first prominent col, then walk down easy but gradually steepening slopes to the north, back onto the moraines at the base of the face. 3-4 hours from the summit.

Ramp Route V 5.8 A1   photo →

FA. J. Lowe, C. Jones and G. Thompson, 1971. FWA. J. Lauchlan and J. Elzinga, March 1977. The first route on the face and in its day one of the hardest alpine routes in the Rockies. Not climbed anywhere nearly as often as the Grand Central. The route takes the obvious ramp line right of Grand Central Couloir and, like its more famous neighbour, is a serious and challenging climb with rockfall hazard. Belays pose a bit of a problem on the ramp due to compact rock. Take along your thinnest knifeblades.

Approach as for Grand Central Couloir, but above the 'schrund trend over to the right-hand of two prominent gullies that come down the face. This is the fastest approach from a bivi site on the moraine. You can if you want take the original start by climbing onto the hanging glacier from the right and heading straight up the slope above.

Climb the right-hand ice slope to its upper right corner below a steep overhanging corner. Bypass the corner on the right and climb a steep pitch to gain the left end of "The Ramp". Eight or so pitches along the ramp lead to the cornice. Anticipate a couple of hours drilling your way through to the summit plateau.

Descend as for Grand Central Couloir.

Photo: James Sevigny

Mt. Kitchener N Face: 1. Grand Central Couloir   2. Ramp Route
a. alternative start   b. Doyle/Blanchard ice strip   c. Cheeseburger   d. alternative finish   195

Little Snow Dome 2672 m

Snow Dome has a ridge that descends eastwards towards the highway. The only summit along the ridge lies at the east end, a 2672 m peak. However, the part of the ridge referred to as Little Snow Dome is the higher, flat section of ridge to the west of the above mentioned summit. The steep north side of Little Snow Dome is split by several large gullies, one of which is taken by Sidestreet. *Map 83 C/3 Columbia Icefield*

Sidestreet II 5.9 AI   photo →

FA. W. Robinson and I. Bolt, April 1986. A short route with only four pitches of climbing and a short approach and descent. Not a good choice for a summer outing (choss/rockfall hazard) but a fun alpine climbing day in winter/spring. It offers a break from the ice-climbing routine that you may have fallen into by the late stages of winter. The climbing is typically mid-5th class except for one section.

The approach is the same as for the famous ice climb "Slipstream" on Snow Dome. Park about 1.5-2 km north of the Icefields Information Centre. Skis may or may not be useful — judge for yourself. Cross the flats to the Dome Glacier and hike/ski up this until below the N face of Little Snow Dome.

The route takes the largest of several gullies splitting the face. The correct one lies in the centre of the face and appears to lead to a headwall just below the summit. Walk up snow slopes to a short, easy mixed pitch (it is possible to avoid this on the right via ledges), then continue up snow slopes for about 300 m until below a roof in the gully. The next pitch is the interesting bit. Climb the slab (maybe ice, maybe aid) to the roof which is turned on the left to gain a corner above (5.9). This leads to more easy snow slopes. Romp up these to where the gully narrows and presents two pitches of mixed climbing. At the top of the second pitch a hidden gully bypasses the headwall above to the left, leaving you just short of the summit on the NE ridge. 4-5 hours.

Descend via the NE ridge on easy snow slopes to a col, paying attention to not getting avalanched over the cliffs to the south. Then drop down slopes on the north side to the Dome Glacier and the car. 1-2 hours summit to car.

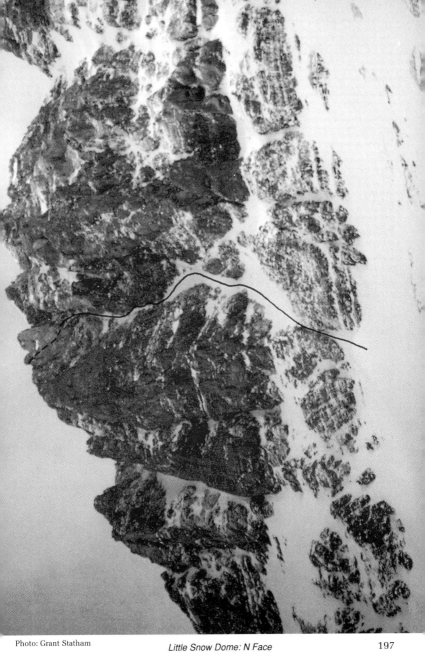

Little Snow Dome: N Face

Mount Bryce 3507 m

Bryce is a huge, isolated mountain sitting all by itself at the south end of the Columbia Icefield. An awesome sight when approaching up the Bush drainage is the mountain's N face, one of the largest in the Rockies, rising over 2000 m out of Bryce Creek and topped by a long stretch of glacier that alone is larger than the N face of Athabasca. However, the jewel of the mountain is undoubtedly the NE ridge traverse, a magnificent ridge climb along a long, high ridge, a route that has always been a popular goal.

For many years Bryce was a very remote peak requiring at least a day and a half just to get there. Now you can drive to within one hour's walk of the base of the N face and a few hour's walk from the NE ridge. Now that vehicle access is possible, the routes on Bryce are undergoing a popularity surge, particularly the N Face route, since its original approach took a minium of two days for a strong team. *Map 83 C/3 Columbia Icefield (83 C/4 Bush R. Approach)*

Access The original approaches to Bryce were up either the Alexandria River valley or the Saskatchewan Glacier. The Saskatchewan Glacier is still a good approach for the NE ridge though it is rarely used nowadays. The logging roads that have been cut into the upper reaches of the Bush River provide vehicle access to the base of the mountain and have become the "modern" approach route. For those who loathe a long walk it is a blessing!

However, both approaches are described as some parties may not have use of a vehicle. In this case they are likely to bus/bike/hitch up the Icefields Parkway rather than up the Bush River! Furthermore, the logging roads may not remain open indefinitely.

Saskatchewan Glacier From a pull-off 800 m south of the "Big Bend" on the Icefields Parkway (6.5 km north of Saskatchewan River Crossing), take the trail to the toe of the Saskatchewan Glacier. From here several approach possibilities present themselves.

The original ascent of the NE ridge was achieved from a camp at Cinema Lake. To reach Cinema Lake walk up the glacier for 3-4 km until a wide valley can be gained on the south side. This is Castleguard Meadows, a beautiful alpine meadow region. Follow the trail down through the meadows below the east side of Castleguard Mtn. and down into the Castleguard River valley. Ford the river (can be time consuming) and climb up into the continuation valley on the south-west side of Castleguard River to Watchman Lake. Continue a little further to Cinema Lake. This is a very healthy day hike from the highway. To reach the col at the north-east end of the NE ridge head west from Cinema Lake towards the glacier descending the east side of Bryce. Work your way up the slopes to the right (east) of the glacier until near the top where the low point of the ridge can be easily reached. Good bivi sites at the col.

The modern approach to the NE ridge from the Icefields Parkway is to walk up the Saskatchewan Glacier to the saddle in the Columbia Icefield just north of Castleguard Mtn. From this point go south-west down the apex of the Icefield towards Bryce to a col just north-east of the mountain. You are now below a

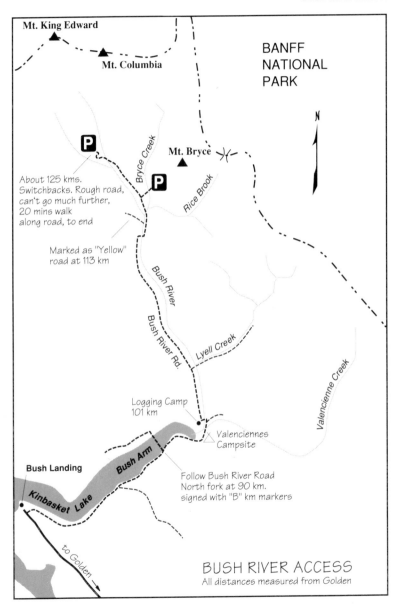

Mt. King Edward

Mt. Columbia

BANFF
NATIONAL
PARK

N

Bryce Creek

Mt. Bryce

Rice Brook

About 125 kms.
Switchbacks. Rough road,
can't go much further,
20 mins walk
along road, to end

Marked as "Yellow"
road at 113 km

Bush River

Bush River Rd.

Lyell Creek

Valencienne Creek

Logging Camp
101 km

Valenciennes
Campsite

Bush Arm

Bush Landing

Follow Bush River Road
North fork at 90 km.
signed with "B" km markers

Kinbasket Lake

to Golden

BUSH RIVER ACCESS
All distances measured from Golden

199

prominent rockwall that forms the north-east end of the NE ridge. Aim for a gully (GR 798681) to the left (south) of the high point in the rockwall and climb it to reach the col at the "start" of the NE Ridge route.

For the N face route, approach Bryce up the Saskatchewan Glacier past Castleguard Mtn. and continue to the col just north-east of Bryce. From here work your way down the headwall of Bryce Creek, picking the easiest line, and bushwhack along the side of Bryce Creek to a large braided creek that leads up to the base of the route. Although this is the original approach to the N face it is not highly recommended since it is much more time consuming than the Bush River approach.

Bush River This is the deluxe access route for all climbs on Mt. Bryce. The only necessity for this approach is a car — any car will do since the road is in good shape (as of Fall 1990). Check with the BC Forestry Service in Golden for the condition of the road. This is also a great approach in the winter via snowmobile.

From Golden drive north along the Trans-Canada Highway until just before Donald Station where a right turn puts you on the Big Bend Highway. Follow the Big Bend Highway which eventually merges into the Bush River logging road. Continue past Bush Landing and the Bush Arm of Kinbasket Lake and follow

the road marked with "B" kilometre markers (in summer 1990) to the Bryce Creek turnoff (unmarked). This is about 115 km from Golden.

To approach the NE ridge, park on the side of the road about 1.5 km south (GR 751620) of the Bryce Creek turnoff. There is a ridge that lies between Bush River and Rice Brook. The objective is to hike directly up and over this ridge via the easiest looking line and drop down into Rice Brook close to the confluence of Rice Brook and South Rice Brook. It's a lot more straightforward than it looks on the map. (DO NOT try and bushwhack up the lower reaches of Rice Brook — it's an experience you wouldn't recommend to your worst enemy. Rest assured that people have tried it!) Continue up Rice Brook and then up into the bowl that leads to the col at the end of the NE ridge. 6 hours to the col from the car.

To reach the N face climb, turn off the main logging road at the Bryce Creek turnoff and cross a bridge over Bryce Creek. Park about 200 m further on at the edge of a clear cut (GR 746641). DO NOT go further up the road. From this point, thrash up Bryce Creek (you should be on its east side) for two hours of hard-core bushwhacking at which time you should emerge at the open, braided creek which leads up to the base of the face. This is the major creek that drains the N face. 1 hour from Bryce Creek.

Mt. Bryce: 1. NE Ridge   2. upper N Face
a. col at start of NE Ridge   b. the 798681 gully

North-East Ridge - Bryce Traverse IV 5.6   photo p. 201

FA. J. Outram and C. Kaufmann, July 1902. FWA. G. Golvach and J.McKay, February 1991. A magnificent ridge route that everyone should climb. The positions on the ridge are superb, and the view of the west end of the Columbia Icefields cannot be matched. Often it is referred to as the Bryce Traverse since it crosses the central summit en route to the main summit. One of the best of its genre in the Rockies, comparable in difficulty to the E ridge of Mt. Temple, for example, but the remoteness of the mountain increases the feeling of adventure. Allow at least four days round trip from the Icefields Parkway and two days from the Bush River. Start from a bivi at the col below the ridge.

Approach the col at the north-east end of the NE ridge by one of the prescribed access routes. From the col climb the NE ridge over loose rock and snow to a grey buttress. Interesting climbing for 25 m (at most 5.6) leads to more mixed terrain and the NE summit. Continue on mixed ground to the centre peak. The continuation ridge drops down into a small col before climbing up to the main summit at the south-west end of the ridge. 7-10 hours from Cinema Lake. Some parties bypass the Centre peak by traversing snow/ice slopes on the south side.

Descend along the same route, except bypass the centre peak by traversing slopes on the south side.

North Face IV 5.7   photo →

FA. E. Grassman and Jim Jones, July 1972. A huge face rising over 2000 m above Bryce Creek. The route starts down below tree-line, has a rocky middle section and finishes with a long ice/snow slope that in itself is as large as the N face of Athabasca. It is technically very reasonable and is now, thanks to the Bush River logging roads, becoming a popular route. Before the logging road it was rarely climbed since it was quite an expedition to get in there, do the route and then get back out. It can now be done comfortably in a three-day round trip.

Gain the base of the face via whichever approach route tickles your fancy. The climb follows the rock well to the left of the waterfalls in the middle of the face. Follow the line of least resistance up trees, cliffs and talus (some 5.7) to ledges (bivi sites) that lead right to the ice that forms the upper part of the face. Climb straight up the ice to the summit ridge. 7-8 hours.

To **descend**, traverse the E ridge back to the col where the approach from Cinema Lake reaches the E ridge (several rappels on the last section).

To reach the Bush River descend westwards onto a glacier which is followed in the direction of Bryce Creek, staying to the right. Eventually, moraines lead down to Bryce Creek. You may need to do some rappelling near the creek, depending on which line you take. Alas, you are in Bryce Creek once again and you'll have to thrash your way back to where you parked your vehicle. Have fun!

If you approached via the Saskatchewan Glacier, locate the gully that leads down through the rockwall northeast of the col (easier said than done). Then head out onto the southern end of the Icefield.

Mt. Bryce: N Face

Mount Columbia 3747 m

Mount Columbia is the highest point in Alberta and an ideal peak for a weekend ski ascent. Furthermore, it is an extremely majestic mountain, sitting on its own at the north-west corner of the Columbia Icefields, overlooking the upper reaches of the Athabasca River valley. The northern aspect is spectacular, dropping almost 2000 m from top to bottom . The E face has a somewhat more mellow angle and is the location of the Normal Route, a non-technical ice/snow climb approached from the Athabasca Glacier. Conversely, the N Ridge is a long, technical alpine climb in a very remote setting. *Map 83 C/ 3 Columbia Icefield, (83 C/4 for the Bush River approach)*

East Face (Normal Route) II   photo →

FA. J. Outram and C. Kaufmann, July 1924. A non-technical route leading to the highest summit in Alberta and a popular route in the spring when the skiing on the Icefields is at its best. It is usual to climb the E face from a camp on the Icefield, usually in the "Trench", a large east-west depression in the Icefield at the base of the face. However, it has been day-tripped from the highway.

The approach to the E face of Columbia is up the Athabasca Glacier. From the Icefield Information Centre approach up the "Snocoach road" as described for Athabasca and Andromeda (pages 185, 189). Continue past the locked gate to the Snocoach parking lot. From there, follow the well-worn dirt road down onto the glacier. Either continue up the south edge of the glacier or just right of centre. Whichever way you choose, you are aiming to get onto a bench below the final icefall. From the north end of the bench a tongue of ice leads up onto the plateau. Be on the look-out for large crevasses. Once on the plateau ski across to the "Trench" at the base of the east side of Columbia.

From the Trench work up the lower slopes to the 'schrund. Most parties leave their skis here. Cross this at its narrowest point and pick the easiest line up the ice/snow slopes to the south of a prominent set of seracs.

Descent is via the same route.

North Ridge V 5.7 W3   photo →

FA. C. Jones and G. Thompson, August 1970. A big climb in a remote setting. An excellent route with lots of variety packed into almost 2000 m of climbing. While not technically desperate, it is still not a route to be taken lightly.

Two long, multi-day approaches have been commonly used in the past but are both almost redundant since the more recent Bush River approach enables you to reach the base of the route in a single day. All three are described for completeness.

Habel Creek access The most common approach used to be the hike-in over Woolley Shoulder and down Habel Creek into the Athabasca River valley. Approach Habel Creek as for the N face of Twins Tower (page 221), but continue all the way down the creek to

Mt. Columbia: 1. E Face (normal) 2. N Ridge a. Columbia-King Edward col g. Scottish gully

the Athabasca River. To reach this point is usually a good day's hike for most people. Continue south up the Athabasca River valley to the glacial lake at the base of the Columbia Glacier. 9 km from the junction of Habel Creek and the Athabasca River. From the drainage below the west side of the mountain, gain talus slopes on the west side of the ridge and cross over to the east side below some rock towers. Bivi sites.

Athabasca River access It is also possible to follow the Athabasca River valley in from the highway, but this is much longer though it has the advantage of little elevation gain compared to the approach over Woolley Shoulder where you gain and lose 1300 m. From the trailhead at Sunwapta Falls on the Icefields Parkway, follow the trail 16 km up the east bank of the Athabasca River until it peters out near the confluence with the Chaba River. Continue along the east bank via gravel flats, the occasional bit of trail and some bushwhacking to the mouth of Habel Creek, 35 km in from the highway. Continue as above to the base of Mt. Columbia. 1.5-2 days.

Bush River access The best approach, without doubt, is from the headwaters of the Bush River which can be accessed by vehicle along the Bush River logging roads. See approach for Mt. Bryce on page 200. From the Bryce Creek turnoff follow the logging road into the headwaters of the Bush River to a prominent ridge dropping down between the Bush River and a tributary. Drive up switchbacks in the ridge (rough road) to a large clearing at roughly GR 704685. This is as far as you could take a car in the summer of 1990. Undoubtedly, the state of the road and the position of clearings will change as logging continues in the area. 3 hours from Golden.

Hike up the road to the last logged clearing, then work your way up through timber to the north-west, following an old stream bed. This trail may be marked with flagging. 1 hour to treeline. Hike northward through beautiful alpine meadows on the east side of the ridge line to a small lake (GR 668733). Gain the glacier and aim for the Columbia-King Edward col. Beware of some big holes. 4-6 hours from car to col. Contour along the base of the W face and the NW face via a prominent ledge system to reach the N ridge just above bivi sites at base of the ridge. It's a rather loose and exposed traverse but it gets you to the base of the ridge. There is only one short section that is of any great concern.

The route follows snow slopes above the bivi site to a narrow gully, the "Scottish Gully", that leads through a prominent rock band (W3) to the upper ice slope on the east side of the ridge. Gain the ridge near the bottom of the ice slope. DON'T climb up the ice slope expecting to gain the ridge much higher up — you'll end up below loose, steep walls that don't offer any easy way on. Rest assured, at least one team has thought this would be an easier way to go. Follow the ridge until below the prominent final tower. Traverse to the right (west) along some ledges until some cracks lead up to the final part of the ridge and the summit.

Descent is dependent on where you started from. To return to the Bush River descend the S ridge to the top of the W ridge, then downclimb the W ridge (some rappels) to the col between Columbia and King Edward. Retrace your approach to return to the car. From the col it's possible to return to the Athabasca River by traversing the W and NW faces (see Bush River approach above) to the base of the N ridge. Otherwise, one can descend the Normal Route and hike out across the Icefield and down the Athabasca Glacier to the Icefields Parkway.

MOUNT ALBERTA AREA

Mt. Cromwell	3330 m	Robinson/Arbic	IV 5.7	p. 210
		Elzinga/Miller	IV 5.7	p. 211
Mt. Woolley	3405 m	N Ridge (normal)	II	p. 212
Diadem Peak	3371	SE Face (normal)	II	p. 214
		N Face - Humble Horse	IV 5.7 W4	p. 214
Mt. Alberta	3619 m	Japanese Route	V 5.6	p. 216
		N Face	VI 5.9 A3	p. 218
		NE Ridge	V 5.10	p. 220
North Twin	3731 m	E Slopes (normal)	I	p. 222
		Lowe/Jones Route	VI 5.10 A4	p. 223
		N Pillar	VI 5.10d A2	p. 224

The mountains accessed by Woolley Creek and Woolley Shoulder are among the most impressive in the Rockies, and in the cases of Mt. Alberta and North Twin, perhaps in all of North America. The placement of a hut at the north end of Little Alberta provides a good base for attempts on both mountains, and has undoubtedly helped make them more popular targets than they were before, by infamy alone. The number of entries in the hut log book is a testimony to this increase in popularity.

The other peaks described may not be as famous as North Twin and Alberta but most certainly they see more successful ascents! Mt. Cromwell is practically unknown from a climbing point of view yet both routes on its N face have had several ascents that have confirmed the quality of the climbing. The Robinson/Arbic route was actually repeated within a very short time after its first ascent, something almost unheard of in recent Rockies alpine history. Diadem and Woolley are the attractions for parties interested in doing something a little more moder-

ate. However, the N face of Diadem has recently come into the limelight after a few years of obscurity with many ascents in the latter part of the '80's.

Come and visit this area. Not only is the climbing at all levels of difficulty excellent, but the hike to Woolley Shoulder is worth it just to savour the view of North Twin and Alberta.

Access via Woolley Shoulder is from the Icefields Parkway by foot. See map page 209. After driving north from Sunwapta Pass to the flats of the Sunwapta River, identify Woolley Creek as the first prominent drainage on the west side of the valley opposite a small pull-out on the east side of the highway (12.3 km north of the Icefield Information Centre). Park here.

To get to Woolley Creek it is necessary to ford the Sunwapta River. It is wise to bear in mind that the river is not only very, very cold but it also tends to rise in the heat of the day which can make for some deep wading (waist deep). A common trick is to take either a pair of neoprene socks and/or an old pair of running shoes. Really smart (and wealthy) climbers take hip waders! Once you have crossed the river just hang your footwear in a tree for the return crossing. Don't forget to hang them up — shoes are favored teeth-proving material for local rodents!

Having survived the awakening rigours of the Sunwapta River, follow the trail up the south side of Woolley Creek. After a short climb through timber, the trail levels out and follows the creek (trail blazes when it enters the trees) to the terminal moraines of the glacier below the north side of Mt. Cromwell. Access to Cromwell is across these moraines.

If continuing to Woolley Shoulder, keep close to the creek and you'll find a faint trail marked by cairns. This is the easiest way up through the moraines. Once above the moraines, the trail levels out in a grassy area — an excellent camping spot. Keep following the trail up the south side of the creek until you reach the glacier below Diadem. At this point you are in an area of very flat sandy soil, a good place to bivi for the normal routes on Woolley and Diadem.

To reach Woolley Shoulder, walk up the glacier and moraines in a southerly direction below the E face of Woolley until you reach a steep, loose talus slope leading up to the shoulder. Unfortunately, it is a two-down-for-three-up kind of slope. Keep at it — the view from the top is worth all the toil to get there.

After soaking up one of the most awe-inspiring mountain views in North America, carry on to the hut by traversing around to the north-west onto the glacier below the west side of Mt. Woolley. Keep traversing the glacier until easy slopes lead down to the hut at the north

end of Little Alberta. Allow the majority of a day to get here, especially with big packs. With a light pack the approach has been done in 4 hours.

Facilities Since this is a backcountry area you have to pack-in all your worldly needs. Shopping has to done in one of the towns, most likely Jasper. Accommodation is simple — either the Mt. Alberta hut or camping/bivi. The hut is a high altitude hut and is unlocked at all times. However, since it is no longer run by the Parks Service, accommodation is no longer a freebie. Contact the ACC for details. Regardless of how the place is run, it is an excellent base to climb from and a great "bolt-hole" in the case of foul weather.

Mount Alberta Hut

Map 83 C/6 Sunwapta Peak
Location End of N Ridge of Mt. Little Alberta. GR 702927
Reservations Alpine Club of Canada
Capacity 6
Facilities Coleman stove & foamies
Water Small spring close to hut or melt water

To register out for climbs in this area the Icefield Information Centre is the place to go. For other details about facilities see the Columbia Icefield section on page 184 and the Jasper section on page 281.

Officialese All the routes are within Jasper National Park and backcountry use comes under the regulations detailed on page 17.

WOOLLEY SHOULDER APPROACH

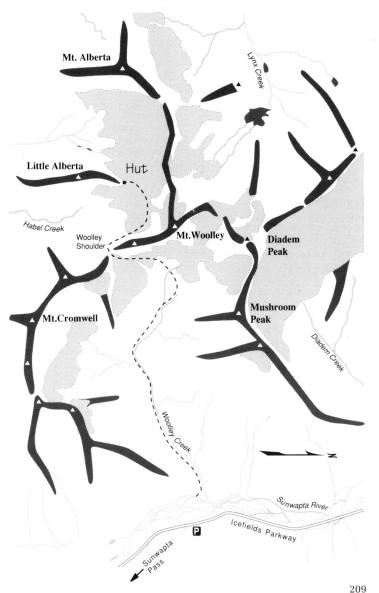

Mt. Alberta

Lynx Creek

Little Alberta

Hut

Habel Creek

Woolley
Shoulder

Mt. Woolley

Diadem
Peak

Mt. Cromwell

Mushroom
Peak

Diadem Creek

Woolley Creek

N

Sunwapta River

P

Icefields Parkway

Sunwapta
Pass

Mount Cromwell 3330 m

The routes on this mountain are not particularly well-known though the N face is very prominent from the highway when travelling south from Jasper. The most notable features of the N face are a hanging glacier immediately below the summit, and a large snow/ice field in the middle. Entry to the icefield is guarded by a high rock band tackled by the Elzinga/Miller route. To the left of these features is a large buttress, the line of the Robinson/Arbic.

This mountain suffers the indignation of being walked past by large numbers of climbers with bigger aspirations on North Twin or Alberta. Well, if those aspirations don't pan out, don't pass up the chance to have a look at either of these routes. The Elzinga/Miller route takes the obvious ice ramp in the middle of the upper face leading directly to the summit, whereas the Robinson/Arbic takes a more unlikely line up the buttress to the left. Both are well worth closer examination. Both routes have required at least one bivi. *Map 83 C/6 Sunwapta Peak*

Access Follow the Mt. Alberta hut approach from the highway until you reach the terminal moraines of the glacier below Cromwell. Work your way up the lateral moraines to the glacier which leads to the base of both routes.

Descents The easiest descent is down the south side of the mountain into the valley below the north end of Mt. Stutfield and out to the highway near the bottom of Sunwapta Pass. The W ridge has been traversed all the way to Woolley Shoulder. However, this is a long and fairly involved traverse and if time is a precious commodity it is not a good choice for a descent.

An alternative is to follow the W ridge to the first major col to the west. Cut diagonally across snowfields on the north side of the ridge (the west edge of the N face) and continue on down to rockbands that can be rappelled to the approach glacier. It is then an easy matter of walking out down Woolley Creek.

Robinson/Arbic IV 5.7   photo →

FA. W.Robinson & P.Arbic, October 1988. The climbing is characterized by tricky, mixed ground with very thin ice. Very much a modern alpine route. Good bivi sites can be found.

To the left of the major icefield on the face is a prominent buttress. This route breaks through lower walls to climb this buttress, breached via a hidden gully.

From the ledge system at the top of the gully, work your way at first to the right and then more or less straight up, following ice-filled grooves until you reach easy ground on the E ridge. Continue to the summit.

Mt. Cromwell N Face:
1. Robinson/Arbic
2. Elzinga/Miller

Elzinga/Miller IV 5.7

FA. J. Elzinga & C. Miller, Winter 1980.
One of the best mixed routes in the Rockies. This route is worthy of many more than the few ascents it has yet received. Best done in the fall.

Begin in the middle of the lower buttress at a weakness directly below the promi- nent ice ramp at the top of the face. Climb up the weakness (5.7) for six or seven ropelengths to reach the large icefield in the middle of the face. Wander up this to the base of the steep ice ramp which is followed along its right-hand edge past a large serac to the summit ridge.

Photo: Urs Kallen

Mount Woolley 3405 m

This is the prominent rock peak with an impressive and unclimbed E face at the head of Woolley Creek. This face would seem an obvious target for a route but no doubt most people are more interested in the big routes over the other side of Woolley Shoulder. The Normal Route is usually combined with an ascent of Dia- dem, an excellent outing for novice al- pinists, though the astounding view of North Twin and Mt. Alberta makes it well worth everyone's attention. The route can be comfortably climbed in a day. The hard part is getting across the glacier and onto the appropriate snow slope. *Map 83 C/6 Sunwapta Peak*

North Ridge (Normal Route) II

FA. J. Ross and D. Wessell, August 1947. A straightforward ascent but with high objective hazard from seracs and rockfall on the ascent to the col. The 'schrund is the crux. Usually combined with an ascent of Diadem. If the serac hazard is too threatening, the SE face of Diadem offers a much safer way of gaining the ridge between Diadem and Woolley via the summit of Diadem. This is the usual way of gaining the summit ridge.

From the toe of the glacier below the E faces of Woolley and Diadem, aim for the right-hand side of the glacier descend- ing from the Woolley-Diadem col. Climb a snow slope/couloir immediately to the right of the glacier to the col and then follow the N ridge to the summit. Pack plenty of film for the view of Alberta.

1. *Mt. Woolley, N Ridge*
2. *Diadem Peak, SE Face*
c. *Diadem-Woolley col*

Photo: John Martin

Diadem Peak: 1. SE Face 2. Woolley N Ridge a. Woolley-Diadem col

Diadem Peak 3371 m

Diadem Peak is the neighbour peak to Mt. Woolley. The SE face is identified by a wide snow slope descending from the summit to the base of the Woolley-Diadem Icefall. This is the line of the Normal Route, a much safer line than that taken by the original ascent party who climbed up the side of the icefall. The N face of Diadem is a route that's become a trade route in the late '80's for local alpinists. Everyone should go take a look at it since it is probably the best route of its type in the Rockies. *Map 83 C/6 Sunwapta Peak*

South-East Face (Normal Route) II   photo p. 213

FA. J. Collie, H. Stutfield and H. Woolley, 1898. The original ascent party stayed on the rock that constitutes the SE ridge of the peak. However, repeating this line is not recommended since the rock is terrible. The snow slope to the left of the ridge is much more pleasant. The route is often combined with an ascent of Woolley.

The snow slope that leads directly up the SE face offers the most straightforward route to the summit. Gain the snow slope from the glacier below Diadem and Woolley and stick to it as much as possible to avoid the chossy rock.

Descend the way you came up. If you intend to include Woolley, descend the S ridge easily to the Woolley-Diadem col, then follow the Normal Route down the N ridge on Woolley (see page 212).

North Face, Humble Horse IV 5.7 W4   photo →

FA. J.Marshall and J.Elzinga, July 1981. An excellent mixed route which everyone raves about. The climbing is never desperate yet it is only easy on some short 50°-55° ice sections. Furthermore, the route finding is simple — just follow the obvious couloir from the bottom to the top of the face.

Start from the Icefields Parkway. Park at the Interpretive pull-out 19 km north of the Icefield Information Centre, where Diadem Creek joins the Sunwapta River. Beware, the Canadian Parks Service has a sign (up to July 1991) mistakenly labelling Diadem Peak as Mushroom Peak! In the past, at least one unfortunate soul has climbed Mushroom instead of Diadem on account of this sign. Use a map!

Ford the river (see advice for Woolley Shoulder approach) to Diadem Creek and then follow Diadem Creek (no trail) onto the crest of a long and elegant moraine on the right side of the valley that leads to the headwall at the head of the drainage. To bypass the headwall hike up the north side of the valley up grassy terraces and ledges, then contour around above the headwall to the glacier below the face. Some parties bivi here. 3-4 hours from the highway.

The 'schrund at the base of the N face is a horseshoe shape below and right of the base of the obvious couloir. Cross the glacier directly to the short ice slope below the bend in the 'schrund and climb this to its upper left corner, aiming for the base of the couloir that runs the

Photo: Karl Nagy

height of the N face. Cross the 'schrund and climb up and left across 55° ice to the base of the couloir. Two straightforward mixed pitches lead up to a short section of more 55° ice. A 40 m W3/4 ice pitch gains yet another stretch of 55° ice and the base of the best bit of the route — two pitches of interesting mixed climbing up a slightly less than vertical gully with a narrow smear of ice in the back. To top it all off, 5 m of 5.7 climbing gains the ridge just below the summit.

To **descend**, traverse to the "other" summit of the mountain, then descend either the SE face (Normal Route) or the S ridge into the Woolley Creek drainage.

Mt. Diadem: Humble Horse. Spot the line!

Mount Alberta 3619 m

A majestic mountain with a most elusive summit. Many people have wanted to "bag" this peak but unlike many mountains there is no easy way up the back. The Normal Route was a tour-de-force for the day by six Japanese on a climbing holiday with three Swiss guides. Today it is still a very healthy day out for a strong team from a bivi at the base of the route. Despite some bad rock, the regular route is still a popular target during the summer months. In particular, this route has been a perennial favorite of visiting Japanese alpinists. The N Face route was a tremendous effort by George Lowe and Jock Glidden in the early '70's and is rightly one of the "grand cours" routes of the Rockies. Unfortunately, it gained a bad reputation, perhaps because of the death of Tobin Sorenson during a solo attempt at a second ascent, and there were few attempts at a repeat until the early '80's. As of the end of 1990 it has only been climbed five times. Another, more recent route is also described. The NE Ridge route is a very aesthetic line with a magnificent steep headwall. It isn't quite as committing as the N Face route and will appeal to a larger number of climbers. *Map 83 C/6 Sunwapta Peak*

Japanese Route (Normal Route) V 5.6   photo →

FA. S.Hashimoto, H.Hatano, N.Okabe, Y.Maki, Y.Mita, T. Hayakawa, J.Weber, H.Fuhrer, H.Kohler, July 1925. This route takes a system of gullies on the SE face of Alberta. It is sometimes climbed in a long day from the hut and back, but most parties spend the night out at the base of the upper part of the route so as to be in a good position to finish the climb and return to the bivi the next day. The rock is a little rank in places but is tolerable by Rockies standards. 12-15 hours return to the bivi at the base of the roped climbing.

From the hut drop down onto the glacier between Little Alberta and Mt. Alberta, aiming for low-angled talus ledges and small cliff bands at the far left (south) end of the E face of Mt. Alberta. These slopes lead up to two wide ledge systems 200 m apart, the upper one running around the whole mountain. Follow the upper ledge system to the right (north) past three "elephant's asses". These are huge, bulbous grey rock masses in the buttress above the ledge that look remarkably as named, tails included! At this point you will be below a line leading up into a wide gully system that reaches to the right-hand of two large notches in the summit ridge. This is where the roped climbing starts. The best bivi site is on top of a buttress-cum-pedestal 70 m down and 200 m left (south) of this point.

Start directly below the gully line. Visible rappel points above provide good landmarks. Climb up via the easiest line into the gully system to gain the notch in the summit ridge in about eight full ropelengths. The rock is typically loose so take care not to drop too many rocks on the second! The position in the notch is wild, especially looking down the W face. Old bivi site here. Follow the ridge towards the summit over rock steps and occasional cornices to an obvious 25 m step. Rappel or downclimb (leave a rope to facilitate the return journey) and continue over similar ridge terrain to the summit.

Descent is back down the same way.

Photo: Glen Boles

Mt. Alberta: 1. Japanese Route   2. NE Ridge   a. 25 m step

North Face VI 5.9 A3   photo →

FA G. Lowe and J.Glidden, 1972. Perhaps the most sought-after of the Rockies "grand cours" routes, with a reputation for superb hard climbing on good rock with sound belays, yet with a very remote feel. The fact that this 1000 m face has had only five ascents as of the end of 1990 is a testimony to its difficulty. An incredible tour-de-force for 1972. Though it comprises in part an icefield, it is predominantly a hard alpine rock climb and as such requires dry conditions for an attempt. The best time is most likely late July - early August when the face is usually driest. However, it has been climbed as late as September. Don't attempt an ascent lightly since escape from the face is a difficult and memorable exercise! Expect at least 3 days from a bivi at the base of the face back to Mount Alberta Hut. Enjoy — this is one of the finest hard alpine climbs the Rockies has to offer.

From the hut, cross the glacier in the direction of the base of the NE ridge of Mt. Alberta. Once on the ridge that overlooks the valley to the north of the mountain find the spur which overlooks the N face — roughly 200 m from the base of the NE ridge. Walk down to and out onto the spur to its furthest point. At the east side of the very end you will find a rappel point. A single 50 m rappel will reach the talus slope below. Drop down the talus to the glacier which is followed down and then across some moraines onto the glacier that extends below the N face. Most parties take a day from the highway to this point and bivi on the moraine before tackling the face the next day.

From the bivi cross the glacier to below the face. Start quite a way right of the prominent icefield that comes down the face. Cross the 'schrund to the rock where two straightforward pitches reach an easy ledge system that leads back left to the base of the icefield. Climb straight up the icefield, aiming slightly left of a yellow rock band located left of the centre of the face. Three mixed pitches through this rotten band lead to the base of the headwall where a steep crack indicates the way ahead. Climb one or two short pitches up the crack to small butt-sized ledges where people have bivied. Not recommended! A crack (mixed free and aid) leads up to a roof where a traverse or a pendulum to the right gains some aid climbing through the right end of the roof (A3). Above is an icy alcove. (Possible bivi ledge down and right from the roof.) Continue up to a good belay in a few metres. Ice screws could be useful. Two more rock pitches (5.7 and some aid) with a jog to the right reach a good ledge. Another free pitch leads to a better bivi ledge. Above are three often iced-up pitches up a crack system that lead up and right to easier ground and a little respite on the summit icefield. A few ropelengths gain the summit ridge which is followed to the top.

Descend via the Japanese route.

Mt. Alberta: 1. NE Ridge 2. N Face

North-East Ridge V 5.10

photo p. 217, 219

FA. K. Swigert and S. Tenney, August 1985. A route that is said to have climbing equal in quality to that on the N Face climb. The lower pitches of the headwall provide some spooky, unprotected and exposed climbing that provides substantial cerebral exercise, but they lead to great climbing on immaculate rock on the upper part of the headwall. 18 pitches of climbing were done on the first ascent, with lots of 3rd class, particularly near the bottom of the ridge. Dry conditions are mandatory for an ascent since verglas would make the spooky pitches a very difficult proposition. The first ascent team bivied once near the summit.

From the hut, contour around the glacier to gain the base of the NE ridge. Picking the line of least resistance up the lower sections, gain a long horizontal stretch of ridge that marks the end of the easy climbing (lots of 3rd class with the odd section of 5th class). At the end of the flat part of the ridge scramble up talus-covered ledges to two pinnacles. Pass these on the left (east) side, then take on the prow directly for two or three pitches to a small amphitheatre with a waterfall. These three pitches offer largely unprotected climbing up to 5.10 on delicate, loose ground. Furthermore, belays are poor to non-existent, all-in-all making this section a true test of nerve and ability. It is the key to success on the route. Persevere, since the upper headwall has beautiful, solid limestone offering climbing more akin to that found on granite.

From the amphitheatre cross the line of the waterfall and gain the ridge on the left. You should now be below a prominent chimney, right on the prow of the NE ridge. Climb the chimney to above a large chockstone (belay). Continue upward on superb rock for four pitches of good climbing (5.8/9) to reach the snow and mixed ground near the top of the ridge. Five ropelengths of mixed climbing lead to a big, wide ledge where a troop of scouts could spend a comfortable night. Three more pitches gain the summit.

Descent is via the Japanese Route.

North Twin 3631 m

North Twin consists of two summits: North Twin itself and the lower North Tower known as Twins Tower. Without doubt, the N face of Twins Tower is one of the most impressive faces in the Canadian Rockies if not in North America. The N face is over 1500 m high and is unusually steep, rising in three main steps: a steep lower rock band, a middle section only slightly lower-angled, and a final impressive vertical headwall. For an appreciation of the atmosphere of the face take a look at Chris Jones' article in the 1975-76 edition of "Ascent". Climbers strong in both mind and body should be prepared for very sustained difficulties on these extremely steep routes. A healthy dose of long Rockies alpine rock routes would be a big help. Dry conditions are another aid to a successful ascent; five days of good weather is what you're looking for. Both routes were first climbed in late July - early August, the period when best conditions are most likely. The rockfall hazard on the lower part of these routes, particularly the North Pillar, is quite high. As of 1990 both routes were unrepeated though the Lowe/Jones has seen several attempts, one reaching within a few pitches of the easy ground at the top. Most flounder in the first rock band.

At a more down-to-earth level is the Normal Route up the SE slopes of the mountain, a popular ski mountaineering outing. *Map 83 C/3 Columbia Icefield*

Access to Twins Tower The usual method is to first get to the Mt. Alberta Hut. Gauging by the likely size of the loads you'll be carrying, this is as far as most climbers will get in a day from the road. From the hut drop down onto the glacier and moraines below the east side of Little Alberta. This leads down onto some flat meadows just north of the steep descent into Habel Creek and directly opposite the base of North Twin. A good place to view the face. Pick up an indistinct trail marked by small cairns at the south-west edge of the meadows. This leads steeply down through timber to Habel Creek. Cross the creek, then work your way through moraines and crevasses to reach the glacier that sits below the face. Easy walking leads to the base of the face. There is an excellent bivi site by a small lake in the moraines immediately to the west.

Descent of Twins Tower Once on the summit of Twins Tower, going home will be foremost in your mind! Start by traversing over the summit of North Twin or, alternatively, traverse across the north side of the summit (once above the serac barrier) onto the col between North Twin and Stutfield. Of three known trips up the N Face, three different descents were taken from this point so pick the one most suited to your needs.

The longest descent route traverses the Columbia Icefield to the head of the Athabasca Glacier, then returns you to the Icefields Parkway via the Athabasca Glacier. This is perhaps the most straightforward descent but takes a long time (see page 222). The other two descents contour round the east slopes of the summit of Stutfield (West Stutfield), then head north towards the summit of Cromwell. Pass one icefall that drops down into Habel Creek and keep going towards a col between the second summit of Stutfield (East Stutfield) and the summit of Cromwell. This is also at the head of a second icefall that drops down into Habel Creek. You have a choice of descents from here: either descend into Habel Creek or descend eastwards into the drainage south of Cromwell. Descending into Habel Creek is a little complex. Start down the middle of the icefall and when it becomes broken head for the north edge to the right. Scramble down rocks on the right-hand side until this too becomes impossible. Cross back to the centre of the glacier and meander down until able to cut across and onto the lateral moraine. Descend to the upper reaches of Habel Creek and thus to Mt. Alberta Hut.

North Twin, East Slopes (Normal Route) I

FA. W.S.Ladd, J.M.Thorington and C. Kain, July 1923. A popular ski mountaineering target since it is possible to ski all the way to the summit. From there it is not uncommon for parties to also ascend either South Twin or Stutfield. An ice axe (at least) is recommended for the narrow ridge on South Twin. A long day trip from the road, it is often split into two days with a camp near the base of the east slopes of North Twin.

Approach up the Athabasca Glacier as for Mt. Columbia on page 204, then contour around the western slopes of Snowdome. Head north-west along the narrow north arm of the Icefield to the col between Stutfield and North Twin. Stutfield is an easy ascent from here. The east slopes of North Twin present little difficulty on skis. If you wish to climb South Twin, descend south slopes to the col between North and South Twin, then follow the N ridge to the summit. Remove your skis; the narrow ridge to the top is hardly a ski route! Return back down the N ridge to the col and traverse the south-east side of North Twin back to the saddle east of North Twin.

Photo: Glen Boles

South Twin: N Ridge   a. Yes, this face has been climbed!

Twins Tower, Lowe/Jones Route   VI 5.10 A4   photo p. 225

FA. G. Lowe and C. Jones 1974. An incredible ascent of undoubtedly the hardest alpine route in North America at that time. It was completed in atrocious weather and with rapidly dwindling hardware. A typically bold ascent by George Lowe. Objective hazard is highest at the base of the face where serac fall threatens the route. The upper part of this route is steep and offers continuously difficult climbing up to 5.10 A3/4. Anticipate a lot of nailing in thin cracks.

Begin at the left edge of the face, just right of an avalanche cone resulting from icefall down the gully at the junction of North Twin and Stutfield. Scramble rapidly up the right edge of the avalanche cone and over rocks to the base of a slabby face. Climb this and a short steep wall above in about two pitches. Traverse right on a large ledge to the base of an inside corner with a good crack in the left wall. Jam the crack (5.8) and continue up to a belay. Above is a vertical corner which is hard to start. Sustained climbing leads up to a small roof that puts up a short battle (hard 5.10 or A2). Above the roof is a ledge where the angle

eases. Easy scrambling now leads up and right to the hanging glacier of the N face. Stay high to minimize rockfall hazard. Good bivi sites can be found at the top of the icefield. Cross the 'schrund and continue up and right to the crest of the buttress. Tricky climbing up good cracks for about six pitches leads to the icy ledge below the final wall. Bivi sites with some chopping of ice. It is possible to traverse off to the left along this ledge and "escape" up the north-east side of the face. The "Traverse of the Chickens" is a useful escape if the upper face is wet.

Starting slightly left of the prow of the buttress, follow a vague line (5.9 A1/2) almost directly above on steep and strenuous ground. After about 200 m small bivi ledges are reached. Continue up and slightly right, following shallow cracks which lead in four to six pitches (rumoured A4 in places) to small ledges where the first ascensionists spent another night. Break out left towards an ice runnel and either tension or rappel into this. Climb out of the top of the runnel to easier-angled slopes. Much easier climbing leads up to the summit of the North Tower.

North Twin: 1. E Slopes   2. N Ridge, South Twin   a. return from S Twin

Photo: Glen Boles

Twins Tower, North Pillar VI 5.10d A2   photo →

FA. D. Cheesmond and B. Blanchard, August 1985. A quintessential Cheesmond ascent — a radical climb put up in impeccable style during one of the longest good weather spells in recent times. A more aesthetic line than the Lowe/Jones and mostly a free climb with the odd move of aid. It will undoubtedly see more attempts than the Lowe/Jones because of these features. A training diet of big limestone rock routes would be very useful. You should anticipate some rockfall, especially on the lower part of the route. The first ascent party spent 4 nights on the face.

Climb 4th class snow slopes and small rock steps at the right side of the face until below and right of a steep, smooth corner in the lower band of the face. There are several "steep, smooth" corners. Pick the easiest and the driest! Climb up and left for one pitch into the corner. Three short or two long pitches (5.10c) lead up to ledges at the top. Continue up and right, then back left towards an ice slope. Traverse left along the top of this to a large, sinister looking gully. Rockfall is severe in this part of the face. Cross the gully and belay in a protected alcove before climbing up and left to bivi ledges. These are approximately 500 m from the top of the first corner.

Continue to a higher ledge and move right to a steep corner. Climb this (5.10c) to a roof. The roof (A1) gives access to a large corner. Eventually, take the crack in the right-hand wall of the corner to a position overlooking the large sinister gully (four pitches). A wide and strenuous crack (5.10d) leads up through a roof to the top of the second band. Move up onto the ice, then descend diagonally left to a small bivi ledge.

Climb straight up the crest of the ice slope to the base of the headwall and belay on the left below a corner crack. Move up the crack and exit on the left. Continue up left to a belay in a deep inside corner (5.10a). Climb the steep finger crack on the left to a huge platform and block belay (5.10d). Move left and up into the base of a chimney/gully and climb a further pitch up the chimney. Continue up to a hanging belay (5.10a). One or two moves lead up to a roof, above which is an excellent belay (5.10a). Carry on up the break for two pitches, ending in a cave across on the right wall. Good bivi inside with ice on the floor.

Return to the main break and climb this for three steep and serious pitches (5.10d). Difficulty with belays. Take the left-hand crack where the line splits, finally exiting onto a ledge on the left. Easier climbing leads to a higher ledge (first ascent bivi ledge). Climb a chimney above to belay near a pinnacle. Move right and launch up a thin flake and crack in a sensational position, eventually trending left to exit onto easier ground (5.10d) and relief from the incredible exposure. Four more pitches lead up to the ridge and another ten or so will reach the summit of the Twins Tower. At this point give yourself a well-deserved pat on the back before commencing with the long descent.

Mt. North Twin, Tower
1. Lowe/Jones
2. N Pillar

CLEMENCEAU ICEFIELD

Pic Tordu	3210 m	W Ridge	II 5.3	p. 228
Tusk Peak	3360 m	S Ridge (normal)	II 5.3	p. 230
		NW Ridge	II 5.4	p. 230
Mt. Clemenceau	3658 m	W Face (normal)	II	p. 232
		NE Ridge	IV	p. 234
		N Face	IV	p. 234
Mt. Shackleton	3330 m	NW Ridge	II	p. 236
		N Face	II	p. 238
		Traverse	III 5.5	p. 238
Duplicate Mtn.	3150 m	N Ridge of NE Peak	II	p. 239
Tsar Mtn.	3424 m	N Ridge (normal)	II	p. 240

The mountains of the Clemenceau Icefield are the most remote peaks described in the book. For those people looking to get "far from the maddening crowd", then a trip to the Clemenceau may be the answer. Most likely you will be quite alone in this remote place.

The big peaks in the area were climbed in the early twenties like so many other large mountains in the Rockies. However, the main development didn't take place until the early '70's when the ACC ran several very successful camps in the area. The development at this time was very much like that of the Columbia Icefield area at the turn of the century — many straightforward routes climbed by only a handful of climbers. The legacy of this development is that there is now a large number of excellent moderate mountaineering routes. The development of extreme routes has yet to get underway though the ascent of the N face of Clemenceau in recent years is a pointer to future possibilities. The large walls on the north side of Tusk are obvious candidates for modern, new routes.

The ACC felt that more people should be enticed into visiting the area, and to this end, the Lawrence Grassi Hut was erected in the summer of 1981. Since the Clemenceau region is predominantly glacier, the hut had to be located at the west side of the area on one of the few rocky ridges with a water supply. This creates a few logistical problems for doing routes on the east side of Tusk and Pic Tordu. Nevertheless, the hut is palatial and makes an excellent base for climbing.

Access

The remoteness of the area poses a few problems for overland access. Some parties relish the experience of a long approach by foot to a beautiful area. For those climbers more concerned with time, then air access is possible since Clemenceau is not inside a National Park boundary.

By foot For those climbers who relish a three or four days' expedition-style walk-in, this has got to be the ultimate approach in the book! Be prepared for lots of wading and bushwhacking. Start from Sunwapta Falls on the Icefields Parkway 65 km south of Jasper. From the parking lot at Sunwapta Falls, cross the Sunwapta River and follow the trail up the Athabasca River valley as far as it goes. Continue up the Chaba River to Fortress Pass at the east end of Fortress Lake.

In winter, skiing across Fortress Lake into the upper reaches of the Wood River and then south up Clemenceau Creek valley is the quickest way to go. When entering Clemenceau Creek contour around the north shoulder of Ghost Mountain to avoid as much bushwhacking as possible.

In summer, this is not the recommended route since getting around Fortress Lake is a miserable affair. At this time of year it is best to keep following the Chaba River up its western fork to the Chaba Icefield. Swing north-west around the south side of a spur of an unnamed peak on the Continental Divide and climb up to a 2650 m col about 1.5 km south-west of the unnamed peak. This leads over to Misty Glacier at the head of Chisel Creek. Pass through a 2850 m col just south-east of Brouillard Mountain and drop down into the Clemenceau drainage. Continue up the Tusk Glacier and across the Cummins Glacier to reach the hut.

By air There is a choice of aircraft depending on how much money you want to spend: ski-plane or helicopter. For the ski-plane you'll be departing from Golden. Contact Amiskwi Air for further details. If going in by chopper then there are three likely take-off points: Golden (Canadian Helicopters), Valemont (Yellowhead Helicopters) or possibly Mica Dam. In summer, large groups will most likely drive to Mica Dam from Revelstoke, then follow the south shore of McNaughton Lake to either Red Harbour or Yellow Creek, both of which can be used as staging areas. From here it is a 15 minute flight to the Grassi Hut. Do bear in mind, however, that you'll have to pay for the time it takes the chopper to get to Mica Dam and back to its base. In winter it may be possible to co-ordinate a flight with Canadian Mountain Holidays heli-ski operation. Contact their main office in Banff.

Facilities If you fly in the last town you pass through is the last place you'll be able to pick up stores, which will be either Golden, Revelstoke, or Valemont. Jasper is the nearest town to the trailhead for the walk-in. See Jasper area information on page 281.

For accommodation the ACC has kindly provided a hut. As mentioned above, it is located on the west side of the range so not all routes are possible in a day trip. Many people will prefer climbing from camps or bivis at other locations in the range. However, the hut is unlocked at all times and provides a good base for a trip and a very palatial bolt-hole in bad weather.

Lawrence Grassi Hut
Map 83 C/4 Clemenceau Icefield
Location Cummins Ridge 2100 m, 8km SSW of Mt. Clemenceau. GR 320813
Reservations Alpine Club of Canada
Capacity 20
Facilities Propane & Coleman stoves, oilfired heater, foamies, dishes & utensils
Water Little tarn to north

Officialese The Clemenceau Area is not within a National or Provincial Park, but is under the jurisdiction of the RCMP in Valemont.

Pic Tordu 3210 m

Pic Tordu is the nearest peak to the Lawrence Grassi Hut. As viewed from the doorway, the mountain is a mass of exposed, contorted strata, part of the ridge line that extends eastward over Cowl Mtn. to Mt. Shackelton. It offers an excellent first day out from the hut. *Map 83 C/4 Clemenceau Icefield*

West Ridge II 5.3   photo →

FA. H. Microys and M. Rosenberger, August 1972. The nearest route to the hut. The W Ridge route is not difficult — in fact, it is never necessary to rope up. It is recommended that you combine Pic Tordu with a traverse to Shackleton to make a very worthwhile outing. Unfortunately, the usual descents all go down the other side of the mountain and require a long walk back. However, an alternative descent to the hut may be possible.

From the hut cross the Cummins Glacier to the base of the W ridge. Follow an ill-defined rib to a subsidiary peak. From there a relatively exposed and serrated ridge rises to the summit.

Most parties continue from the summit over Cowl Mtn. (a small bump in the ridge) to the Pic Tordu-Shackleton col, and either go up the W ridge on Shackleton or down the south side of the col onto the glacier south of Shackleton. It's a long way to the hut from here!

Descents From the summit the quickest way back to the hut is the way you came up.

However, it may be possible to drop down onto the glacier immediately north of Pic Tordu and walk down to the head of the icefall overlooking the Cummins Glacier. Descent from here is most likely easier on the south side of the icefall but will involve rappels. It cannot be confirmed whether this route has ever been descended but it has been used as an approach to the NW Ridge of Mt. Shackleton (see page 236). This glacier can also be reached from the Pic Tordu-Shackleton col.

The other descent option from the Pic Tordu-Shackleton col requires a long, long glacier hike around Duplicate and up the Tusk Glacier to get back to the hut. Definitely an overnight trip.

*Pic Tordu: 1. W Ridge   2. Traverse of Shackleton
3. approach to Shipton-Irvine col or descent from Pic Tordu
s. Mt. Shackleton   c. Cowl Mountain*

Tusk Peak 3360 m

This is the large pyramidal rock peak sitting across the Tusk Glacier from Mt. Clemenceau. It certainly looks appealing, though in the true tradition of the Rockies, the rock quality lowers the appeal! The north side of the peak is one of the most impressive rock faces in the area and is still unclimbed. Immediately south of Tusk are three summits, Irvine (GR 358833), Chetten (GR 350829) and Shipton (GR 344828) that provide an interesting traverse. *Map 83 C/4 Clemenceau Icefield*

South Ridge (Normal Route) II 5.3   photo →

FA. J. DeLaittre, W.R. MacLaurin and A.J. Ostheimer, July 1927. The easiest way to the top. A scramble.

The original approach to the S ridge was via the Duplicate-Tusk icefall. However, quoting the AAC-ACC guide, "the original approach....is no longer sensible" Quite! Considering the position of the hut this approach is now defunct. From the hut you now approach by crossing the Cummins Glacier up onto the Tusk Glacier. Ascend the glacial cirque between Shipton and Tusk, then climb a snow couloir to gain the Tusk-Irvine col.

From the Tusk-Irvine col you can take two routes. Either ascend the S ridge directly with one small step to liven up the day, or traverse onto the south-east slopes. Take your pick.

Descend via the same route. 8-10 hours.

North-West Ridge II 5.4   photo →

FA. G.I. Bell and J.R. Rousson, July 1951. A very aesthetic line to the summit marred somewhat by poor quality rock in the lower sections. The ridge is a scramble except for a section near the summit where many parties use a rope. Thankfully, the rock improves as you get higher.

From the hut gain the Tusk Glacier and cross to the base of the ridge. Climb the ridge throughout to the top.

Descend the Normal Route.

A challenging end to a day on Tusk can be had by continuing from the Tusk-Irvine col along the ridge over Irvine, Chettan and Shipton. The route is not technical and provides a more interesting way back to the hut. Descent off Shipton is down its long N ridge. This outing has been done in 16 hours.

Tusk Peak: 1. S Ridge (normal) 2. NW Ridge a. Tusk-Irvine col b.to Irvine, Chettan & Shipton

Mount Clemenceau 3658 m

The fourth highest mountain in the Canadian Rockies and unquestionably the main attraction of the area. It is a huge, bulky mountain, each face presenting a different perspective of the peak. The Normal Route up the W face is a classic glacier outing, sufficiently mellow it is possible to ski almost to the summit! The views of the Clemenceau Icefield area (and the mountains beyond) make an ascent a very worthy escapade. The other two described routes on the northern aspect of the peak are much more climber's climbs. Both these climbs would not be out of place on Mt. Robson. The S and E faces are the two predominant rock faces on the peak. They beckon.... *Maps 83 C/4 Clemenceau Icefield, 83 C/5 Fortress Lake.*

West Face (Normal Route) II   photo →

FA. D.B.Durand, H.S.Hall, W.D. Harris and H.B.DeVilliers-Schwab, August 1923. FWA. G.Bruce and D.James, February 1976 The most popular route in the area and a classic climb to the top of a high mountain. The route is essentially a non-technical glacier hike that avoids the steepest parts of the face. It is similar in character to the Normal Route on Mt. Athabasca though longer and more interesting.

From the hut cross the Cummins and Tusk glaciers to the base of the Tiger Glacier, the glacier that descends the west side of the mountain to join the Tusk Glacier at the base of the south-west slopes. The first objective is to reach a col between the upper W ridge and a small subsidiary bump on the ridge itself. To do this, gain the glacier below the southwest corner of the mountain and work your way through crevasses to the col. Continue up the rounded W ridge at the left (north) side of the steep W face until just below steep slopes leading to the summit ridge. Traverse a bench below these slopes to the north to gain the NW ridge which is followed to the top.

Descend the same way you came. 11-15 hours hut-to-hut.

Mt. Clemenceau W Face: a. Tiger Glacier b. the "bump" c. the "bench"   233

North-East Ridge IV   photo →

FA. D. Eberl, P. Jensen, T. Kelly, G. Thompson and J. Wilson, August 1980. A relatively new route. There is no doubt that if Clemenceau was closer to a road this route would have been climbed many years earlier. It is very similar in character to the Emperor Ridge on Robson. The climbing on the heavily corniced part of the ridge at its very end is far from straightforward. Proceed carefully. Expect to take three days round trip.

From the hut, cross the Cummins and Tusk glaciers to the terminal moraine of the Clemenceau Glacier. Gain a small flat alpine meadow area below the east side of Clemenceau via one of several easily climbed drainages. Bivi sites. Climb straight up an ice slope on the E face of the NE ridge, just to the north of a rock buttress. Some mixed climbing at the top of the slope exits onto the ridge. Continue up the straightforward ridge to a summit, the most southerly point on

the ridge. Press on along a snow/ice crest until just short of the main summit where you come face-to-face with hideous, large cornices and gargoyle formations. And when I say large, imagine 10 m overhanging cornices! This is more like Alaska than the Canadian Rockies. The remaining 200 m to the summit is the crux and can be quite a test of nerve and judgement. In the heat of the day these formations are very unstable. To overcome this problem, the first ascent party bivied and tackled the cornices first thing in the morning when the snow was consolidated after a cold night. Whatever way you choose to proceed, you'll have to work your way very carefully through this section.

Descend the W Face route or the NW ridge. This latter descent takes you back down to Clemenceau Creek via easy downclimbing and scrambling.

North Face IV   photo →

FA. K. Wallator, T. Thomas, G. McCormicke, February 1989. A classic ice face in the same class as the N face of Mt. Robson. The first ascent was done over 16 days road to road, in winter with NO air support. A tremendous effort by this young team. Done in this fashion, it is highly recommended for the alpinist looking for a remote experience. During the summer months the route could be climbed to the summit in a day by a strong team.

Gain the NE ridge route as described under that climb. Once you have gained the ridge follow it a short way until a traverse below some seracs gains the snow and icefield of the up-

per N face. An obvious, beautiful ice ramp that screams out to be climbed leads up the middle of the face directly to the summit.

Descent The first ascent party descended the NE Ridge route which they described as "airy...scary". Not recommended. The Normal Route is much easier and safer. However, if you want to return to Clemenceau Creek, the NW ridge can be downclimbed with few complications.

Mt. Clemenceau: 1. NE Ridge   2. N Face   g. the gargoyles

Mount Shackleton 3330 m

A splendid mountain that presents quite a formidable approach challenge, particularly from the north. The Duplicate-Tusk icefall is more reminiscent of a Himalayan glacier than one in the Rockies. The mountain can be climbed from the hut, either over Pic Tordu or up the glacier to the north of Pic Tordu, but is usually tackled from a camp either below the Duplicate-Tusk icefall or on the south side of Duplicate, typically near the base of the S ridge. Obviously your approach is dependent on your anticipated ascent route. *Map 83 C/4 Clemenceau Icefield*

North-West Ridge II   photo →

FA. G.I. Bell and D. Michael, July 1951. If approaching from the north, the crux of the route is undoubtedly finding a safe route through the spectacular Duplicate-Tusk icefall. The ridge is exposed but cornices are not too much of a problem and the climbing is straightforward.

Via Duplicate-Tusk Icefall The original approaches from the north side navigated the icefall on the left (east) side near a prominent streak of lateral moraine where the threat of falling seracs used to be quite low. However, icefalls change and this route may now be threatened. It is still most likely that the safest routes through the icefall are close to either the west end of Duplicate or the base of Tusk's E face. Use your own judgement and be careful! Much less intimidating approaches are possible from the hut. Once in the glacial bowl between Shackleton and Duplicate gain the NW ridge just below where it steepens, about 200 m below the W summit. The 'schrund just below the ridge may put up a fight!

Via the Shackleton-Irvine col This approach is the recommended one for the NW Ridge and the N Face since objective hazard is low and it may be possible to climb Shackleton in one long day from the hut via this route. From the hut climb the rock headwall to the right (south) of the icefall between Pic Tordu and the Shipton-Irvine ridge (5.5) to gain the glacier above. Ascend the glacier and climb up to the Shackleton-Irvine col. 3-4 hours from the hut.

Climb the step in the NW ridge of Shackleton (5.4) to gain the upper part of the ridge. Follow the north side of the ridge to the W summit. It is usual to continue along to the main summit of the mountain via the narrow and exposed summit snow ridge.

Descent is typically via the same route. However, the descent of the SW ridge to the Pic Tordu-Shackleton col is not difficult; a small rock step near the top is the only obstacle. This gives access to the glacier north of Pic Tordu and the approach route for the Shackleton-Irvine col. This route has two advantages: it keeps you out of the Duplicate-Tusk icefall and it takes you directly back to the hut. The step in the NW ridge of Shackleton is climbed at first on the W side and then at about half height on the N side (5.4) to gain the upper part of the NW ridge. Traverse across the base of the N face to reach the N Face route.

Mt. Shackelton: 1. NW Ridge d. via Duplicate-Tusk Icefall s. via Shackelton-Irvine col
2. N Face 3. Traverse n. North Summit m. Main Summit
e. SE Peak f. Shackelton-Sir Ernest col

Photo: Glen Boles

Mount Shackleton

North Face II   photo p. 237, 239

FA. M. Heath and W. Summer, August 1971. Similar in character to the N face of Athabasca but with a much more challenging approach.

Approach as for the NW Ridge either via the Shackleton-Irvine col or the Duplicate-Tusk icefall (see page 236). Start at the base of the prominent rocks leading up to the main summit of the mountain. The route follows the snow and ice slopes immediately to the right (west) of these rocks. After the 'schrund, keep going uphill until there is no more slope. Continue easily to the main summit.

Descend as for the NW Ridge.

Traverse III 5.5   photo p. 237, 239

FA. H. Microys and M. Rosenberger, August 1972. The first traverse of the mountain was quite a tour-de-force that also included the first ascent of the W ridge of Pic Tordu. A highly recommended outing if traverses are your big thing. The first ascent party bivied once but two nights out would be necessary if you plan on the long walk back to the hut around Duplicate.

From the hut you can gain the Pic Tordu-Shackleton col either by climbing the W ridge of Pic Tordu and traversing along the ridge line (page 228) or via the approach route to the Shackleton-Irvine col (page 236). Alternatively, from a camp on the south side of Duplicate or Shackleton you can gain the col by climbing easy snow slopes on the south side of Cowl Mtn.

From the Pic Tordu-Shackleton col scramble up the W ridge of Shackleton to the W summit. A small rock step near the summit provides some interest. From the W summit continue along the narrow summit snow ridge to the main summit.

The next section to the SE peak is most definitely the interesting part of the whole outing. Breathe in, tighten your belt and get stuck in! Just east of the main summit is an impressive rock tower. Traverse the north side of this across very rotten rock to gain the east side. Drop into a sharp notch and climb a short vertical wall of the usual Rockies highest-quality loose rock to gain a long flat stretch of ridge. At the end of it climb steep ice to gain the SE summit. 3 hours from the main summit.

Descend steep snow and rock of the NE ridge to the Shackleton-Sir Ernest col. Sir Ernest is the small peak between Shackleton and Duplicate (GR 391822). The original traverse party finished by descending through the Duplicate-Tusk icefall. However, it is possible to return to the hut via the Shackleton-Irvine col. Dropping down to the south side of Duplicate is easy but makes for a long walk around that mountain to get back to the hut. Preferably, traverse around the west side of Sir Ernest to the Duplicate-Sir Ernest col, then descend to the glacier south of Duplicate.

*Duplicate: 1. N Ridge, NE Summit
Shackleton: 2. N Face 3. Traverse
g. Duplicate-Tusk Icefall s. Sir Ernest*

Duplicate Mountain 3150 m

A three-peaked mountain with the highest peak being the middle summit. This summit is easily reached from the col between Duplicate and Sir Ernest. However, the interesting route on the mountain is on the NE peak — a long ridge that extends north-east and then north to the Clemenceau Glacier. The N ridge lies at the head of the glacier that descends from the north side of Duplicate to the west of this ridge. *Map 83 C/4 Clemenceau Icefield*

North-East Summit, North Ridge II

FA. H. Microys, M. Rosenberger and T. Turner, August 1972. The lower section is a rock ridge of the usual quality rock leading up to a steep final ice slope below the summit. The majority of the climbing is on snow and ice.

Typically, this route is climbed from a bivi somewhere between the Clemenceau and Duplicate glaciers. From the bivi, approach the climb up the glacier to the base of the prominent rock ridge.

Avoid the vertical lower section of rock by climbing up snow to the right (west). Scramble up the rock ridge over several small vertical steps to the base of a prominent ice slope (45°) that leads to the NE summit.

Descent Continue over the NE summit and scramble down the rock of the S ridge onto the Clemenceau Glacier. Hike back to your bivi site. 9-12 hours.

Photo: Glen Boles

Tsar Mountain 3424 m

Tsar is a very prominent landmark in the area, being a large pyramidal peak that sits head and shoulders above the surrounding mountains. Though it is somewhat separated from the rest of the Clemenceau group, it has to be included since it is a high mountain and will be a target for many parties coming to this area to climb. *Map 83 C/4 Clemenceau Icefield*

North Ridge (Normal Route) II   photo →

FA. G.I.Bell, W.V.G.Matthews, and D. Michael, July 1951. A very prominent ridge rising from the Tsar Glacier directly to the summit. Not a technical route but rather a steep snow walk especially towards the top. From a camp under Mt. Ellis anticipate a good day to gain the summit and return to camp.

From the Lawrence Grassi Hut the first objective is to circumvent the Tusk, Shackleton and Duplicate massif. Cross the Cummins Glacier and descend the Tusk Glacier to reach the Clemenceau Glacier. Ascend this through the shallow col between Duplicate and Apex, and continue in a south-south-east direction to below the south-east side of Mt. Ellis, the peak to the north-east of Mt. Somervell. Descend the glacier south of Ellis through an icefall onto the Tsar Glacier and the Tsar-Somervell col.

From the Tsar-Somervell col work your way up a face between the N ridge and a spur descending to the north-west. Gain the crest of the spur and follow it to a junction with the N ridge. Continue up the ridge until below the steep summit block. Traverse across the north-west aspect of the summit block and cross the 'schrund to gain the W ridge. Surprisingly steep snow leads to the summit.

Descend via the same route.

Tsar Mountain: N Ridge   c. Tsar-Somervell col

Photo: Glen Boles

FRYATT CREEK

Mt. Brussels	3161 m	NE Ridge (normal)	III 5.7	p. 244
		N Face	IV 5.10	p. 246
Mt. Christie	3103 m	NE Face	III 5.6	p. 248
Mt. Lowell	3150 m	S Ridge	II	p. 248
Mt. Fryatt	3361 m	SW Face (normal)	II 5.4	p. 250
		W Ridge Direct	III 5.8	p. 250
Mt. Geraldine	2910 m	N Ridge	II 5.5	p. 252
Mt. Belanger	3120 m	N Face	II	p. 255
Mt. Olympus	2940 m	NW Ridge	II 5.6	p. 255
		NW Couloir	II	p. 255

Even though Mt. Fryatt is the highest mountain in this group, the "fame" of the area is due to the outcry arising from the first ascent of another peak — Mt. Brussels, by Garner and Lewis in 1948. Not only did they use many pitons and aid but also bolts and sneakers. What outrage!! It may all seem a little amusing in the 1990's, but back then it was obviously "terribly bad form, what?" to be involved in such escapades. However, to Garner and Lewis's credit they not only climbed the peak but made a movie and put up with foul weather throughout!

While Fryatt and Brussels are the major attractions, there are other mountains well worth doing. This is one of the better mountaineering areas within Jasper National Park with routes of varying though generally moderate difficulty and short approaches from a hut. All the routes can be completed from the Fryatt valley in a single day. The Sydney Vallance Hut provides an excellent base; hence, the hut is a fairly popular destination during the summer months.

Access to Hut From the Athabasca Falls turn-off, 31 km south of Jasper on the Icefields Parkway, follow Highway 93A (Athabasca Parkway) for 1.1 km to the Geraldine Lakes road. Drive along this road for 2.1 km to a signposted fire road leading left (east) toward the Athabasca River. Park here in a small parking area on the left side of the road.

Hike the fire road which heads south, paralleling the river for 11.4 km to Lower Fryatt campground. (Mountain bikes are allowed to this point.) A trail then swings away to the west towards Fryatt Creek. It leads steeply up into the valley, passing Brussels campground (approach Brussels from here), winding through a cairned boulder field, and then around Fryatt Lake to Headwall campground. Above is Fryatt Creek Falls. The trail climbs about 150 m right of the falls and tops out at the Sidney Vallance Hut. This is a healthy distance of 22 km from the trailhead.

Facilities You are going to have to carry all your goodies into this area. Groceries and supplies can be obtained in Jasper, the nearest town. For further information regarding the facilities in Jasper see page 281.

Once in the Fryatt valley there are two forms of accommodation: the Sydney Vallance Hut and camping. The hut is administered by the ACC and is locked. For further details on using the hut see page 20.

Many climbers are going to be interested in camping. There are two designated campgrounds in the valley that are likely to be of use to climbers: Brussels campground below Brussels, and Headwall campground at the base of the headwall just before the hut. Routes can be done in a day from either of these two locations. Camping near the hut and bivis at the base of the routes are not allowed.

Officialese The routes are all within Jasper National Park and backcountry use comes under the National Park regulations detailed on page 17.

Sydney Vallance Hut
Map 83 N/12 Athabasca Falls
Location Above headwall at head of Fryatt Creek. GR 403174
Reservations Alpine Clubs of Canada
Capacity 16
Facilities Coleman stove and lamp, wood stove, tick mattresses for 6, pots and utensils
Water Creek few metres east of hut
Notes Locked when hut custodian not present

Mount Brussels 3161 m

A very impressive rock tower easily identified from the highway. The first ascent via the NE ridge caused quite an uproar because of the use of four bolts and a "bucket full of pitons". Tut, tut! The first instance of the use of bolts in the Canadian Rockies. The N face has a much more modern route, offering steep, interesting climbing with rock of all qualities and long run-outs. Uniquely Rockies! *Map 83 C/12 Athabasca Falls, 83 C/5 Fortress Lake*

North East Ridge (Normal Route) III 5.7   photo →

FA. R.C. Garner and J. Lewis, July 1948. By today's standards this is not a particularly hard climb. However, there is a lot of steep, rotten rock that will keep many seasoned alpinists on their toes. The majority of the interesting climbing is contained in two pitches, the "First Step" and the "Lewis Crack". The rest of the route is relatively straightforward and can be comfortably climbed in a day from Fryatt Creek.

Approach to both routes is up the drainage that leads directly towards Brussels from the Brussels campground. Once above treeline, contour below cliff bands until directly below the Christie-Brussels col. Go straight up to the col.

From the Christie-Brussels col traverse around the east side of the peak until easy scrambling leads up to the base of the steep upper part of the NE ridge. Gain a notch in the ridge via a 12 m-chimney, then continue up a short steep wall and another chimney to the top of the first pinnacle. Scramble along the ridge beyond to the base of the "First Step", a 40 m-high buttress. Diagonal 12 m across the face on the right (north) side of the ridge to a roof which is turned on the right into a chimney. Follow this for 12 m to a chockstone. Traverse further right into another chimney leading to the top of the first step. Climb around onto the left (east) side of the ridge to the base of the "Lewis Crack". Surmount this infamous fissure (5.7) and continue to the top of the first of the four summit pinnacles. Tackle the second pinnacle direct, traverse the right side of the third and climb easily over the fourth to the summit. 3-6 hours from the col.

Descend via the same route.

Page 246 *Mt. Brussels: 1. NE Ridge a. the "First Step"   2. N Face c. Christie-Brussels col*

Mt. Brussels: NE Ridge   a. the "First Step'   b. the "Lewis Crack"

245

North Face IV 5.10

FA. G. Randall and D. Waterman, August 1979. An improbable route with some steep and poorly protected climbing. Very much a modern alpine rock route. With an alpine start, it can be done comfortably in one day from Fryatt Creek.

Approach as for the Christie-Brussels col, but instead of going to the col scramble up talus slopes to the base of the N face.

Start at the left side of the face below a large roof about 70 m up. Zig-zag up a poorly protected wall immediately below the roof to a shallow left-facing corner (5.8). Climb this until about 10 m below the roof. Traverse around the right side of the roof, then move up and back left into a prominent groove/chimney (loose 5.9). Continue more easily up and left for two pitches to the large scree-covered ledge about halfway up the face. Scramble left across the ledge until below the last dihedral system before the junction of the N and NE faces. This is different from the other dihedrals — it looks like it can be free climbed! Climb the dihedral in two sustained pitches (5.10 & 5.9), then ascend easier ground for two more ropelengths to gain the summit.

Descend the NE Ridge.

Photo: Greg Horne

Mt. Christie: NE Face

Mount Christie   3103 m

Mount Christie is the northern end of a ridge of peaks including Brussels and Lowell. The NE face is the impressive rock face overlooking the Athabasca Valley and has, no doubt, been examined by many climbers as they drive past on the highway. *Maps 83 C/12 Athabasca Falls, 83 C/5 Fortress Lake*

North-East Face III 5.6   photo p. 247

FA. R. Berg and P. Ford, July 1977. An excellent outing up the prominent rib in the middle of the NE face.

Near the end of the climb into Fryatt Creek valley, a creek enters Fryatt Creek from the south. (GR 436229). Follow this drainage up to a secluded small lake below and right of the NE face. Bivi sites. 1.5 hours from the Fryatt Creek trail.

Go diagonally leftwards up slopes to gain the small glacier below the NE face. Follow the glacier to its southern end and the base of the rib. 2 hours from lake.

The route follows the prominent rib above all the way to the summit, approximately 20 rope lengths of 5th class climbing. 9-12 hours.

Descent is down the SW ridge initially and involves little more than walking. Arriving at the Brussels-Christie col, head down through a weaknesses in the cliff bands (loose rock) to easier ground. From here, head south below the cliff band into the first drainage leading down to Fryatt Creek.

Mount Lowell   3150 m

This is the rocky peak immediately south-west of Mt. Brussels. The crenellated summit ridge between the two summits is about 600 m long, providing a fairly lengthy extension to the climb to the south summit. *Map 83 C/12 Athabasca Falls*

South Ridge II   photo →

FA. A.J. Ostheimer, H. Fuhrer and J. Weber, July 1927. A good moderate route to the south (main) summit of the mountain. For hearty souls, the seemingly endless ridge to the N summit adds a little extra to the day.

From the hut cross Fryatt Creek and follow the drainage up toward the peak just south-west of Lowell, the eastern most peak of the Three Blind Mice ("Minnie"). Cross the NW ridge of Minnie to the col between Lowell and Minnie. Scramble up through shaley cliffs above to gain the W buttress which is followed to the S ridge. A scramble along the crenellated ridge leads to the S summit. If desire grabs you, continue over more crenellations to the N summit.

Descend the way you came up. 8-10 hours for a north summit trip.

Photo: Glen Boles

Mt. Lowell: S Ridge

Mount Fryatt 3361 m

This rocky summit is the highest of the group of peaks around the Fryatt valley. As a result, the Normal Route to the summit is one of the more popular outings in the area, even though it is little more than an involved scramble. The W ridge of the peak is a prominent line,

only recently climbed directly to the summit. The new direct finish takes in some of the best rock on the peak. As yet, the N face and the SE face remain as unclimbed challenges. *Map 83 C/12 Athabasca Falls*

South-West Face (Normal Route) II 5.4   photo →

FA. J.W.A.Hickson, H.Palmer and H. Fuhrer, July 1926. The most popular of the easier routes in the mountains around Fryatt creek. Expect lots of scrambling over talus. A full day round trip from the hut.

From the hut follow Fryatt Creek a few hundred metres, then head up the valley to the north-west to open meadows. Aim for the 2680 m col to the south of Fryatt and north of the 2900 m peak mentioned in the approach to Belanger. Follow the talus-covered ridge towards the southern subsidiary peak of Fryatt until just below its summit where a traverse to the

left (north) gains a broad shoulder overlooking the steep SE face. There is often snow or ice here — take your crampons and axe. From the shoulder work your way diagonally up and left across the SW face to gain the W ridge at a prominent shoulder below the summit block. Break through the first cliffs via a couloir (easy 5th class) and continue up the W ridge to the final summit step. Traverse across a ledge on the south-west side to the S ridge which is followed to the summit.

Descent is via the same route.

West Ridge Direct III 5.8   photo →

FA. P.Fehr and K.Wallator, summer 1985. The best route on the mountain; an excellent long climb in a very spectacular setting. The majority of this route was climbed by A.D. Abrahams and H. von Gaza in 1972. However, this party avoided the upper part of the route by traversing onto the SW face and finishing up that climb. The upper part of the route offers the hardest and best quality climbing on the whole route. Expect to take a day for a round trip from a bivi at the base of the ridge.

There are two possible approaches to the route. From the Fryatt Hut approach as for the SW face. From the 2680 m col below the SW face drop down the glacier on the north side of the col to the base of the W ridge.

The most expedient approach is from a road, however. From Highway 93A, follow the Geraldine Lakes road for 5.5 km to the Geraldine Lakes trailhead. A signed trail leads for 6 km to the second of the two Geraldine Lakes. Keep following the creek upstream past two more lakes into the drainage below the SW face of Fryatt and climb up to the base of the ridge. 3-4 hours from the trailhead. Bivi sites.

Mt. Fryatt: 1. SW Face   2. W Ridge   c. 2680 m col

Photo: Glen Boles

Follow the ridge in its entirety. It consists of a series of rock steps. The lower steps are 5.6 at most while the steps in the upper part of the route offer a lot of steep climbing (up to 5.8) on solid rock. You may find some 5.7 mixed ground, depending on the season and time of year. It is possible to avoid the upper part of the route by following the final section of the SW Face route, as did the first ascent party. However, this alternative is much less aesthetic and the quality of the rock is lower than on the ridge itself.

Descend by the SW Face route.

Mount Geraldine 2910 m

Before you rush off to find this peak on the map you should know that this is the Canadian Parks Service name for an unnamed summit (GR 353288) just to the west of the northernmost Geraldine Lake. The N Ridge up to this summit is a little-known and little-travelled gem. *Map 83 C/12 Athabasca Falls*

North Ridge II 5.5   photo →

FA. Unknown. The rock is quartzite and is typically excellent. An excellent choice for a fun day out on a moderate route. Not to be missed.

From Highway 93A follow the Geraldine Lakes road for 5.5 km to the Geraldine Lakes trailhead. Park here. Start along the signed trail to Geraldine Lakes, but before reaching first Geraldine Lake, turn right (still on the fire road) towards the site of the old Geraldine Fire Lookout. Just before the road flattens out (approximately 1 km before the lookout site) take a faint trail up through the bush to treeline and the base of the ridge.

Follow the ridge throughout (one pitch of 5.5) to the summit.

The **descent** gully starts immediately below the summit block and drops down the east side of the peak directly to the north end of the second Geraldine Lake. Follow the valley trail out to the parking lot. 12 hours round trip.

Mt. Geraldine: N Ridge

Photo: Tony Daffern

Mt. Belanger: N Face

Photo: Glen Boles

Mount Belanger 3120 m

The N face of Mt. Belanger presents an impressive, "steep looking" face of snow/ice when viewed from the summit of Fryatt. However, when you rub up against it the angle is much more reasonable. *Map 83 C/12 Athabasca Falls*

North Face II

photo p. 254

FA. W.R. Hainsworth, J.F. Lehmann, M.M. Strumia and N.D. Waffl, July 1930. 400 m of ice! It must have been quite the step-chopping experience for the first ascent party. Today, the route is a good introduction to this genre of climbing and is similar in standard to the Skyladder on Mt. Andromeda. Difficulty is determined by the amount of snow cover on the ice slope.

From the hut, walk a few hundred metres up the creek, then head north-west up a low-angled valley to the col between Belanger and the 2900 m peak to the north. Climb the ice slope above to the N summit. The ridge to the main summit gives some interesting climbing on mixed ground.

Descent is back down the same way.

Mount Olympus 2940 m

This long, low peak lies at the head of the Fryatt valley. The long summit ridge extends from the top of the NW face, where the two described routes top out, to a high point to the east above the col between Olympus and Xerxes. For both routes approach from the hut across the glacier at the head of Fryatt Creek to the Olympus-Parnassus col. *Map 83 C /5 Fortress Lake*

North-West Ridge II 5.6

photo p. 256

FA. A.D Abrahams and H. von Gaza, July 1972. Originally climbed in 1936 with a detour around the gendarme high on the ridge. The described route takes up the gauntlet and challenges the gendarme directly. The rock is somewhat loose.

From the col follow the ridge throughout. At the large gendarme make an ascending traverse to the right (west), then regain the ridge above (5.6). The gendarme can also be passed on the east side. Continue over rock and then snow to the summit.

To **descend**, traverse the mountain and scramble down the E ridge to the Olympus-Xerxes col. Romp down the glacier back to the hut.

North-West Couloir II

photo p. 256

FA. A cast of many ACC members, July 1960. The obvious wide snow/ice couloir in the NW face, a speedy ascent route best climbed early in the day.

From the col contour across the snow and ice to gain the base of the couloir. The summit is upward!

Descend as for the NW Ridge route.

Photo: Glen Boles

Mt. Olympus: 1. NW Ridge   2. NW Couloir   d. descent

TONQUIN

Mt. Geikie	3270 m	SE Face (normal)	IV 5.5	p. 260
		N Face	VI 5.10b A3	p. 263
Bastion Peak	2970 m	E Face	IV 5.7	p. 265
Redoubt Peak	3120 m	NW Ridge	III 5.6	p. 266
		E Face	IV 5.7	p. 266
Dungeon Peak	3130 m	E Face	IV 5.7	p. 267
Oubliette Mtn.	3090 m	E Ridge, S Summit	IV 5.7	p. 272
		E Face, N Summit	IV 5.9	p. 273
Paragon Peak	3030 m	E Ridge	I	p. 274
Bennington Peak	3265 m	E Ridge	III 5.4	p. 276
		N Face	IV 5.7	p. 276
Outpost Peak	2830 m	SW & NE Peaks	II	p. 277
Mt. Erebus	3119 m	N Ridge	III 5.6	p. 278
		SE Ridge	III 5.4	p. 278

The Tonquin Valley is the most frequently visited area in Jasper National Park. Deservedly so. The scenery at Amethyst Lakes is astounding with the southern Ramparts forming a spectacular backdrop. The Astoria Valley and Maccarib Pass access trails make a loop popular with weekend hikers and used frequently by two packtrain companies running fishing camps at Amethyst Lake.

Surprisingly, it is rare to see many climbers at Tonquin, perhaps because the weather is often quite inclement and the climbing is AT LEAST a two-day affair due to the walk-in taking up a major fraction of one day. This is an unfortunate state of affairs since the Tonquin Valley has some superb routes of all standards of difficulty that few climbers know about. For example, the N Ridge on Erebus and the N Face of Bennington are excellent routes for their grade, yet are rarely climbed.

From a rock quality point of view there is no comparable area in the Canadian Rockies. The majority of the Canadian Rockies is composed of sedimentary rock, typically limestone, that has the capability of fraying ones nerves due to its loose and highly fractured nature. However, the peaks in the Tonquin Valley are mostly composed of quartzite which gives excellent protection, solid belays and pitches that are rarely loose, unprotected horror-shows. For climbers who are looking for something a little less unnerving, this is the place for you.

Approach Routes
The two most common approaches are via the Astoria River valley and Maccarib Pass trails. Both are well-maintained and give very easy hiking. Mountain bikes are NOT allowed on either of these trails.

If you are interested in routes at the eastern end of the Ramparts, i.e. the Amethyst Lake rockwall and the peaks around the Fraser Glacier, the Astoria Valley is the recommended approach. The Maccarib Pass trail is ideal for approaching routes near Moat Lake or beyond, i.e. Bastion and Geikie. Approaching the area from the Yellowhead Highway via Meadow Creek is a bad idea — the trail is largely overgrown and if you miss it, the bush is brutal.

There are other methods of approaching the Tonquin: on horse-back or by helicopter. I've not heard of anyone riding in on horseback but the packers who run the fishing camps have been approached for carrying gear into the valley. The chopper is only an option for the peaks at the west end of the Ramparts. Geikie is outside the National Park boundary and a helicopter ride is an ideal solution to the long approach, particularly if you are interested in climbs based out of Geikie Meadows. For information about helicopter travel, contact Yellowhead Helicopters in Valemont.

Astoria River valley approach The shorter of the two approaches. To access the Astoria trail follow the Icefields Parkway for 7.5 km south of Jasper, turn right onto Highway 93A for another 5.5 km, then right again onto the Edith Cavell road which leads in 14.5 km to the trailhead for Cavell meadows below Mt. Edith Cavell. About 2 km before the road ends is the Youth Hostel and a parking lot at Cavell Lake. From here walk down a track across the creek draining Cavell Lake and past some stables onto the trail proper which is unmistakable — it's about 2 m wide! Follow it over one bridge across the Astoria river and past the Astoria River campground to a log bridge at 8 km. From the log bridge the way on depends on your destination.

For Amethyst Lakes, continue along the trail on the north side of the river, up switchbacks and across the side of Old Horn Mountain to a junction at 17 km. To get to north Amethyst Lake take the right-hand trail, and for south Amethyst Lake keep to the left.

For the Wates-Gibson Hut, cross the log bridge and follow the trail on the south side of the Astoria River to Chrome Lake. Go around the north shore of the lake to a junction with a trail from Amethyst Lakes. Pass this and continue across meadows in a westerly direction towards Penstock Creek. Follow the creek on its north side until you can access the south side of the creek. The trail climbs steeply through timber to a bench above Outpost Lake and the hut. 4.5-6 hours from the trailhead.

Maccarib Pass Approach From the junction of Icefields Parkway and 93A 7.5 km south of Jasper, follow 93A for 2.5 km to the junction with the Marmot Basin Ski Area access road. Turn left and drive the Marmot Basin Road for 6.6 km to a parking lot at Portal Creek. Another highway of a trail leads up and over Maccarib Pass to the west end of Amethyst Lakes in 20 km. If you are going to Moat Lake take a trail that leads around the north end of the lakes, past one of the fishing camps. There is no maintained trail to Moat Lake.

Facilities The nearest town is Jasper. See Jasper for details about supplies, accommodation etc. (page 281). A trip to the Tonquin will necessitate either taking your own shelter or staying at the ACC Wates-Gibson Hut. On both the walk-in trails there are several campsites. The hut makes an ideal base for climbs at the southern end of the valley around the Fraser Glacier. For other routes you are best working from one of the designated campgrounds, Suprise Point campground being the best bet. Bivis in the moraines below routes are not permitted. At Amethyst Lakes there are two fishing camps but don't expect too much from these quarters. In the event of pouring rain (yes, camping and eating trips in here are quite frequent) you are going to have to stick it out in your own shelter.

For permits, registration, weather and information regarding the backcountry go to the Jasper National Park Information Centre in Jasper.

A tip. Take plenty of mosquito repellent; the mosquitoes have to be seen to be appreciated. Rumor has it they have sabre-teeth!

Officialese The routes are all within Jasper National Park and backcountry use comes under the National Park regulations detailed on page 17. If you have any problems (accident, rescue etc.) head for the Warden Cabin near the south-east end of S Amethyst Lake (GR161383). A warden is in residence throughout the summer season.

Wates-Gibson Memorial Hut

Map 83 D/9 Amethyst Lakes
Location NW corner of Outpost Lake GR 152353
Reservations Alpine Club of Canada
Capacity 40
Facilities Fully equipped, summer custodian
Water Outpost Lake
Notes Locked when custodian is not present

Mount Geikie 3270 m

This big bulk of a mountain is the dark horse of the Canadian Rockies. Everyone who crosses Maccarib Pass is struck by the size of the mountain and yet it seems many climbers don't even know of its existence, most likely since it is tucked away at the north end of the Ramparts and lacks the magazine exposure of peaks like North Twin and Kitchener. Having said this, the N Face is undeniably one of the "grand-cours" routes of the Rockies, and certainly the most solid! The normal route is on the "back side" of the peak and involves a long approach. The mountains around Geikie Creek are bristling with unclimbed lines and are sufficiently tempting to encourage people to visit the back side of the Ramparts. *Map 83 D/9 Amethyst Lakes*

South-East Face (Normal Route) IV 5.5   photo →

FA. A.W. Drinnan and L. Grassi, August 1926. A remote climb. However, if you make the effort to get there, you'll find a very reasonable route to the top of the highest mountain in the Tonquin. It is also a long climb, being almost 1500 m from the Blue Inkwell to the summit. 8-12 hours up and a similar time for the descent. Most likely if you make the effort to do this route you will also be interested in other possibilities on this side of the Ramparts.

The approach is either over Maccarib Pass and around the west end of Barbican Peak to Geikie Meadows or over Drawbridge Pass between Drawbridge and Bastion, a long and tiring day via both routes. Alternatively, shell out the money and take a chopper into Geikie Meadows (expensive but expedient).

From Geikie Meadows hike up to a small lake (Blue Inkwell) below the SE face. Above the lake a large open couloir extends to the E ridge. Follow this gully to about the halfway point where it forks to the left (west). Take the left fork and gain ledges and rock steps on the SE face proper. Carry on scrambling up the face, following the easiest line to reach the summit ridge just east of the summit.

Descend by the same route.

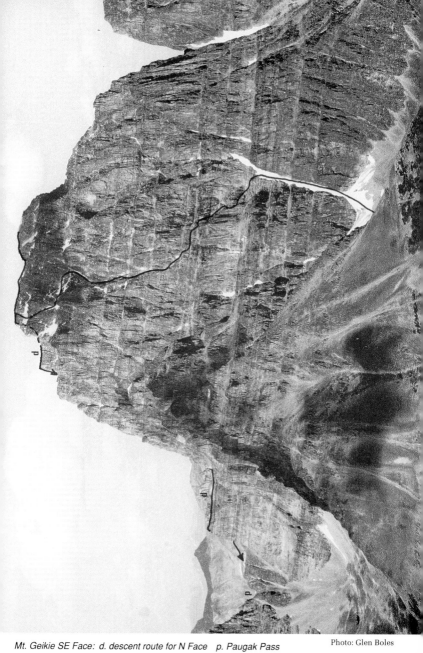

Mt. Geikie SE Face: d. descent route for N Face   p. Paugak Pass

Photo: Glen Boles

Mt. Geikie:N Face: 1. original start 2. alternate start

Photo: Glen Boles

North Face, Lowe/Hannibal VI 5.10b A3   photo p. 262

FA. G. Lowe and D. Hannibal, August 1979. Alternate start: S. Dougherty and J. Sevigny, August 1989. A 1500 m face that is split in two halves: a lower 750 m rock face below a 750 m mixed alpine face. The Lowe/Hannibal takes the obvious, aesthetic rib in the middle of the rock face; an uncompromising line which gives interesting and sustained climbing throughout. Being another of the "grand-cours" routes, the climb is involved and technical, particularly the headwall of the lower face. However, the protection and belays are solid, unlike on so many other grand-cours. The rock throughout the lower half is solid quartzite, offering steep climbing on good holds with some wild exposure. The upper face is at a much lower angle and involves quite a bit of scrambling followed by various bits and pieces of ice. Pack your rock rack and your ice gear — you'll use all of it. Rock shoes are highly recommended. Water is a problem on the headwall so grab it when you can. The first ascent party took almost six days. It has since been climbed in two days. A reasonable estimate is two bivis on the face and one on the descent.

The most expedient access is by chopper to the base of the face, and considering the likely size of your packs you'll be grateful for the ride! For those on foot, follow indistinct trails from from N Amethyst Lake to Moat Lake, then continue through marshy meadows to the moraines at the base of the face. A recommended bivi site is on the west side of the moraines at the base of the face.

Two starts are described since the 'schrund crossing of the original start is somewhat more difficult than it used to be in August 1979. Immediately below the prominent rib in the face is a large pillar of rock detached from the main face. Somehow cross the 'schrund and gain the ice behind this pillar, then move up onto another, smaller pillar at the base of the main rib. Follow cracks (5.9, some aid) just to the left of the rib for four or five pitches until at the upper right corner of a large depression in the middle of the lower face immediately below the headwall. The last water until quite a way up the headwall is found at the base of this depression.

This point can also be gained by an **alternative start** about 100 m left of the base of the ridge where the 'schrund is very easy to cross. Climb up a corner (5.8) to a large ledge. Traverse left 20 m to below a wet overhang. Pass this on the left and continue up a prominent corner system (5.8) for two pitches to easier ground. Wander up ledges and gullies for a pitch until two more pitches (5.6) lead up into the depression in the middle of the face. Fill up on water and wander up talus-covered ledges to the right to the base of a steep corner. This is the start of the headwall.

Climb the corner (5.8) for a pitch to a loose ledge (possible bivi). Traverse 10 m to the right and tackle a prominent vertical crack (5.10a) for another pitch (superb climbing) to a large ledge system (possible bivi). Climb the wall above over a small roof (5.10b or A2) to another small roof. Bypass this to the left and move up a few metres to a hanging stance in a corner (A1). Traverse right into the main corner and climb this for 10 m until a traverse back to the left is possible (5.9). Gain a slab up on the left and cross this diagonally to a small stance. Climb straight up for 10 m, then traverse left (5.9) around the corner to a hidden crack

263

that gains a ledge. Traverse along the ledge to the right until directly above the small stance (possible belay). Drop down 2 m and continue right until a tricky move gains the base of a slab. Either pendulum 10 m over to a crack and climb up to a prominent ledge, or climb up to another small ledge (5.10b) from which a pendulum gains the same prominent ledge (excellent bivi site).

Traverse easily around the corner to the right for one ropelength (water), then go straight up moderate rock to a crack in a short wall. Climb the crack (5.8) to a small ledge below a roof. Avoid the roof via a ramp leading up and right to the base of a short chimney (bivi site at the top of the chimney). Traverse right to a wide ledge at the base of a steep dihedral. Take the left-hand of two possible cracks (A3) until the left end of a large ledge can be reached (possible bivi). Either climb up to the left to regain the ridge and continue up cracks and walls for three pitches to the upper face, or traverse the ledge and the continuation break around the corner to the right to a huge ramp system that leads easily (5.5) up to the upper face in three ropelengths.

Scramble up talus and ledges as far as you can go. The upper face is split by a large rock band. A gully in the middle of the band offers a direct route but is usually a raging torrent. More pleasant are the ice slopes which lead around the left-hand end of the rock band and up to a snow ridge below a small band of rock immediately below the summit ridge. Breach the small band in two pitches of interesting climbing (at most 5.8) to the summit ridge.

Descent The quickest descent to the Tonquin Valley is to traverse the summit ridge to the top of the W ridge. One rappel gains a large flat area. Some downclimbing leads to two or three more rappels down a rib of rock to the south of a large ice gully. Rappel into the gully to its far side and then rappel back across the ice to the rock rib. One more rappel across the ice leads to talus ledges. Follow these down until stopped by a 50 m-high steep buttress. Rappel from the northern end of the buttress to more talus ledges.

Traverse the ledges along the south side of the ridge past some remnants of a bivi site, then cross to the north side of the ridge. Rappel down and traverse west to a large step in the ridge. A 50 m rappel brings you to a large flat area in the ridge. Don't scramble over to the top of the couloir between Geikie and Barbican (Paugak Pass) — the couloir is death on a stick (trust me!). Instead, hike down talus slopes on the north side of the ridge to the top of a large buttress. Two rappels gain easy ground and eventually the bottom of the face.

Bastion Peak 2970 m

A large rock peak with a double summit overlooking Moat Lake. The north side of the peak is quite spectacular, featuring steep rock faces, some glacier and several large subsidiary buttresses.

The S face is split by several gullies, one of which provides an expedient descent route to Drawbridge Pass, the col between Bastion and Drawbridge Peak. *Map 83 D/9 Amethyst Lakes*

East Face IV 5.7

FA. F. Beckey and J. Fuller, August 1965. A bit of a misnomer calling this the E face considering that the bulk of the climbing is on the N face. Nevertheless, it is one of the better climbs in the Tonquin, offering a little of all types of climbing. It starts off up some snow slopes that face east (the E face bit), then gains the rocks on the north side of the E ridge. A long day out.

Start on the moraines below Drawbridge Pass. Climb up ice/snow slopes to the east of a prominent buttress ("The Ramrod") to a saddle behind the buttress. Traverse across and up more ice to its high point at the base of a rock buttress. Climb the buttress to a higher snowfield. Traverse along a series of rock ledges on the north side of the ridge until you eventually end up in a notch immediately below and east of the summit. A 30 m traverse onto the south side is followed by interesting climbing up cracks which lead to easier ground just below the summit.

The **descent** is accomplished by regaining the notch below the summit block and descending a snow couloir in the SE face all the way down to talus-covered ledges. Traverse the ledges back to Drawbridge Pass.

Mt. Bastion: E Face a. "The Ramrod"

Photo: Don Beers

Redoubt Peak 3120 m

This is the northernmost of the group of three peaks which form the impressive rockwall above Amethyst Lakes. (The other two are Dungeon Peak and Oubliette.) The first ascent of the mountain by F.H. Slark and F. Rutishauser in the summer of 1927 ended tragically when both climbers went missing and were never found. *Map 83 D/9 Amethyst Lakes*

North-West Ridge III 5.6   photo p. 269

FA. D. LaChapelle, R. Jones and D.K. Morrison, July 1957. This is the moderate route to the top of Redoubt and a good day outing. The proximity of the E Face routes on Oubliette, Dungeon as well as Redoubt distracts many parties from this climb.

The first task is to get to Lookout Pass. From the south end of S Amethyst Lake follow a faint trail around the west side of the lake to the moraines below Lookout Pass, the pass between Redoubt and Drawbridge. Two obvious snow couloirs lead up to the pass. Scramble up rocks between the two couloirs until almost at the pass, then climb the right-hand of two chimneys (it looks harder than the left-hand one) to gain the pass. If conditions are good then the left-hand couloir is the best bet since it brings you out some way up the NW ridge. Stick to the sides to minimize rockfall hazard.

Traverse talus slopes to a prominent patch of snow on the W face. Scramble up easy ground to the base of a narrow snow couloir that leads to the notch below the NW ridge. From the notch, follow the ridge to easier ground about 100 m from the summit.

Descend the way you came up.

East Face IV 5.7   photo p. 269

FA. F. Becky and J. Fuller, August 1965. One of three prominent buttresses on the east side of the rockwall above Amethyst Lakes. Of the three routes, the E Face route on Redoubt is the least popular, in part because of some rockfall hazard.

Approach along the trail on the west side of Amethyst Lake until below Redoubt Peak. After crossing the moraines gain the low-angled bottom section of the E face via snow slopes and the 'schrund. Easy climbing (mostly scrambling) on the face just to the right (north) of the crest of the buttress leads to the prominent ledge system that runs across the face. Above the ledge, the line generally follows the crest of the buttress. Two steep pitches on excellent rock gain more reasonable ground. By traversing back and forth following ledges it is possible to find straightforward climbing through steep steps. Continue in this vain all the way up the rounded ridge crest to the summit.

Descent is down the NW Ridge.

Dungeon Peak 3130 m

The centre summit of the rockwall and highest of the three summits above Amethyst Lakes. The buttress taken by the E Face route gains the pocket gla-cier on the E face, then follows the crest of the rock buttress above. *Map 83 D/9 Amethyst Lakes*

East Face IV 5.7   photos p. 269, 270-271

FA. F. Beckey and D. Eberl, August 1967. Another of the prominent east-facing rib routes. Not quite as aesthetic as the E Face of Oubliette but still a very worth-while outing. Mostly a rock route but take ice gear for both the ascent and descent.

From the south end of S Amethyst Lake, take the trail along the west shore until below Dungeon Peak. Cross the moraine to the base of the spur on the E face. Follow a chimney system up and left to the hanging glacier between Dungeon and Oubliette. Skirt around the edge of the glacier onto the prominent ledge system that extends across the face. Easy climbing just to the south (left) of the rib crest on excellent rock leads in about 150 m to steeper climbing. Continue up corners and grooves (some 5.7) to a large ledge system that is followed back to the crest of the buttress. From here on, the crest offers easy climbing all the way to the summit.

The two **descent routes** are quite long, taking you on a magical mystery tour of the west side of neighboring peaks. From the summit you can descend the NW ridge to a prominent ledge that leads across the W face to the Redoubt-Dungeon col and across the W face of Redoubt to the NW Ridge, which is descended as for that route via Lookout Pass (see opposite page).

Alternately, descend the west slopes of the summit block to a ledge system that traverses to the Dungeon-Oubliette col. From the col continue along the ledge system across the west side of Oubliette to a short snow/ice slope that leads up to the Oubliette-Paragon col. Descend easy snow slopes to the valley or continue even further(!) along the ledge to the col between Paragon and Parapet known as Para Pass and then drop down to the valley.

Amethyst Lake Rockwall
Oubliette: 1. E Ridge   2. E Face, N Summit   d. descent

Photos: Glen Boles

Dungeon: 3. E Face
Redoubt: 4. E Face   5. NW Ridge

W Face of Dungeon Peak - the descents
1. NW Ridge   2. W Face   a. to Redoubt

Photos: Glen Boles

W Face of Oubliette Mtn. - the descents
3. S Ridge b. Oubliette-Paragon pass c. N Summit, Oubliette

Oubliette Mountain 3090 m

Oubliette Mtn. is the name for the southern pair of summits making up the Amethyst Lakes rockwall. The E buttress leading directly to the southern and higher summit is a very noticeable line that screams out to be climbed. It is no wonder that Fred Beckey returned to climb the companion ridges on Dungeon and Redoubt after ascending this beautiful line. The recent E Face route up to the N summit is similar in character to its older and more famous partner. *Map 83 D/9 Amethyst Lakes*

East Ridge, South Summit IV 5.7 photo p. 268, 271

FA. B. Greenwood, F. Beckey and D. Gordon, July 1962. The most popular route in the Tonquin Valley and one of the most aesthetic routes in the Rockies takes a very prominent ridge line almost all the way from Amethyst Lakes to the summit. The positions on the route are superb and the climbing never harder than 5.6/7. A must-do route. Allow a full day. Crampons and axe are useful, at least for the descent.

From the south end of S Amethyst Lake, make your way over the moraines directly to the base of the buttress. The first order of the day is to gain the base of the prominent ridge above the prominent ledge that traverses all the peaks at Amethyst Lake. There are two possible starts. The easier start ascends snow slopes south of the ridge to gain the prominent ledge system which is then followed easily to the base of the ridge line. The start followed by the first ascent party gains the rock below the centre of the E face, about 200 m north of the ridge line. This gives straightforward climbing until just below the ledge system. A harder pitch (5.7) up a steep wall and crack gains the ledge. Traverse south (left) to the ridge. The direct start up the rocks immediately below the main ridge line awaits a first ascent.

In general, the route follows the ridge crest, climbing predominantly on the left (south) side. Continue up into a gap behind a gendarme on the ridge. (A lot of this climbing can be done unroped.) A short steep pitch leads to easier ground that continues to the summit.

Descend the S ridge with two short rappels to the Paragon-Oubliette col, then descend a wide snow slope almost to the moraines. A short rappel reaches easy ground at the bottom. 5 hours from the summit.

East Face, North Summit IV 5.9   photo p. 268, 271

FA. *K. Christakos and T. Coe, August 1990.* A recent addition to the rockwall, that takes the buttress leading directly to the N summit of Oubliette. Like the Greenwood route to the S summit, the crux is on the face below the prominent ledge that runs across the face. Very similar in character to the Greenwood route though a little more difficult. Crampons and ice axe are very comforting on the descent. 25 pitches and a full day for an ascent.

From the south end of S Amethyst Lake make your way directly over the moraines to the snow cone at the base of the route. Climb the snow cone and scramble a couple of ropelengths to the base of a series of left-facing corners. Climb four pitches up these corners and past several small roofs (5.9) to gain the easier angled ground just below the long snow covered ledge that runs across the face.

Above the snow-covered ledge stay on the prow for about 200 m of easy 5th class. An awkward chimney brings you out on the right side of the ridge line where several pitches of cracks and chimneys interspaced with short sections of face climbing lead to the upper part of the route (5.7/8 and lots of 4th class). Continue upward just to the right of the ridge line all the way to the summit cornice. The first ascent team bivied on ledges just to the south of the summit.

To **descend** pick up wide ledges that traverse the west side of Oubliette and lead to the S ridge. After a couple of rappels to gain the Paragon-Oubliette Col, and then continue the descent as described for the North Summit route.

Paragon Peak 3030 m

A pointed peak immediately south of Oubliette. The E ridge descends from the summit and extends some way out into the valley, ending in a feature known as Surprise Point. *Map 83 D/9 Amethyst Lakes*

East Ridge I

FA. A. Carpe and H. Palmer, August 1919.
The perfect route if a short approach from a hut is your thing. A pleasant introduction to the climbing in the Tonquin Valley.

From the Wates-Gibson Hut head northwest across moraines to the south side of the E ridge. Work your way up the easiest possible line to gain the crest of the ridge. Walk along the ridge crest until at the base of the upper part of the E ridge. Scramble up rock and snow slopes to the summit, always picking the easy line.

To **descend** it is easiest to just retrace your steps. However, it is possible to descend the E Ridge about 100 m, then traverse the NE face along a prominent snow ledge and drop down to the Paragon-Oubliette col. An easy snow slope can then be descended to the moraines.

Paragon Peak: E Ridge
c. Oubliette-Paragon col   Photo: Glen Boles

Bennington Peak 3265 m

This is the prominent mountain immediately east of the Wates-Gibson Hut. The N face looks very spectacular and sits above an equally impressive approach glacier. The E ridge takes the left-hand skyline of the peak when seen from the hut. Both climbs are excellent for their standard, both reclusive gems. *Map 83 D/9 Amethyst Lakes*

East Ridge III 5.4   photo p. 275

FA. R.C. Hind and party, July 1945. A classic line that offers an excellent moderate day out. The positions on the ridge are airy and exciting in a few spots.

From the hut, walk over seemingly endless moraine to the Fraser Glacier, then contour round into a shallow basin at the base of the E ridge. Gain the crest of the ridge along an obvious diagonal ledge system. Follow the ridge in its entirety over small rock steps (5.4) to just below the summit step. Climb up to the summit by following rocks on the south side of the ridge.

To descend, drop down the south side about 70 m to a ledge system that leads onto the SW ridge. Descend the ridge to the McDonnell-Bennington col, then bumble down snow slopes and ledges on the south side of the col to the Fraser Glacier. Follow this down to the endless terminal moraines and eventually the hut.

North Face IV 5.7   photo p. 275

FA. F. Beckey and H. Mather, August 1963. For its time this was an impressive ascent up the steep triangular face seen from the hut. An alpine endeavor typical of Fred Beckey. The climbing on the upper face is on excellent rock with sound belays and protection. Unfortunately, the lower approach glacier is riddled with crevasses that have been known to turn back parties because of routefinding problems. The easiest approach would be in spring, or even winter when the crevasses are more likely to be filled with snow.

From the hut gain the glacier to the east between Parapet and Bennington. Follow this glacier up into the cirque below the N face, weaving through a large number of crevasses. The route takes the rock face to the right of an impressive quartz wall.

Cross the 'schrund and continue over mixed ground or rock (depending on the season) for 400 m to the base of the upper headwall. From here a number of lines exist, all on excellent quartzite and generally in the 5.6-5.7 range with a few moves of 5.8. Take one of these lines to the top.

Descend as for the E Ridge route.

Outpost Peak: 1. NE Peak   2. SW Peak 3. N Ridge, Erebus   4. SE Ridge, Erebus

Photo: Glen Boles

Outpost Peak 2830 m

This twin-peaked mountain south of Outpost Lake is an ideal peak for an easy day out. The original route to the NE peak ascends the glacier between the two peaks to a col and from there either one or both summits can be easily attained. *Map 83 D/9 Amethyst Lakes*

South-West & North-East Peaks II

FA. (SW peak) R.B.M Bibby, J.M. Hoag, W.W.Maclaren, H. Fuhrer, P.Prescott, G. Tollington and F. Rutis, August 1926. FA. (NE peak) B. Cautley, E.R. Gibson and W.E. Streng, August 1930. Though little more than a strenuous hike, travel on the glacier between the summits makes this much more of an mountaineering outing than, for example, the SW Ridge on Mt. Temple.

The glacier that occupies the bowl between the two summits has two tongues dropping down toward the Fraser Glacier. From the hut cross the moraines and scramble up easy rocks between the two tongues to gain the glacier. Cross this to the col between the two summits. To the left is the SW ridge of the NE peak and to the right is the E ridge of the SW peak. Most parties ascend both peaks in a day and get back to the hut in time for afternoon tea.

Descent For a different descent route (that is, different from the ascent route) it is recommended that you bag the NE peak, then the SW peak and descend via the slabby north-west slopes of the latter peak to the Fraser glacier. If this doesn't appeal, just go back down the way you came up.

Mount Erebus 3119 m

Immediately south of Outpost Peak is the pyramidal rocky summit of Mt. Erebus at the crest of the Fraser Glacier. The N ridge of this peak is a distinctive, sharp-edged ridge, another relatively unknown Rockies classic route. *Map 83 D/9 Amethyst Lakes*

North Ridge III 5.6   photo p. 277, →

FA. G. Crocker and K. Hahn, August 1965. The N Ridge is very much in the same class as the E Ridge of Oubliette — very aesthetic and highly recommended. Another little known gem. Allow a long day for the round trip.

From the hut, gain the crown of the Fraser Glacier at the base of the northwest slopes of Outpost. Contour around the head of the glacier that drops down into Simon Creek, then scramble up rocks to the col between the SE peak of Outpost and Erebus. Amble along the N ridge over the first knob to a small step that is assaulted directly with no problem. Continue easily to the base of a big step about three pitches in height. This wall is climbed (5.4) on the right (west) side of the ridge crest. Another horizontal bit leads to another step. Traverse left (east) to a chimney that is followed back to the ridge (5.4). A light-colored band of rock is climbed just to the left of the ridge (5.6) and leads to easier ground and the summit.

Unfortunately, the **descent** takes you in the opposite direction to the hut at first. However, it is without complications. Descend slabs for about 50 m, then continue down the SSW ridge until an easy descent is possible down slopes to the left (east) . Contour around the base of the SSW ridge onto the Fraser Glacier, and hence back to the hut. About 3 hours from summit to hut.

South-East Ridge III 5.4   photo p. 277, →

FA. C. Beattie, E.R. Gibson, M. McNeil and W.J. Watson, July 1934. A pleasant ridge route at a moderate standard. The crux is gaining the Erebus-Eremite col, but thereafter enjoyable climbing takes you to the summit.

From the hut drop down towards Chrome Lake and take a trail south up the Eremite Creek valley towards Arrowhead Lake. From the lake cross moraines and climb up onto the Eremite Glacier.

Cross the glacier to the rocks immediately below the Erebus-Eremite col. Climb a prominent rib (5.4) to the col. From here turn right and follow the ridge to the summit. The ridge is mostly scrambling apart from the summit block which has a steep step (5.4).

Descend the SSW ridge as for the N Ridge route. 7-10 hours round trip.

Mt. Erebus: 1. N Ridge 2. SE Ridge

JASPER				
Mt. Edith Cavell	3363 m	W Ridge (normal)	II	p. 283
		E Ridge	III 5.3	p. 284
		N Face E Summit	IV 5.8	p. 284
		N Face Colorado Spur	IV 5.7	p. 284
		N Face Main Summit	IV 5.7	p. 286
		McKeith Spur	IV 5.7	p. 286
Roche Miette	2316 m	N Face	IV 5.8 A3	p. 288
		W Face	IV 5.9 A2	p. 289
Mt. Charlton	3217 m	N Glacier	II	p. 290
Mt. Unwin	3268 m	N Glacier	II	p. 290
CR2	2600	Meisner Ridge	III 5.6	p. 292
Mt. Colin	2687 m	Colin Traverse	III 5.6	p. 294
		SW Face Direct	III 5.7	p. 296
	SW Face Central		III 5.7	p. 296

From Jasper townsite the most prominent mountain is Mt. Edith Cavell with its large snow-covered N face and distinctive E ridge. In this area the only other alpine climbing involving snow and ice is found on Mts. Charlton and Unwin by the shores of Maligne Lake. To the east of Jasper are a number of lower altitude rock peaks offering high quality rock climbing similar to that found on the big limestone faces above Canmore but with better rock generally. They offer longer rock climbs when high mountains are out of condition. They are especially useful for climbers fed up with sitting out bad weather at the Columbia Icefield campground. In little over an hour's drive you could be rock climbing in the sunshine.

Roche Miette lies at the eastern boundary of the National Park where the weather is often better than in the main ranges. It may be warm and sunny here while Jasper townsite is being deluged by rain. The peaks of the Colin Range can be seen to the east from Jasper. Colin is the easiest to recognize with its slabby SW face.

For the rock routes a standard Rockies rock climbing rack is all the gear you require. However, bear in mind that while the southern aspects of the peaks may be free of snow, the north sides may still be snow bound, especially in the spring. Pack ice axe/crampons appropriate for the conditions.

Access Jasper is located on the Yellowhead Highway (Highway 16) 362 km to the west of Edmonton near the northerly terminus of the Icefields Parkway (Highway 93) 232 km north of Lake Louise. It is also served by Via Rail if you fancy coming in by train.

All routes in this area are accessed from the Yellowhead Highway, the Maligne Lake Road (which branches off Highway 16 5 km east of Jasper) and the Edith Cavell Road off Highway 93A (the Athabasca Parkway).

Facilities Jasper is a tourist town very similar to Banff though not quite as busy. Thus, it is possible to find almost everything you require: groceries, restaurants, accommodation, campsites, bike rentals, information centres, 24 hour gas stations, etc. Totem Men's Wear & Ski Shop sells a limited amount of climbing gear. There are showers in the coin laundromats in town. And if you have a vehicle you could treat yourself to Miette Hot Springs at the end of the Miette Hot Springs Road which leaves the Yellowhead Highway at Pocahontas, 41 km east of Jasper.

For accommodation choose from countless hotels, motels, guest houses, campsites and youth hostels. The nearest hostel to town is Whistlers Hostel located close to the Jasper "Sky Tram". Drive south along the Icefields Parkway for 2 km to the first road to the right, Whistlers Road, and follow it for 3 km to the hostel. The other hostel in the area, near Cavell Lake, is located at the trailhead for the Astoria River valley trail into the Tonquin. It is close to routes on Mt. Edith Cavell. There are two large campgrounds, Whistler and Wapiti, located 2 and 4 km south of Jasper along the Icefields Parkway. These campgrounds are incredibly busy and noisy during summer months so you may be more interested in other smaller campgrounds scattered throughout the area.

Inquire at the Jasper National Park Visitor Centre, opposite the railway station, about campgrounds, permits, weather and conditions. Information regarding hotels, motels etc. can be obtained from Alberta Tourism.

Officialese All the routes in this section are within Jasper National Parks and back-country use comes under the National Park regulations on page 17.

Rock Climbing Around the Jasper area is a selection of rock climbing for those days where you don't feel like exerting yourself for 12 hours or more. No guide-book exists but, certainly in the Rock Gardens, the routes are relatively short and the lines reasonably obvious. Local climbers could be of help; ask at some of the local outdoor suppliers or bike shops. Otherwise, this information is it.

Close to Jasper are the "Rock Gardens" near the 5th bridge in Maligne Canyon. From Jasper go east along the Yellowhead Highway for 5 km, then turn right across the Athabasca River onto the Maligne Lake Road. Take the second road on the left to a parking lot by the 5th bridge. Cross the Maligne River and climb a little way up the hillside on a good trail to the cliffs. You'll find a good selection of limestone routes of all grades.

Further afield there is Ashlar Ridge near the east boundary of the National Park where there is a chance the weather might by fine. Until recently this big limestone face was essentially only known by the local climbers in Jasper. To get there, turn off the Yellowhead Highway 41 km east of Jasper onto the Miette Hot Springs Road which is followed for approximately 8 km. Park at the riverside, directly below the cliff viewpoint. Cross the Miette River via the cable crossing (an adventure in itself!) and hike up to the cliff. The face is off vertical, more like a slab. Only a few routes a few pitches high have been developed up to 5.10. The sky is the limit on possibilities.

If you are looking for something a bit more "granite-like", then some quartzite cliffs near Cavell Lake at the base of the N face of Edith Cavell may fit the hill. To the right of the Angel Glacier is a thick band of quartzite; the developed lines are the clean ones. Undoubtedly there is scope for a lot more routes.

Mount Edith Cavell 3363 m

The typically snow-covered north face of Mt. Edith Cavell, the highest mountain in the immediate vicinity of Jasper, dominates the southern skyline from the townsite. The routes are amongst the most accessible in the Rockies and can be completed comfortably in one day given an early start from the parking lot. The E Ridge is a classic Rockies route, offering mixed climbing at a moderate standard, and sees a large number of ascents each season. Hence, it is not uncommon to meet another party on the route, an unusual occurrence in the Rockies.

The N face of Cavell is one of those faces that lends itself to ascents almost anywhere. Testimony to this fact is the large number of different lines that have been put up over the years. Only four routes are described in this book but the number of possible variations is infinite. The character of the climbing on all routes is very similar with the possible exception of the N Face of the E summit, which offers more sustained climbing than the other routes. Rockfall is particularly prevalent on the face since it is topped by a thick band of shale. Interestingly, though the first ascent was in 1961, the first winter ascent happened as recently as March 1988. Probably the 19 km ski approach from a highway had something to do with the lack of interest!

Map 83 D/9 Amethyst Lakes

Access for all routes on the mountain start from the parking lot at the Cavell roadhead near Cavell Lake. Follow the Icefields Parkway south from Jasper for 7 km, turn right onto Highway 93A for another 5 km, then turn right again onto the Edith Cavell road. Follow the road for 14 km to the roadhead parking lot, about 2 km beyond Cavell Lake.

Descent for all routes is down either the E Ridge or the easier W Ridge. The former is certainly the quickest. However, if you don't feel up to it, here is the W Ridge descent description which is the Normal Route in reverse. Traverse the summit ridge over the main summit to the top of a steep shale step. Descend the SW ridge a short way until it is possible to traverse below the shale step back to the W ridge. Continue down the W ridge by easy scrambling to the col between Cavell and Mt. Sorrow, the next mountain (a small bump in the ridge would be more accurate) to the west. DON'T try and angle down to the south-west once below the shale step — there are steep cliff bands low down.

Once at the col drop down talus slopes to the south into a large cirque from where a well used trail leads down the Verdant Creek valley to the main Astoria River trail. 4 hours to the roadhead from the summit.

West Ridge (Normal Route) II

FA. A.J.Gilmour and E.W.D.Holway, August 1915. The easiest route up the mountain and a commonly used descent route. The initial part of the climb is a hike to the base of the ridge followed by a scramble up to the ridge crest. Crampons are typically necessary for the upper ridge and the ridge between the two summits. A long day trip, taking 7-9 hours car to summit.

Start from the parking lot near the Cavell Youth Hostel, as for the Astoria River valley approach to the Tonquin valley (page 258). Hike along the Astoria trail until just before Verdant Creek where a well used, though unmarked trail leads off to the left (south). Take this trail towards Verdant Pass and up into the cirque below the west side of Cavell. Walk to the back of the cirque and climb up talus slopes and small rock bands to gain the col at 2930 m on the W ridge of Cavell.

The ridge to the W summit of Cavell is quite narrow but straightforward. Just below the summit a short, steep shale step presents a barrier. Either climb the step directly or traverse right to the SW ridge and climb this to gain the top. The step offers a few steeper scrambling moves, but nothing alarming. From the W summit the E summit is reached by following the narrow and often corniced ridge.

Photo: Greg Horne

East Ridge III 5.3 photo →

FA. J.W.A. Hickson and C. Kain, August 1924. One of the classic routes of the Rockies and certainly the most recommended route on the mountain. Another of the must-do routes. It is necessary to take crampons and ice axe even though it may look clear of ice and snow from below. There is at least one patch you have to climb across. It can be comfortably done in a day.

From the parking lot follow the signed trail for Cavell Meadows. When the trail makes a switchback into trees take to the moraines and climb talus and snow slopes to the col at the base of the ridge (possible bivi sites). Ascend the rocks to the immediate right of the snow couloir by easy scrambling to a short snow/ice slope that leads to a shoulder. Above the shoulder the ridge is followed directly to the E summit (5.3).

North Face, East Summit IV 5.8 photo p. 287

FA. Y.Chouinard, J. Faint and C.Jones, July 1967. The longest and most involved route on the face. It offers the most interesting climbing and avoids the trepidations of the Angel Glacier — something in its favour.

From the roadhead hike along the interpretive trail towards the Angel Glacier and past the small moraine lake below

the N face. Start immediately below the E summit. Climb up the lower buttress just to the right of a prominent snow patch (5.8) to gain the ledge system that runs across the face about 400 m from the base. If it gets any harder than 5.8 you are not following the easiest possible way! Continue up mixed terrain to a buttress that aims straight for the E summit. Follow the crest of the buttress to the top.

North Face, Colorado Spur IV 5.7 photo p. 287

FA. M. Hesse, J. Kraukauer and J. Laddock, July 1978. Takes the rib between the upper part of the E Summit route and the original N Face route.

Approach as for the N Face, Main Summit route but continue to the east end of the upper Angel Glacier. Start up mixed terrain towards the rib which is some-

what better defined towards the summit. Above the ledge system that runs across the face at about half-height, deke around a steep buttress on the left on easier ground to gain the rib above (keep an eye out for rockfall). Follow the rib to the summit slopes and eventually the summit ridge.

Mt. Edith Cavell: 1. E Ridge   2. N Face, E Summit (upper part)   3. Colorado Spur (upper part)

Mount Edith Cavell

North Face, Main Summit IV 5.7 photo →

FA. F. Beckey, Y. Chouinard and D. Doody, July 1961. The original route on the face and still the most popular. Originally, the approach route was to the left of the Angel Glacier. However, this presents climbers with tremendous icefall hazard. Thankfully, some sane guys found a much safer route to the upper glacier that most parties now use. The route up the face above follows the prominent rock buttress directly to the summit snow slopes and offers good climbing on excellent quartzite.

From the parking lot, cross the creek by a "bridge" and gain the lateral moraine that leads to the rocks right of the Angel Glacier. There is a well-worn path these days. Scramble up the rocks (4th and easy 5th class), staying well to the right of the glacier to minimize the danger of icefall until the flat upper part of the glacier is reached. Cross the glacier and gain the rib that leads directly to the main summit. At first the climbing is straightforward and all to the left of the crest. Work your way up about 50 m left of the crest through small bands of rock to the large snow ledge that runs right across the face. Continue up for another 200 m to the base of a steep buttress. Traverse back right to the crest of the rib and climb three short pitches (5.7) on excellent rock up steep corners and cracks. Continue up several pitches of mixed climbing, trending left to another rib. Break through steeper steps onto the final snow/ice slopes. A rotten band of rock immediately below the summit is bypassed most easily to the left. 10-13 hours.

McKeith Spur IV 5.7 photo →

FA. L.Bruce and H.Kent, July 1978. Climbs the spur to the west of the original route to the W ridge.

Approach as for the N Face, Main Summit route. Above Angel Glacier scramble up rocks below the prominent rib right of the original N Face route.

Avoid the steepest climbing by climbing the lower-angled rocks to the right (watch for rockfall) to gain the crest of the rib which is followed over mixed ground to the W ridge. The summit is then easily gained by following the last bit of the Normal Route.

Mt. Edith Cavell North Face: 1. E Ridge 2. N Face, E Summit 3. Colorado Spur 4. N Face, Main Summit 5. McKeith Spur 6. W Ridge

Photo: Tony Daffern

Roche Miette 2316 m

A formidable rock tower overlooking the Yellowhead Highway just west of Pocahontas. It is sufficiently impressive to make you want to stop the car to look at it. The routes here are well worth more than just a look! While the N Face route is the big centrepiece route, the W face offers a route that is just as spectacular, though a little easier. A word of warning: watch out for packrats, especially if you bivi below the routes. The favorite diet of the local habitues is rope. At least one party has had their ropes chewed up! *Map 83 F/4 Miette*

Access for all routes Park at the side of the Yellowhead Highway (Highway 16) 3.4 km west of Pocahontas. Walk up the obvious drainage below the N face to where it starts to become a canyon. Take to the talus slopes, avoiding rotten cliff bands by going up to the right to below the west side of the mountain. Continue up talus to the large ledge system at the base of the W face. Traverse left around the NW nose of the mountain to reach the start of the N Face route.

To **descend,** walk south over the summit and descend the east slopes. Just beyond the obvious col between Miette and the next ridge east, look for a trail leading down the north side of the ridge back to the highway. This descent is loose but straightforward.

North Face IV 5.8 A3   photo →

FA. P. Charkiw and P. Paul, May 1980. This climb takes on the impressive N face. An alpine rock route that starts off at a moderate standard (5.6-5.8) and ends up with some A3 thrown in near the end for a complete Rockies rock experience. The rock is excellent throughout, belays are good and the pitches are generally full 50 m affairs. Originally climbed with a bivi but this no doubt was a result of a 4 pm alpine start! It CAN be climbed in a day, though you will have to be slick to complete a round trip road to road in this time.

The route follows the obvious line of weakness leading diagonally up and left from the bottom right corner of the face. A 5.8 hand traverse just off the deck leads up past a bolt to ledges. Continue (5.7) to more large ledges. Climb the left edge of a large slab, then move up and left for two wandering 5.6 pitches to some huge ledges that can easily be seen from the highway.

Above, follow a chimney with some loose blocks inside for a short way, then go right along a hand traverse to the left edge of a flake. Shinny up this, then move back left past the chimney to a belay at the left end of a roof. Continue up a steep layback (5.8) in a corner to the top of a pedestal. Two bolts give access to a thin crack leading up through a roof to easier climbing (A3 5.6) — the short pitch (25 m). Traverse left to a chimney that leads (5.7) to easy ground and the summit.

West Face IV 5.9 A2

R. Costea and K. Wallator, April 1989. A modern route up a crack system in the middle of the W face. A true 5.9 A2! Very spectacular. Originally climbed on a cool, clear day in April which resulted in the first ascent party requiring quite a lot of aid. The route has excellent potential for a free ascent.

Start in the middle of the W face. The first pitch follows the easiest break in the face. Ascend past ledges to an overhang that is surmounted (5.9) to gain a left-leaning crack. Climb the crack for 45 m (5.8 A1) to a small ledge. The next two pitches ascend a dihedral (5.9 A0) to a prominent ledge half-way up the face. Bivi site on the first ascent. Climb a crack leading up from the middle of the ledge (5.7 A2) to a small overhang, above which is a ledge. Continue over "blocky" rock for another 10 m to a large ledge. Traverse along the ledge to a very prominent dihedral which is followed for three ropelengths on excellent rock (5.7-5.9) to the top.

Mount Charlton and Mount Unwin

The view from the north end of Maligne Lake is one of the many "calendar" scenes that pervade the Rockies. On the right of lake are the twin snow-covered summits of Mt. Charlton and Mt. Unwin.

These two summits are usually climbed in a single day, giving one of the better outings in the Jasper area. *Maps 83 C/ 12 Athabasca Falls, 83 C/11 Southesk Lake*

North Glacier II   photo →

FA. W.R. Hainsworth and M.M. Strumia, July 1928. The described outing is the one taken by Hainsworth and Strumia on the first ascent of Mt. Charlton. As is usual today, they also climbed Mt. Unwin via the E ridge. The route is technically straightforward but has "magnificent ambiance". About 12 hours return trip from the lake.

From Jasper drive east along the Yellowhead Highway for 5 km, then turn right across the Athabasca River onto the Maligne Lake Road. Follow the road for 44.5 km to the roadhead at the north end of Maligne Lake. From the dock take a charter boat to Samson Narrows at the south end of the lake. Prior reservation of the boat is not required, though you are advised to check beforehand. Remember that you'll also need to book a return trip! Some parties have been known to forget

and have had to make the long trek around the lake to get back to the roadhead. Get ashore on the delta formed by the creek draining from the Charlton-Unwin N glacier. Bivi sites.

Bushwhack through the trees, then climb up onto the lateral moraine on the left (east) side of the creek. Cross the tongue of the glacier and continue up and right into the W basin of the glacier. Continue up the glacier between Mt. Unwin and the prominent rock pinnacle to the base of the final steep snow slope leading up to the Charlton-Unwin col. From the col follow the easy snow slope to the east to gain the summit of Mt. Charlton. Return to the col, then climb up the E ridge of Unwin. 1.5-2 hours col to col.

Descend to Maligne Lake by the same route. 7-10 hours round trip from lake.

1. Mt. Charlton: W Ridge   2. Mt. Unwin: E Ridge

Photo: Greg Horne

CR2 2600 m

The six summits of the rocky ridge extending north from Roche Bonhomme to Mt. Colin don't have names and are identified by the initials CR (Colin Range). Of all the routes on these peaks the Meisner Ridge on CR2 is by far the best. This peak is roughly 1.5 km north of Roche Bonhomme (GR 353682). The prominent Meisner ridge can be easily identified from the Yellowhead Highway. *Map 83 C/13 Medicine Lake*

Meisner Ridge   III 5.6   photo →

FA. Unknown. One of the most popular outings in the Jasper area on a very prominent ridge line. Good rock, good moderate climbing which is always interesting, excellent position and the aesthetics of the line are undoubtedly the reasons. A long day for a round trip.

Follow the Yellowhead Highway eastwards out of Jasper for 5 km. Turn right onto the Maligne Lake Road and drive along it for another 5 km to a turnoff leading to the parking lot for the 6th bridge. From the parking lot by the bridge, cross the Maligne River and walk along the "Overlander Trail" on the east side of the Athabasca River for about 4 km to the outwash of the first main canyon. This canyon can be recognized by prominent hoodoos. Hike up the canyon, following the creek until past a tributary that comes down the drainage just west of the ridge. This hike used to be quite straightforward until heavy rain in July 1989 dramatically changed the character of the canyon. You may have to make a few short (at most 10 m) rappels in a few spots to make progress. Once in the drainage to the west of the ridge, take the first avalanche slope up through the trees to the north end of the ridge.

Follow the ridge throughout. The difficulty is reasonable (5.6) and the rock on the narrow ridge is generally good. To stay on the ridge it is necessary to climb a very prominent tower. You'll have to rappel off this on its left side to regain the ridge (20 m rappel). Continue in much the same way as before to the summit.

Descend the NE ridge of the peak on moderate but very broken rock to the col between CR2 and CR3. Descend the drainage to the north-west which leads down into the approach canyon.

CR2: Meisner Ridge

Mount Colin 2687 m

The highest peak of the range. For the most part, the rock is quite clean and the climbing interesting. The SW face consists of numerous steep slabs with at least four routes and unbounded scope for more. Only the two most popular (and the best as yet) are described.

Unfortunately, the approach to the hut is quite a deterrent for some parties, but don't give up — the climbing here is very enjoyable. The boating approach option across the Athabasca River can provide hilarious fun. *Maps 83 F/4 Miette, 83 D/16 Jasper, 83 C/13 Medicine Lake*

Access to Mt. Colin Centennial Hut
The usual approach is to cross the Maligne River at the 6th bridge (as for the approach to CR2 on page 292) and follow the "Overlander Trail" to Garonne Creek (about 7 km). Alternately, for those with a seafaring bent, you can boat across the river from near the south end of Jasper airfield. Whichever way you choose, hike up Garonne Creek for about 1 km, avoid-ing thick bush to the north. Where the trees thin out and open slopes are obvious to the north, take to the slopes. Follow the crest of these slopes, heading upstream until a sharp drop-off forces you to turn north. Find cairns and bits of progressively better trail as you continue, keeping high above the creek. After contouring east across several drainages the trail descends back down into Garonne Creek. A good trail leads from the creek up to the hut which is placed on a bench directly below the summit of Colin. 3.5-5 hours.

Mount Colin Centennial Hut

Map 83 C/13 Medicine Lake
Location Near treeline below SW face of Mt. Colin GR 333724
Reservations Alpine Club of Canada
Capacity 4 plus 3 on floor
Facilities Coleman stove & lamp, large cook pots, foamies
Water Creek in front of hut

Colin Traverse III 5.6   photo →

FA. N.E. Odell, J. Ross and F.S. Smythe, August 1947. FWA. J.Moss, P.Ford, P.Gibb and B.Howell, 1970. The original classic of the range. It has the notoriety of having made the hardware-scorning Frank Smythe resort to placing his first and, as legend has it, only piton. It was originally climbed in a SE-NW direction but is now commonly traversed in the opposite direction. A popular outing.

From the hut gain the Colin-Hawk col by traversing over talus below the SW face. Scramble up the NW ridge until stopped by an overhanging step a few hundred metres short of the summit. Follow a ledge system on the right (west) side of the ridge into a corner. Continue traversing around an outside edge and across a slab on the SW face to a second corner. Climb up the corner in two pitches (5.6) to regain the ridge line. Continue to the summit. 3-5 hours.

After a snack on the summit, **descend** the SE ridge to the Colin-CR 6 col. This is mostly scrambling though there is one half-rope rappel off a large block. Continue easily down talus to the hut.

Mt. Colin: *1. Traverse   2. SW Face Direct   3. SW Face Central   a. Colin-Hawk col   b. Colin-CR6 col*

Photo: Greg Horne

South-West Face Direct III 5.7   photo p. 295

FA. W. Pfisterer and A.N. Other, some time in the past. A bit of a misnomer calling this the direct since the central route is much more direct. Nevertheless, an excellent choice for a 5.6-5.7 rock climb. This route generally follows the left edge of a buttress which leads up to the summit.

From the hut wander up open slopes to the face directly below the summit of Colin. Start at the bottom left corner of the buttress and work your way up a series of prominent corners and cracks to the top of the buttress (5.4-5.5), a point about 100 m directly below the summit. The next 10 m is the crux. Climb up the slabs above, first to the right and then to the left via some thin cracks (5.7). The route finishes up loose blocks to the summit. 4-8 hours.

Descend via the SE Ridge (see Traverse page 294).

South-West Face Central III 5.7   photo p. 295

FA. R. Bandfield and B. Hagen, July 1975. A bit harder than its companion, though very similar in character.

At the base of the central buttress is a big hole. Start at the fourth dihedral right of this hole. Climb straight up to gain the dihedral that leads directly from the hole itself. Continue up two harder pitches (5.7) to a large groove that curves up and left. This is the "Sickle Blade" that belongs to the "Handle", a chimney that starts about 70 m above the hole. Climb the "Blade" to the "Handle" (taking care not to cut yourself of course). Two easier pitches lead straight to an arete which is followed to a fractured zone of small dihedrals. Climb over teetering blocks and up to a junction with the Direct Route below its crux, which is also the crux of this route. Follow the Direct Route to the summit. 6-10 hours.

Descend via the SE ridge (see Traverse page 294).

MOUNT ROBSON PROVINCIAL PARK

Mt. Robson	3954 m	S Face (normal)	IV	p. 302
		Wishbone Arete	IV 5.6	p. 304
		Emperor Ridge	V 5.6	p. 305
		Stump/Logan	VI 5.9 A2	p. 306
		Cheesmond/Dick	VI 5.9 A2	p. 308
		N Face	IV	p. 308
		Fuhrer Ridge	IV 5.4	p. 310
		Kain Face	IV	p. 310
Resplendent Mtn.	3426 m	NW Slopes (normal)	II	p. 312
		Ice Arete	III	p. 314
		E Ridge	IV 5.7	p. 314
Whitehorn Mtn.	3395 m	N Ridge	III 5.3	p. 315

The big attraction in this area is undoubtedly Mt. Robson, the highest peak in the Canadian Rockies and an impressive mountain from every direction. Its first ascent was a much sought after prize and the object of several major attempts, particularly by G.B. Kinney and D. Phillips who were turned back close to the summit in 1909. The first ascent by the guide A.C. Kain and his clients W.W. Foster and A.H. McCarthy in 1913 was one of the most celebrated ascents in the history of climbing in the Canadian Rockies, a fine testimony to Kain's ability both as a climber and a guide.

Today, the mountain is a major attraction for climbers from all over the world, partly because of its height but also because all the routes offer excellent challenges of differing degrees of difficulty. There are no non-technical routes on this peak!

The other two mountains in the area with described routes, Resplendent Mtn. and Whitehorn Mtn, were originally climbed around the same time as Robson by Kain, who climbed them both in 1911. They are both spectacular mountains (though Mt. Robson steals the show), being technical outings which require a lot of glacier travel. Perhaps the easiest route of all is the Normal Route on Resplendent. Hence, it sees a lot of traffic, particularly during the years that the ACC has mountaineering camps at Berg Lake.

Access Mt. Robson lies within Mount Robson Provincial Park in British Columbia which extends eastwards to the Jasper National Park boundary. The trailhead for all routes in the area is reached by turning north off the Yellowhead Highway (Highway 16) at the Robson Services gas station, located 82 km west of Jasper and 44 km east of Valemont. The routes are all accessed from the Berg Lake trail which leads to (surprisingly) Berg Lake, via the Valley of a Thousand Falls. Mountain bikes are allowed 10.5 km along this trail as far as the Whitehorn campground. Beyond this point you are on foot. For the wealthy there is also the possibility of helicopter transport (see Officialese).

Facilities Next to Robson Services is the Mt. Robson Visitor Centre and the Provincial Park Ranger Office. Any information regarding the park (camping, trails, conditions) can be obtained here. The Visitor Centre is open only during the summer months. However, the Ranger Office is open year round.

For groceries and other needs the nearest town is Valemont, 44 km to the west. Almost all your needs can be obtained here — even hot showers at the laundromat! If you are coming from the east, then you can purchase all necessities in Jasper as well as some limited climbing gear (see page 281). Gas is no problem at Robson — the gas station is next to the Visitor Centre. The gas station is also a coffee shop-cum-grocery store with limited supplies. 24 hour gas is available in Valemont or Jasper.

For accommodation, you will either be camping or using the Ralph Forster Hut (see pages 300, 301). There are seven campsites to choose from along the Berg Lake trail.

Officialese Unlike the National Parks, backcountry permits are not required. However, if you are going to use any of the campsites along the Berg Lake trail you are required to get an overnight permit from the Visitor Centre.

To register out for climbs, a voluntary registration scheme is in place. At the Berg Lake trailhead is a box with a registration book inside. Just fill out the necessary details of your trip so that rangers can check to see if you are overdue. Don't forget to register back in!

Mountain bikes are allowed along the Berg Lake trail for the first 10.5 km, as far as Whitehorn campground. Beyond this point bikes are NOT allowed.

At present there are no restrictions on landing locations for helicopters in Mount Robson Provincial Park as there is in Mount Assiniboine Provincial Park. If you wish to use a helicopter for access to such far-flung routes as the E Ridge of Resplendent, then contact Yellowhead Helicopters in Valemont.

In emergency either raise help at the Visitor Centre or at one of the two ranger cabins on the Berg Lake trail: at the north end of Berg Lake and at Whitehorn campground. These huts are staffed during the summer months.

Mount Robson 3954 m

The south and west aspects of the mountain are very spectacular, rising over 3000 m from the valley floor. Facing the highway is the south side of the peak with its S Face route and Wishbone Arete. The former route winds its way up the mountain, first to the east and then back west to a subsidiary summit known as Little Robson and then onto the summit underneath the seracs of the summit glacier. The Shuswap Indians used to call the mountain Yuh-hai-has-kun — "the mountain of the spiral road", a name which is also very appropriate for the S Face route! A hut high up the SSW ridge, the Ralph Forster Hut, provides a good starting point for a summit attempt. The west skyline of the mountain is the Emperor Ridge, famous for the final section of ridge with its double cornices and gargoyle formations.

The north aspect of the peak is heavily glaciated with glaciers descending all the way into Berg Lake. Rising above Berg Lake is one of the most daunting faces in the Rockies, the Emperor Face. To the east of this face is the N face of Robson and the Fuhrer Ridge. Continuing eastward you come to the Resplendent-Robson col and the ice face taken by the Kain route.

The Emperor Face is the big daddy of faces in the Rockies, rising 2500 m from Berg Lake, almost 1500 m of which offers difficult climbing. It presents such an awe-inspiring sight from Berg Lake that several well-intentioned souls intending to climb the face have immediately turned around and walked back out again! The two routes on the face are both typical of the upper echelon of alpine routes in the Rockies — difficult, runout, mixed climbing that requires exceptional ability to succeed. Four serious attempts

were required before Mugs Stump and Jim Logan succeeded. Both routes are unrepeated as of the end of 1990. Besides being 5.9 A2 they are on rock that is certainly not above suspicion. Falling rock is a major problem on both routes and cold nights and days are a big boon to reducing this hazard. Retreating in poor weather can be a nightmare.

The remaining three routes on the north side of the mountain each represent an advance in alpine ice climbing in North America. In 1913, the Kain route was by far the hardest ice climbing outing on the continent. Kain chopped steps all the way to the summit until he is reported to have said to his clients, "Gentlemen, that's as far as I can take you". A major tour-de-force for its day. In 1938, Fuhrer and companions chopped steps up the steeper N ridge of Robson. Such a sustained ice face had never been climbed before in North America. And lastly, the ascent of the N face by P. Callis and D. Davis in 1963 represented another level of steepness and difficulty. Today, both this route and the Kain route are very popular ascent routes, no doubt due to the relatively low objective hazard from serac fall compared to the S Face route, and the fact that these routes received magazine exposure in the '70's when ice faces were the vogue of the day.

Being a big mountain and so much larger that the neighbouring mountains, Robson often creates its own weather. It can be hot, sunny and calm in the parking lot while the summit is enshrouded in cloud often accompanied by high winds. Hence the formations on the Emperor Ridge! You have to be prepared for whiteout conditions on the summit glacier — otherwise the descent could be a nightmare. Wands, snow stakes, fluorescent surveyors' tape are all very useful. The usual season for climbing the mountain is August-September when you are most likely to have a low freezing level and little loose snow. Some years the right weather and conditions just don't happen and the mountain goes without any ascents. Hopefully, you'll have good conditions — the ascent of this peak is a memorable experience. *Map 83 E/3 Mount Robson*

Ralph Forster Hut

Map 83 E/3 Mount Robson
Location On rock step at 2470 on SSW ridge of Mt.Robson GR 457893
Reservations First come first served
Capacity 8
Facilities Coleman stove and lamp, foamies, water buckets. Best to take your own stove
Water Run-off stream horizontally across screes from hut

Access All routes are approached from the trail to Berg Lake. From Yellowhead Highway (Highway 16) at the gas station, follow an access road north for 2 km to the trailhead. Park here. The trail reaches Kinney Lake in 4 km, then continues around the east shore and up over a heavily treed shoulder. When the trail descends back to lake level it runs across a gravel bar, following markers across the outlet of the "Great Couloir" on the SW face of the mountain. The trail to the Ralph Forster Hut and the S Face and Wishbone Arete routes starts a short way up the right bank of this drainage. This not-so-obvious approach defies description so check out the approach topo opposite!

If you are doing any of the other routes, continue along the Berg Lake trail, past the Kinney Lake campground and on to the Valley of a Thousand Falls and Emperor Falls. Just past the campground above Emperor Falls is a stretch of gravel flats. Cross the Robson River at this point for the Emperor Ridge, Emperor Face and N Face routes. For the Kain Face continue along to Berg Lake.

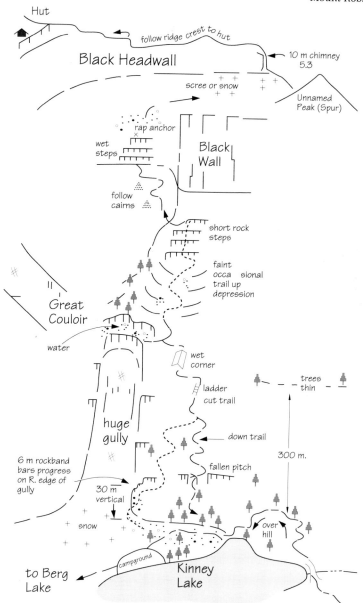

Hut

follow ridge crest to hut

Black Headwall

10 m chimney
5.3

scree or snow

Unnamed
Peak (Spur)

rap anchor

wet
steps

Black
Wall

follow
cairns

short rock
steps

faint
occa   sional
trail up
depression

Great
Couloir

water

wet
corner

ladder
cut trail

trees
thin

huge
gully

down trail

300 m.

fallen pitch

6 m rockband
bars progress
on R. edge of
gully

30 m
vertical

over
hill

snow

campground

Kinney
Lake

to Berg
Lake

Topo courtesy of Murray Toft

301

South Face (Normal Route) IV

photo →

FA. M.D. Geddes, T.B. Moffat, M. Pollard and C. Kain, July 1924. This is one of the two most popular routes on the mountain, the Kain Face being the other. However, the approach to this route is much shorter and less technical than that for the Kain Face — it's a walk, though a grunt of a walk! The route itself isn't particularly technical (at most easy 5th class) but it is long, committing and subject to quite high objective hazard from the S glacier. There are two reasons why this route is so popular: a hut high up and the fact that it is the fastest route to the summit. Typically, three days are taken but a fit team could do it in two.

Approach the Ralph Forster Hut on the SSW ridge as shown in the topo on the previous page. From the hut follow a trail up to a ridge below the seracs of the lower S glacier. Traverse to the left below the seracs along easy ledges and then scramble up the rock ridge (3rd and 4th class) past cairns and various bits of trail to the summit of Little Robson. After gaining the summit of Little Robson, the next objective is to cross a gully below the seracs of the upper S glacier. Attempt to pick out the way ahead from Little Robson — it's a lot healthier than romping around looking for the route while standing below the seracs! Start off by following a rib towards the seracs, then take to a ledge system about 75 m below the seracs that runs right around the back of the gully and out the other side.

The seracs directly above the rib have been climbed though the ice is up to 90° and often overhanging — not particularly recommended. After the gully, hurry across leftward-rising ledges to the prominent rib that runs up the left side of the seracs. At this stage take a breather — the nasty bit is behind you.

From the top of the rib you can either work your way up snow/ice slopes and ice bulges straight towards the summit, or traverse across the S glacier to the SE ridge and climb this to the summit. 6-10 hours from the hut.

An alternative used in the past to by-pass the seracs is a feature known as the Hourglass, a snow slope at the right end (SE) of the seracs. However, the glacier has changed to such a degree that this is now a particularly hazardous route to follow — it is not recommended.

Descent is by the same route you came up. There is an alternative to re-crossing the ledges below the upper seracs. It is to make a 50 m rappel off the end of the serac barrier directly down to the rib leading to Little Robson. In white out conditions this descent is not recommended because of the difficulty in finding the correct place to rappel. 4-6 hours summit to hut.

Mt. Robson: 1. S Face 2. Wishbone Arete a. Little Robson g. Great Couloir w. W Bowl y. Yellow Bands

Photo: Don Beers

Wishbone Arete IV 5.6

FA. D. Claunch, H. Firestone and M. Sherrick, August 1958. This is the prominent "wishbone" ridge leading directly to the summit when the mountain is viewed from the Yellowhead Highway. The route follows the right-hand bone in the wishbone. The gargoyles of crappy snow at the very top are usually the technical and mental crux. The climb is somewhat overrated considering the amount of loose rock and the long approach. Three days is the usual time taken.

Both approach alternatives are long, taking a major part of a day to reach the base of the ridge. The shorter (in distance, though perhaps not time) approach is to traverse north from the Ralph Forster Hut along the "Yellow Bands", the wide talus ledges that run right across the south side of Robson and across the Great Couloir to the base of the Wishbone Arete. The other route follows the Berg Lake trail to the gravel flats above Emperor Falls. Easy scrambling below the Emperor Ridge via small steps and loose couloirs leads to the "Yellow Bands". Follow these right (south) past the Fan Glacier at the base of the W bowl to the ridge. Bivi sites are plentiful.

Follow the ridge throughout with the usual deviations to left and right at difficult bits. It should never get harder than 5.6. Once you get to the stem of the wishbone, things ease off for a short while before the final corniced and gargoyled ridge. Work your way carefully to the summit.

Descent is via the Normal Route.

Emperor Ridge V 5.6

FA. R. Perla and T.M. Spencer, July 1961.
One of the big ridge climbs if not the biggest in the Canadian Rockies. A great proving route if you are thinking of ridge routes in the greater ranges. The final ridge is more reminiscent of Alaska than the Rockies. The rock ridge lower down is not too technical but loose. The major difficulty can be bypassed via a gully on the Emperor Face. Two days to the summit is outrageously fast on this route. Three days up is more common.

From the gravel flats above Emperor Falls scramble up loose gullies and rock steps to gain the "Yellow Bands". The original route takes the left-hand ridge (NW ridge) bordering the Emperor Face though some parties choose the SW rib (it's easier!).

For captions, see next page

The NW ridge is followed to the base of a big, steep step (bivi sites). Move on to the Emperor Face side of the ridge and into a gully which leads to easier ground above the step. Continue up the ridge above until the angle of the ridge drops off markedly at the beginning of the infamous gargoyled ridge stretching the final 1 km to the summit. This bit can seemingly take forever, depending on conditions. Typically, belays in the rotten snow/ice are pathetic and the safest way to proceed is to keep as much rope as possible weaved in and out of the gargoyles. If someone falls off, for whatever reason, the other guy had better jump down the other side — it's the most reliable belay you'll have. Undoubtedly the crux of the route. Enjoy!

Descent is via the Normal Route.

Emperor Face, Stump/Logan VI 5.9 A2

photo →

FA. T. Stump and J. Logan, July 1978. This route takes the most prominent rib in the middle of the face all the way up to the Emperor Ridge. The rib offers some protection from rocks falling from the upper face. If foul weather interrupts your ascent high on the face and you decide to bail out, contemplate traversing to the Emperor Ridge — at least there the rockfall hazard is less. The first ascent required three bivis on the route and one on the Emperor Ridge. Probably best in late August/early September when the temperatures are lower (hence less rockfall) and the face is relatively free of snow.

Approach the route by crossing the Robson River at the gravel flats above Emperor Falls, as for the Emperor Ridge. Once across the river, follow the edge of the Mist Glacier which drops down from the N face below the Emperor Face. Continue up to below the centre of the face. Cross the 'schrund and climb initial ice slopes through a number of rock steps to where the face steepens. The next section follows the rock on the right of a deep gully, the gully normally being an excellent rockfall chute. Move up in a steep ice runnel until able to cross over right into an easier groove. This leads to a steep rock pitch and then a small snow slope (bivi site). The upper section of the rib consists of small vertical rock steps, many requiring aid, interspersed with relatively easier slopes. At the very top of the rib is a steep headwall that succumbs to one pitch of hard mixed free and aid climbing. Once you are on easier ground above, four rope-lengths take you to the Emperor Ridge at the beginning of the upper, gargoyled ridge. 28 pitches in total.

Descent If you are still keen, you can follow the remainder of the Emperor Ridge to the summit and then descend either the Normal Route or the Kain Face. However, most parties will be mentally fried by this stage of the climb and all you'll want to do is go home. The quickest way off is to drop straight down the other side of the Emperor Ridge, down the edge of the W bowl to the "Yellow Bands". Be aware that the W bowl is a likely avalanche bowl, though by late summer this is an unlikely turn of events for this slope. Follow the talus ledges out to either the Ralph Forster Hut or to the base of the Emperor Ridge and then escape to the bars in Jasper for a well earned celebration.

Photo p. 304: Greg Horne
Mt. Robson gargoyles - uugh!
e. Emperor Ridge
w. Wishbone Arete

Photo p. 305: Leon Kubbernus
Mt. Robson W Side: 1. Emperor Ridge
a. approach to N Face
b. approach to Wishbone Arete
c. Emperor Face

Emperor Face close up: 1. Fuhrer Ridge   2. N Face   3. Cheesmond/Dick   4. Stump/Logan

Photo: Leon Kubbernus

Emperor Face, Cheesmond/Dick VI 5.9 A2   photo p. 307

FA. D. Cheesmond and T. Dick, August 1981. A route established in the true Cheesmond tradition. They were on the mountain for a week and climbed the Wishbone Arete, descended to the Ralph Forster Hut, traversed the Yellow Bands all the way around the mountain and finished off with this route — and the weather was never a problem! Not a lot of details are known about this route but what follows is the best that can be dug up. The difficult section on this route is much shorter than that on the Stump/Logan since a lot of height is gained up an ice ramp at the base. The first ascent required two bivis on the face and another near the summit.

Approach as for the Stump/Logan. Cross the 'schrund below an obvious ramp that leads up and left to an icefield about a third of the way up the face. Follow the ramp to the icefield. At the top of the icefield, exit up rock steps to the right to gain lower-angled ground. Keep going up this to reach more rock steps (bivi on first ascent). Continue up to another short section of easier ground, then diagonal up and right to a ledge that runs across the whole face (bivi site). Keep going up and right and then back left to gain easier ground leading up to the Emperor Ridge.

Descent Either continue along the ridge to the summit and descend either the S Face (Normal Route) or the Kain route. OR descend the Emperor Ridge to the end of the gargoyled bit and drop down the rib at the edge of the W bowl, as described for the Stump/Logan route on the previous page.

North Face IV   photo →

FA. P. Callis and D. Davis, August 1963. FWA. T. Sorenson and A.Henault, Winter 1978. This remote and elegant ice face is one of the most popular north faces in the range. A classic north face route on a big mountain. The approach is somewhat lengthy but don't let this deter you; the route is well worth the grunt to get there. It's best to get a very early start so you climb the majority of the face at the coldest part of the day and get down as far as possible before nightfall. The difficulty is determined by the depth and condition of snow on the face. The route has been climbed in two days car to car but three or four days are more usual.

The first objective is to get to the Helmet-Robson col. Cross the Robson River about 0.5 km from Berg Lake and grovel up talus slopes at the base of the Mist Glacier to the rock buttress between the Mist and Berg glaciers. Start off to the left of Mist Glacier and work your way up ledges to the top of the buttress, finishing off just west (right) of the prow. Cross the Berg Glacier to the Helmet-Robson col. 4-6 hours from Berg Lake. Most parties bivi here and start the face early the next morning.

From the col walk across to below the face and ascend right up the middle of the snow/ice slope (50°-55°), going to the right at the top to avoid the usually large cornices. Wrestle with the last stretch of the Emperor Ridge to the summit.

Descent is usually via the Kain route, though some parties go down the Normal Route.

Photo: Don Beers

Mt. Robson N Side: 1. Fuhrer Ridge 2. N Face 3. Cheesmond/Dick 4. Stump/Logan
5. Emperor Ridge b. Berg Lake h. The Helmet m. Mist Glacier

Fuhrer Ridge IV 5.4   photo p. 309

FA. J.W. Carlson, W.R. Hainsworth and H. Fuhrer, July 1938. A rarely climbed route, no doubt because of the proximity of both the N Face and the Kain Face routes. This is a shame since it would get climbed regularly if it were on any other mountain.

Gain the Helmet-Robson col as for the N Face route. Cross the col to the base of the

rounded snow/ice slope that forms the ridge. Ascend this to mixed climbing higher up near the summit. At the top, follow shallow gullies and snow and ice slopes to the right of the ridgeline, at the very left edge of the N face.

Descent is via the Kain Face.

Kain Face IV   photo →

FA. W.W. Foster, A.H. McCarthy and C. Kain, July 1913. FWA. L.Patterson, a.Bertulis, F.Beckey and T.Stewart, March 1965. The line of first ascent of Robson. A tour-de-force for the day, and perhaps the crowning achievement for guide Conrad Kain. The story goes that Kain chopped over six hundred steps during the climb, a point to ponder as you front-point your way up the NE face! This is another route with a reasonably adventurous approach. Typically, parties take a day to reach the Dome from Berg Lake, a day to reach the summit and get back down to the Dome, and a half-day back down the Robson Glacier the following morning. One thing to consider is that snow on the glacier is much firmer in the very early hours and even if you get back to the Dome early in the afternoon, stop for a breather and descend the glacier during the night. A full moon would be an obvious aid.

From the trail beyond Berg Lake, cross moraines to gain the Robson Glacier which descends to the east of Rearguard Mountain. Follow the glacier towards the col between Robson and Resplendent, aiming for the base of a prominent icefall to the left (south) of the Dome. Either angle up through the icefall area towards the Dome or traverse under the icefall (the "Mousetrap"), climb up slopes to the left of it and then traverse above the icefall area to the Dome. Some parties go to the Robson-Resplendent col before traversing across to the Dome. This is much further and not really necessary. Most parties bivi on the Dome.

The NE face is usually climbed left of the prominent ice bulge up to the SE ridge. The slope is at most 45 degrees and presents little technical difficulty. The SE ridge is followed to the summit with perhaps a few deviations onto the south side to bypass the odd bulge.

Descend by the same route.

Mt. Robson NE Side: *1. Kain Face   2. Fuhrer Ridge   d. The Dome   g. Robson Glacier   h. The Helmet*

Photo: Leon Kubbernus

Resplendent Mountain 3426 m

A shapely snow peak somewhat dwarfed by its neighbour. The west side consists of snow slopes and glaciers in various stages of movement. The Normal Route goes up this way. The east side is an impressive 1000 m-high face with the E ridge forming an obvious, beautiful line up the middle. *Map 83 E/ 3 Mount Robson*

Descent for all routes Descend as for the Normal Route by walking down the north-east slopes to the Robson-Resplendent col and then down the Robson Glacier to Berg Lake.

North-West Slopes (Normal Route) II

FA. B. Harmon and C. Kain, August 1911. The original route up the mountain. A pleasant day outing from Berg Lake with excellent views of the south-east side of Robson. The glacier approach is by far the most taxing part of the climb. 8 to 12 hours round trip.

From Berg Lake, cross moraines to gain the Robson Glacier. Follow the glacier all the way to the Robson-Resplendent col. From the col easy, open snow slopes lead to a narrowing snow ridge just before the summit. Watch for cornices.

Resplendent Mtn: 1. NW Slopes   2. Ice Arete (upper part)   Photo: Glen Boles

2

Photo: Greg Horne

Resplendent Mtn.: 1. E Ridge   2. Ice Arete

313

Ice Arete III
photo p. 313

FA. C.H. Mitchell, H.H. Prouty, J. Watt and W. Schäuffelberger, July 1913. The Ice Arete is a magnificent narrow ridge with an impressive drop to the east. A much finer climb that the Normal Route up the south-west slopes. The route follows the ridge that descends north-north east, north and finally north-north west from the summit.

Approach up the Robson glacier as for the Normal Route until just beyond the Extinguisher. Head south-east to gain the rocky rib of the NNW ridge leading up to the beginning of the Ice Arete. Scramble up the rib past a few pinnacles on the right side of the rib to the saddle below the Ice Arete. Follow the Ice Arete to the steep, final slopes which are normally climbed on the right to gain the final bit of the Normal Route near the summit.

East Ridge IV 5.7
photo p. 313

FA. J. Lowe and M. Weiss, July 1973. A very aesthetic route that, unfortunately, has a very long approach. An ideal candidate for heli-alpinism. The climbing is very reasonable to begin with; all the difficulties are packed in at the end.

From Berg Lake head up the Robson Glacier and then up to Snowbird Pass, the col between Lynx Mountain and Titkana Peak. This gives access to the upper part of the Reef Icefield. Contour around past the E ridge on Lynx into the upper reaches of Resplendent Valley.

Drop down and then climb back up again to the base of the east side of Resplendent. A good day hike to this point or a quick chopper ride from Valemont.

The rib is followed throughout after starting on the right (south) side. Small rock steps are interspersed with snow slopes. The climbing is never harder than 4th class until you reach the upper part of the ridge where a few pitches of steeper climbing (up to 5.7) gain the summit snow. Follow the ridge to the main summit. 7-10 hours.

Whitehorn Mountain 3395 m

This is the prominent peak west of the Valley of a Thousand Falls with an impressive E face. This face has no routes as yet, although the neighboring and elegant NE face glacier has been climbed. The N Ridge, however, is the more aesthetic line. *Map 83 E/3 Mount Robson*

North Ridge III 5.3   photo p. 316

FA. J.C. Glidden and D. Hamre, July 1973. An interesting route with excellent views of the north side of Robson.

The best approach is to follow the Berg Lake trail into the Valley of a Thousand Falls and then head up the drainage through BC bush to the moraines below the glacier on the east side of Whitehorn. Bivi sites are numerous. To reach the N ridge cross the glacier east of the peak to a snow/ice-covered ramp leading to the col just to the north of a small subsidiary peak on the N ridge. Drop down the other side and contour around to the NE corner of the NW face. 2-3 hours from the E glacier, 5-6 hours from the Berg Lake trail.

Gain the ridge as convenient below some prominent seracs on the west side of the ridge. The first section of the ridge is over easy rock to the left of the seracs. Climb the rock to gain the upper ice slopes above the seracs. Follow the ridge line all the way to just below the summit. Avoid the "White Horn" by traversing steep snow to the left (south) to the SE ridge and then climb up to the summit. 3-4 hours.

Descent is via the W ridge, the line of the first ascent and the Normal Route. Between the upper part of the W ridge and the SE ridge is a snow couloir. Descend this until it is possible to traverse towards the W ridge. Continue down the south side of the ridge line until able to contour around the base of the NW face back to the west side of N ridge and the subsidiary peak. From here, return to the Valley of a Thousand Falls the same way you came up.

Photo: Greg Horne

Whitehorn Mtn.: 1. N Ridge   2. W Ridge descent

Park Administrative Offices

Kananaskis Country Office, Canmore	(403) 678-5508
Parks Canada Regional Office	(403) 292-4440
B.C. Parks, East Kootenay Office	(604) 422-3212

Information Centres

Barrier Lake Information Centre	(403) 673-3985
Kananaskis Lakes Visitor Centre	(403) 591-7722
Banff	(403) 762-4256
Banff (French language information)	(403) 762-4834
Lake Louise	(403) 522-3833
Yoho	(604) 343-6324
Columbia Icefields	(604) 761-7030
Jasper	(403) 852-6161
Mount Robson Visitor Centre	(604) 566-4325

Travel Alberta

Travel Alberta (summer)	1-800 222-6501
(May to mid Oct)	(403) 678-5277
Field	(604) 343-6446

Weather Reports

Banff	(403) 762-2088
Jasper	(403) 852-3185

Reservations

Alpine Club of Canada Huts	(403) 678-5855
Banff National Park Huts	(403) 762-4256
Lake O'Hara Bus & Campground	(604) 343-6433

Helicopter Companies

Canmore Helicopters	Tel (403) 678-4802
PO Box 2069, Canmore, AB T0L 0M0	Fax 678-2176
Canadian Helicopters Canmore	Tel (403) 678-2207
PO Box 2309, Canmore, AB T0L 0M0	Fax 678-5600
Canadian Helicopters Golden	Tel (604) 344-5311
PO Box 482, Golden, BC V0A 1H0	
Yellowhead Helicopters, Valemont	Tel (604) 566-4401
PO Box 190, Valemont, BC V0E 2Z0	Fax (604) 566-4333

Fixed Wing Companies

Amiskwi Air:	Tel (604) 344-2534
PO Box 1589, Golden, BC V0A 1H0	Fax (604) 344-5808

Index

In an Emergency

In an emergency, contact
the Royal Canadian Mounted Police (RCMP) or
the nearest Ranger or Warden Office

RCMP Offices

Canmore	678-5516
Banff	762-2226
Lake Louise	522-3811
Jasper	852-4848
Valemont	566-4466

Park Ranger or Warden Offices

Kananaskis Country Emergency	591-7767
Banff	762-4506
Lake Louise	522-3866
Field	343-6324
Sunwapta	852-6181
Columbia Icefields	761-7030
Pobokotan Creek	852-5383
Jasper	852-6156
Mount Robson	566-4325